S0-AKC-617

GROWING SOFTWARE

GROWING SOFTWARE

Proven Strategies for Managing Software Engineers

by Louis Testa

no starch press

San Francisco

GROWING SOFTWARE. Copyright © 2009 by Louis Testa.

All rights reserved. No part of this work may be reproduced or transmitted in any form or by any means, electronic or mechanical, including photocopying, recording, or by any information storage or retrieval system, without the prior written permission of the copyright owner and the publisher.

13 12 11 10 09   1 2 3 4 5 6 7 8 9

ISBN-10: 1-59327-183-2
ISBN-13: 978-1-59327-183-1

Publisher: William Pollock
Production Editor: Megan Dunchak
Cover Design: Octopod Studios
Developmental Editors: Tyler Ortman and Adam Wright
Technical Reviewer: Clayton Greer
Copyeditor: Lisa Theobald
Compositors: Riley Hoffman and Kathleen Mish
Proofreader: Gabriella West
Indexer: Lori Bell

For information on book distributors or translations, please contact No Starch Press, Inc. directly:

No Starch Press, Inc.
555 De Haro Street, Suite 250, San Francisco, CA 94107
phone: 415.863.9900; fax: 415.863.9950; info@nostarch.com; www.nostarch.com

Library of Congress Cataloging-in-Publication Data:

Testa, Louis.
  Growing software : proven strategies for managing software engineers / Louis Testa.
       p. cm.
  ISBN-13: 978-1-59327-183-1
  ISBN-10: 1-59327-183-2
  1. Computer software industry--Management. 2. Computer software industry--Technological
innovations--Management. I. Title.
  HD9696.63.A2T47 2009
  005.068'4--dc22
                                                    2008046171

No Starch Press and the No Starch Press logo are registered trademarks of No Starch Press, Inc. Other product and company names mentioned herein may be the trademarks of their respective owners. Rather than use a trademark symbol with every occurrence of a trademarked name, we are using the names only in an editorial fashion and to the benefit of the trademark owner, with no intention of infringement of the trademark.

The information in this book is distributed on an "As Is" basis, without warranty. While every precaution has been taken in the preparation of this work, neither the author nor No Starch Press, Inc. shall have any liability to any person or entity with respect to any loss or damage caused or alleged to be caused directly or indirectly by the information contained in it.

To my wife, Edie

BRIEF CONTENTS

PART V: PLANNING THE FUTURE

CONTENTS IN DETAIL

PART II
PRODUCT AND TECHNOLOGY

5
DEFINING THE PRODUCT 85

6
DRIVING RELEASES 109

PART III
OUTSIDE OF ENGINEERING

PART IV
MAKING WORK FLOW: PROJECTS, PROCESS, AND QUALITY

17
UNDERSTANDING QUALITY ASSURANCE   301

PART V
PLANNING THE FUTURE

18
SETTING THE DIRECTION   337

19
PRODUCT ROADMAP AND STRATEGY   349

ACKNOWLEDGMENTS

Pulling together my first book has been fun but has taken a huge amount of effort. However, no matter how much effort I put in individually, this book would not be worth reading without the help and advice I received from many people, including family and friends.

I would not have written this book without encouragement from my wife, Edie, and from my four children, Logan, Kevin, Kerry, and Brady. Edie's advice and suggestions for clarity led me to rewrite many of the sections and fill in the gaps.

I would like to give special thanks to Clayton Greer for his careful technical review of the book and really great suggestions; to Anita Maria Gutierrez for her extensive review of the entire draft of the book, as she provided editorial insight and suggestions for ideas for improvement; to Jef Bell for his exhaustive review, recommendations, and ideas that made the book stronger; and to Mike Portwood for his insightful advice on topics for the book and the considerable amount of time he spent reviewing the material.

Additionally, I am very grateful to Bob Tidwell, Curt Frye, Paul Irvine, Gordon Huntsman, Miki Tokola, Rick Sanstrom, and Dylan McNamee for their useful information and recommendations.

Finally, it has been great working with the team at No Starch Press: Megan Dunchak, Tyler Ortman, Lisa Theobald, and Adam Wright. I would recommend them to any aspiring technical author. (I guess I just did.)

INTRODUCTION

In many small and growing companies, engineering managers are often in the unique position of having to deal with the technical team and other senior managers, while simultaneously taking direction from the CEO. Too often, development managers focus only on technology, even though the nontechnical aspects of the job can have the biggest impact on a company's success. As your company grows, problems that once seemed small can grow accordingly, exploding into major disasters. I wrote *Growing Software* to offer advice for newer development managers about how to succeed when faced with these diverse challenges.

The role of a development manager at a small company differs from the same role in a large and stable company in many ways. For example, the development manager at a small company must often work with developers to support an immature product. Development managers must also work with the strong personalities who are attracted to the challenges faced by growing companies. But most of all, a small company's development manager must have a wide focus that includes employees, product, process, planning, technology, and customers.

In contrast, large companies typically support multiple existing products, and their processes are usually well defined and relatively static. Policies in large companies typically limit the choices of tools, techniques, and approaches that a development manager can use. The manager's role is more specific and much narrower in scope than the same role in a small firm.

Growing Software serves as a practical, hands-on guide for development managers at small companies that have moved past the initial survival stage and are trying to grow. It is intended to help the manager look ahead and deal with problems before they become unwieldy. The techniques described here are useful for small firms producing software for sale or for a software-as-a-service offering; they are not directed at software consulting businesses. *Growing Software* provides general advice, specific solutions, and detailed templates and spreadsheets to help development managers put general concepts into direct action.

Because the scope of the book is broad, it is written in a prescriptive style rather than an argumentative one—that is, many recommendations are not supported by exhaustive arguments as to why the techniques work well. Although this information would have greatly increased the scope of the book, it would have made it less readable.

For convenience, I use the terms *development manager* and *development management* throughout this book to describe the *top* software/engineering manager—whether the particular job title is chief technology officer (CTO), vice president of engineering, director of engineering, or senior engineering manager. This person manages software engineers, but he or she might also manage quality assurance, documentation, and project management groups. Although the target audience for this book is the person in charge of all of development, nontechnical managers will also be interested in the problems and solutions described here.

Book Organization and Conventions

This book is divided into the following major sections that make it easy to use as a reference:

- Development Team

- Product and Technology

- Outside of Engineering

- Making Work Flow: Process, Projects, and Quality

- Planning the Future

Although the order of the book allows for each topic to build on earlier ones, you can jump to any section to read about a particular topic of interest.

Company Growth Stages

Companies grow in stages as they progress from startup to full growth mode. The information in this book applies to one or more of these stages. Table 1 defines the stages according to the size and completion of the product.

Table 1: Stages of Startup Company Growth

Stage	Company size	Customers
Startup	Less than 12	0 to 2, with no major customers
Foothold	12 to 40	3 to 5, with one major customer
Growth	40-plus	More than 6, with 2 major customers

Real-Life Accounts

Growing Software offers short narratives of real-world situations that illustrate key points; these narratives are offset from the rest of the text. Although all accounts are written in first person for consistency, the stories are a mix of the experiences of others as well as my personal experiences. Company and individual names have been removed.

Spreadsheets

Spreadsheet examples are used throughout to illustrate techniques for collecting, analyzing, and displaying information to solve specific types of problems. Each is illustrated and described in the text and can be downloaded from *http://www.nostarch.com/growingsoftware.htm* to be used in Microsoft Excel or OpenOffice.org Calc, adjusting for each program's minor differences. The primary purpose of the examples is to teach how to analyze and solve underlying problems with a simple spreadsheet.

Although the spreadsheets can be used as is, many problems will require that you customize the basic spreadsheet layout. You can re-create a spreadsheet by typing all the fields into a spreadsheet program. Arrows point to particular cells to indicate a formula you can enter, with a description to the right or below the example. As appropriate, copy the formula across a row or column as described in the note attached to the spreadsheet. Figure 1 illustrates these conventions.

When entering formulas, pay attention to dollar sign ($) characters that affect how a formula reads data when it is copied from one cell to another. Not including the dollar sign character can result in incorrect calculations after the formulas are copied.

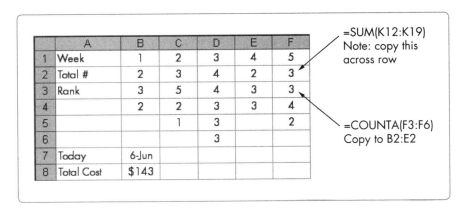

Figure 1: This sample spreadsheet illustrates cell instructions.

Correct formatting is also important for the spreadsheet examples. The default format for an entry is General, which will not display all values in the most appropriate ways. Formatting is implied from the examples: *Dates* should use Date formatting; *currency* amounts should use Currency formatting with zero digits after the decimal; and *numbers* should use Number formatting with the rounding chosen based on how many digits are of interest.

IMPORTANT DIFFERENCES BETWEEN EXCEL AND OPENOFFICE.ORG CALC

- OpenOffice.org Calc uses a semicolon (;) to separate fields in a formula, and Microsoft Excel uses a comma (,). This book uses commas to separate fields in all formulas. If you are working in Calc, use semicolons instead. For example, the Excel formula *=WORKDAY(B3, C3)* looks like this in Calc: *=WORKDAY(B3; C3)*.

- A second important difference is the *inter-sheet reference* used to refer to cells in other worksheets. The inter-sheet reference is an exclamation point (!) in Excel but a period in Calc. For example, a formula that references the *Eng* sheet appears in Excel as *=Eng!H3* but appears as *=Eng.H3* in Calc.

Templates

Growing Software also provides sample templates, surrounded by a dashed box, that you can copy as starting points for your own templates. Template instructions appear in italics; feel free to delete these instructions as you fill out the template.

PART I

DEVELOPMENT TEAM

Development managers often focus solely on the company's technology. Although technology is fun, good managers must first understand the people they work with. Focusing on technology instead of people is like coaching a baseball team and spending all your time testing the latest, greatest bats.

This section covers starting a new job, working with the development organization, and successfully growing your team. No need to worry; we'll talk about technology—just a little later.

1

GETTING STARTED

Imagine you're hiking through the woods, following some new trails. The weather is perfect, and you are relaxed. As you walk along, you notice the landscape beginning to change as you enter unexplored, rugged wilderness. Eventually, you stop to sit on a large rock and eat a snack.

As you are eating, you realize that you have no idea where you are. You forgot to bring a map and neglected to plan a route or mark your path. Now you feel a sudden burst of tension and fear. *You are lost.* You want to move faster—either continuing in the direction you were going or turning around to find your way back. But you know that panicking and running in any direction is a big mistake when you're lost in the woods.

You remember some crucial wilderness advice: When you're lost, stop, assess, and then act. You've stopped moving. You assess your situation and ask yourself a few questions: *What do I know about where I am? Do I have tools, maps, or supplies in my backpack that would be helpful? How much time has gone by since I started out? How much time do I have to get back safely?* Next, you make a plan—and then you act.

Now, a shift of scenery: You are vice president of engineering at a small company that is growing rapidly into unfamiliar territory. Although you have been with the firm since the beginning, it's no longer the little startup you used to know. You feel lost in the woods without a map. Like the hiker, any fast and frantic actions will worsen your situation, so instead of panicking, you stop, assess the situation, gather what information you can, map out a strategy, and then act.

On the other hand, if you are starting a new job at a growing company, you might feel like you've been dropped into the middle of the woods—and you missed the pleasure of the initial hike in. The same approach to the situation applies, however: Stop to survey the landscape and collect what information you can before you act. By following these steps, whether you're new or newly lost, you can find your way.

Finding Your Way in a New Job

As the volatility of technology companies increases, loyalty to company senior staff decreases. As a company folds or changes its focus, development managers often find themselves looking for new jobs. Getting a new job, of course, starts with an interview.

Interviewers paint masterful pictures of their companies during interviews, like a softly focused Monet. But once you start the job, the picture begins to look distorted, somewhat like a Picasso. Small and subtle problems described to you during the interview process become huge crises that you must resolve immediately. Table 1-1 shows a tongue-in-cheek comparison between the interview statements and reality.

After you've joined the company and headed down that formidable path, you need to make the best of the reality.

Table 1-1: The Interview vs. Reality

Interview statement	Reality
We have a *few* minor quality problems.	The product is a disaster. As soon as you come on board, *you* will be blamed for everything that ever went wrong.
We need to improve our delivery on commitments.	Nothing comes out on time. The company needs to make constant changes to its newest product features throughout the development process because marketing and other executives cannot make up their minds. However, they still expect on-time delivery.
We have a great team of engineers, but a little coaching is needed.	Team members are having screaming arguments in the halls. At least one engineer needs to be fired for non-performance.
We are a driven company with highly motivated employees.	Your "lazy" development team is expected to work through lunch, every evening, and most weekends— or you will have to fire them.

Dealing with the Immediate

During your first days as development manager, urgent issues will demand your immediate attention. Some problems will have built up since the last manager moved out of the position, leaving several months' worth of deferred decisions on your desk. *Wading through a swamp* best describes the job of tackling that backlog.

You might feel pressure to focus exclusively on these issues, but that can be hazardous to your long-term success. By focusing only on the pressing concerns, you can miss opportunities to learn about your company, its products, your co-workers, and your team. So take a deep breath and see the bigger picture.

If you split your time between tackling the outstanding issues and handling day-to-day crises, you will eventually reduce some of the reoccurring problems, thus improving the effectiveness of your team. Spending part of each day learning about your company will be more effective than spending all your time clearing out the problem backlog. In addition, you'll better understand the bigger problems faced by your team, which will allow you to start addressing them sooner. Many issues will pop up during the day and continually force you to shift your focus. You can keep this process from becoming too chaotic by creating a system for handling the many demands on your time.

Maintain a List of Issues and Efforts

Careful task management and good record-keeping will help from the start. Maintain a list of your decisions and efforts as well as the big issues, especially those that are presented to you as urgent problems. Organize the list in prioritized sections along with notes about required completion dates. Managing this list will help lower your anxiety about missing any issues, and an assembled list will let you review your priorities and efforts with your boss.

Review your task list daily and target priority issues. For large tasks, target subsets that you can complete in a short time. Focus energy on large, high-priority tasks every week; otherwise, they will continue to be deferred by short-term pressing demands. Assume that you will have only a limited amount of time during the day to work on these issues: Avoid overbooking your time and hindering your progress.

As you complete a task to resolve an issue, mark it as such with a date and archive the task. This archive can be helpful later, when you're asked whether and how you handled specific issues. Checking off completion is also good for your morale.

Delegate When Possible

Delegate responsibility as appropriate for some immediate issues instead of trying to tackle them all yourself. Proper delegation makes you and your team more productive, and the opportunity to tackle new tasks is good for team member morale. When delegating, make sure the delegatee understands the task, its priority relative to other work, any status check-in dates, and a due date. Also make sure that the team members know they can come to you for more information.

If delegating an entire task is not appropriate, you can assign parts of the task to team members. For example, you could assign information collection tasks to others and reserve assessment for yourself. Or you could ask a team member to provide background research on an issue and then coach the person on approaches to analyzing the data. If you give team members an opportunity to take on part of an important job, you all benefit.

As you work through the immediate issues, remember to keep your boss apprised of your progress. This can help prevent misconceptions about your efforts.

Undergoing Initial Training

Success during your initial training period will require focused effort and time. Reserve a fixed amount of time each day for learning about your company's employees, technology, products, market, and process. Find an hour or two when you are most alert and able to focus your attention. Arrive early and spend the start of each day on your training, and continue to reserve this time later to tackle difficult issues.

As a new development manager, you'll probably experience a short "honeymoon period" of three to six weeks, when your boss gives you some leeway to learn about your job and the company culture. You should expect to work some overtime hours during this time, but these extra hours offer you time to learn about and act on important issues. If your boss recognizes your extra efforts, she'll feel satisfied with her decision to hire you in the first place. After you have shown what you can do, you can scale back your hours to a reasonable and sustainable level that works for you.

Know whether you were hired specifically to be a change agent or whether you are expected to make incremental changes to an already effective organization. These expectations will frame how you present issues to your team and your boss. If, for example, you identify significant issues but the expectation is to maintain the status quo, you might waste considerable time and energy trying to convince your boss and team about the importance of some problems.

Your timing on addressing long-term issues is also critical. If, for example, you wait six months or more to discuss big-picture issues, your challenge might be greater: You might have lost an opportunity to present a fresh perspective or even to identify the problem, as it can be difficult to recognize flaws in a system once you become immersed in it. Later on, you might find the development team more resistant to change, as people might be willing to listen to fresh perspectives only from a new manager.

If you propose significant changes, speak credibly about the benefits and the costs to the company. "Selling" your changes can help you avoid making enemies or facing inappropriate behaviors from others who might be resistant to change.

Collecting Information

Collect information about the company's product, people, and process to decide on a strategy for your first three to six months on the job. Talk with your boss and spend time with direct reports and peers to gain a broad perspective on the company. Your goal is to get a big picture view of the company's problems and successes and to learn how development can best serve the company. Begin by asking the following open-ended questions to identify and isolate major concerns:

- What is working well?
- What do you see as major problems?
- What solutions do you propose?

Then pull what you learn into a summary and look for patterns.

Creating a Discussions Summary

As you meet with co-workers, managers, and other staff, take notes; then type up your notes into bulleted statements to keep the ideas organized and fresh in your mind. Paraphrase and summarize comments to make your statements short and succinct.

Next, organize the summary document by categories. Each category can include problem areas as well as successes. After each of the problem areas, list a solution that was identified during your conversations. Here is a list of potential categories in which to collect information (of course, your list might look different):

Technology	Quality problems
People	Internal documentation
Organization structure	Risks
Clarity of goals	Customer service
Policies	Marketing and sales
Process	Financial issues
Planning	Other

Problems and solutions will fall into three categories: issues you and your team can address directly, issues on which you can collaborate with other departments and people in the organization, and issues that you can influence but not directly address. Label each issue accordingly in your summary.

A snippet of the final document might look like this:

4. Technology

- Positive: Our technology is faster and more reliable than our competitors'.

- Positive: Languages and libraries in use are up to date.

- Problem: The system is missing redundancy in subsection A-15 that will lead to "core meltdown." This will require collaboration with Operations.

- Problem: The API has poor error checking. Two flawed data requests will cause the system to erase the database.

    Solution: I can address directly through discussion with development.

Putting Your Summary to Work

Next, set priorities for the successes and problems identified. Ranking successful approaches as well as problems will allow you to think about how to keep the most important positives strong. A simple *A, B, C* prioritization works well for the initial sorting, and it's a good idea to follow this system within each level. Rate your boss's statements high, but do not minimize others' feedback. Ultimately, you must decide which areas to address and how to address them. Create an action plan from your highest priority items. Estimate what you can accomplish in the next three to six months, for example. A realistic plan will help you avoid tackling too many tasks at once and getting little accomplished.

Make sure you understand the acceptable mix of project work versus improvement work before creating a plan. For a small firm, spend at least 10 to 20 percent of your time and 5 to 10 percent of the team's time solving issues that do not deal directly with completing current projects. Such non-project issues include improving productivity, conducting training sessions, advancing technology, planning for the future, improving working relationships, and resolving people issues.

Action plans fail due to lack of company support, so be sure to solicit the support of your boss in your improvement efforts. You need your boss's enthusiastic support—or at least acceptance—if you hope to succeed. If your boss reacts negatively to your suggestions, you need to try to understand his concerns—or, if you still believe in your proposals, do more research and selling. Your boss needs to know that you are addressing company problems in a reasonable way before your approach can be successful.

You should also engage with other department managers, especially in marketing and sales. They'll need to understand why time and resources are required for work not directly related to their short-term goals. Explain the long-term benefits your changes can provide to the company. Since problems you identify might not relate to your department only, feedback and discussion with others will improve your understanding of the scope of problems and help you find the best solutions.

Establish each effort as a project with a timeline and resources. Encourage the continuation of improvement projects or they will lose momentum; failing to improve leads to lower productivity as the company grows.

GETTING AN OVERVIEW AT MY COMPANY

When I joined my last company, I made time to talk to a dozen people in different departments. I took what I heard and coalesced it into a summary document of a few pages. This process gave me valuable insight into what was going on. Talking to everyone was an enlightening exercise that directed me toward the biggest problems to address first.

—New manager

Understanding the People

Understanding your co-workers will make your job much more productive and a lot more fun. Conversely, not getting to know them will be frustrating and can lead to friction. Fortunately, you can find out a lot by talking to people, especially the developers on your team.

Ask the following questions:

- What do you like to do?
- What work assignments do you dislike?
- What do you do best?
- What would you like help with?
- Where else have you worked?
- Why did you join this company?
- What would you like to change?

Answers to these questions will offer hints about how best to work with each person. Learning how developers complete their work and interact with others provides a helpful assessment of behaviors. Reading your team's past performance reviews can offer some insight, as long as the previous manager wrote usable review comments. If that's not the case, it tells you something about how the team was managed before you came on board.

Talk to workers outside your team as well. Strike up conversations with people throughout the company to gain insight into company culture and to determine what methods do and don't work. The benefits of building relationships with others in the company are huge—plus, getting to know people can be enjoyable.

Chapters 2 and 3 provide detailed discussions on working with your team. Chapters 9 and 10 offer advice on how to work with others throughout the company.

Reluctance to Reveal Information

You might encounter engineers or others who are reluctant to reveal information. They can express this in the following ways:

- Claiming to be too busy to answer your questions
- Providing only minimal information with important details left out
- Claiming not to know an answer, even when you believe they do know

- Providing extensive low-level details without providing context for the information
- Leaving out technical details intentionally

These claims appear to close the door to getting the information you need. To overcome this, you need to understand the real reasons behind them. These are some common reasons for people being reluctant to provide information:

- The person's ego requires him to know more than anyone else.
- He is worried about job security and wants to hold on to critical information.
- She is embarrassed by her lack of knowledge.
- He is busy with work and sees little value in educating you.
- She does not like or trust management in general.

Politely persisting in your requests for information usually works. In all cases, explain your interest in the information to build trust, but insist that the engineer provide the information without excessive delay. Make the following points:

- You need to understand the technology and choices to work effectively with the engineer and with others.
- You need complete information in some areas, not a cursory overview. If the engineer pleads lack of time, discuss his time commitments. You can request some overtime efforts.
- If an engineer's answers seem incomplete or ill-formed, ask the engineer to research the topic and report back to you. This shows your confidence in this person and the importance of your request.
- If the person really does not know an answer, ask her to tell you so directly. Ask who would know the answer. If you cannot get the information from that person, assign another engineer to get it for you.
- Tell the engineer that you will be making decisions that affect his job, and those decisions should be well informed.

Hostile engineers will require winning over—or, in the worst case, weeding out. Take time to understand the person and his or her motivations before acting. Chapters 2 and 3 go into more detail about managing a development team.

Identifying the Company Culture

Company culture concerns the ways people interact with each other and what types of behaviors are rewarded by management. To identify the company culture, observe what managers say compared to what they do. Reading the corporate values and mission statement can also help. You can determine how mission and values affect corporate direction by discussing them with peer managers; you should understand how management applies these resources to their staff and work decisions.

HINT *If your boss did not discuss company values during initial conversations about your job, the values are probably basic boilerplate statements.*

Small and growing companies need to think through their values and mission statements carefully. These statements provide a foundation upon which the company culture is built. Management must train employees in the mission and values during orientation, and management should review major decisions that are not in line with these statements. Because of the rapid changes of a small and growing company, mission and value statements are even more important than they might be at a large and established company.

In a well-run company, the values and mission statements define the company. People make decisions based on defined values, which are also used to set company direction and define the organization. For example, a key value of *quality* would direct the CEO to give the quality assurance team a prominent spot in the organization and to emphasize quality training. As the development manager, consider your company's mission and values and do your best to apply them to your management style.

Chapter 9 covers company culture in more detail.

Learning the Technology, Process, and Product

During your first two months on the job, get an overview of company technology, process, and product. Learn about the technology used, how the product works, how the development process works, and how the development team members work together. Assess what you know and identify areas that you don't fully understand. Then fill in the gaps by systematically collecting the missing information.

Know your product inside out. Review, at a minimum, the top-level architecture showing the major component blocks of the product along with data flows. Developers on your team should be able to describe these elements and provide existing overview documents.

WARNING *In many small firms, overview and process documents are often out of date or lacking in detail.*

Document the information and draw diagrams of what you learn to help you absorb the information. (A drawing tool such as Microsoft Visio is great for creating these diagrams.) Your diagrams will contribute to the company's intellectual property (IP). Increasing the company IP in this way creates multiple positive effects: New hires will have a training reference, other groups and potential partner companies will have reference information, and, if the company is sold, the IP has a positive impact on its valuation.

Consider sending your diagrams to the development team for feedback. They can spot problems and provide suggestions for improvement. Correcting and refining process diagrams often requires several rounds of changes. In the process, teams will form a consensus about the details of how the product and process actually work. In addition, the effort can lead to improvements in existing processes.

Thinking systematically about what you learn can help you avoid blind spots in your training and, later on, in your ability to manage. Figure 1-1 illustrates a sample checklist of technical topics for review.

To gain the proper perspective about your company's product, gather information from many sources. Ask sales or marketing managers to train you to use the product so you can learn how they present the product to customers.

Experiment with the product on your own to make the training details easier to remember. Set up your experiment with realistic but hypothetical data—do not use actual customer or production data. Using a safe data

Technology

- ❏ Scaling
- ❏ Risk factors
- ❏ Failure modes
- ❏ System flexibility
- ❏ List of third-party packages
- ❏ Internationalization support
- ❏ API
- ❏ Security
- ❏ System documentation
- ❏ Data reporting/analysis

Tools

- ❏ File backup
- ❏ Source control versioning
- ❏ Build method
- ❏ Software release
- ❏ Defect tracking
- ❏ Customer incident tracking
- ❏ Developer documentation storage
- ❏ Intranet/wiki
- ❏ Development tools: compilers, IDEs, debuggers, profilers

Products

- ❏ Product specifications
- ❏ Product functions
- ❏ Product documentation
- ❏ End of life review
- ❏ Alpha and beta releases
- ❏ List of all testable products and internal tools

Quality

- ❏ Specifications
- ❏ Test plans
- ❏ Quality assessment
- ❏ QA staff
- ❏ Defect process
- ❏ QA measurements
- ❏ QA tools
- ❏ Degree of automation

Process

- ❏ Development process
- ❏ Process measurements
- ❏ Change order process
- ❏ Problems identified

Figure 1-1: Technology review checklist

set lets you experiment without worrying about damaging or exposing data. Try every feature, every button, and every data entry model—and try breaking them. You need a good understanding of the product and its limitations.

You can find more information about products in Chapters 5 and 6. Chapters 7 and 8 cover technology and tools, and Chapter 15 covers process in more detail.

Understanding the Customer

Learning about your company's customers should also be a part of your initial assessment. Talk with sales and marketing teams to understand the company's typical customers. Work with sales to set up visits and listen in on sales calls.

Discuss the following with sales and marketing teams:

- Customer satisfaction
- Customer perception of product qualities and features
- Customer purchasing concerns and value propositions

Spend some time with key customers to understand their use of the product. Communication will provide insights into how customers perceive your product. Learn about the industry served by your product. Information from sales and marketing teams can help.

Chapter 12 covers understanding the customer in more detail.

Understanding the Corporate Business Workflow

To understand how different teams work together to provide products, support, and customer service, learn about the company's business workflow. Many companies employ unique overall workflows that are important for you to understand. Diagram the information you collect to clarify the business workflow and create a useful reference for others to use.

Creating an overall corporate workflow diagram will clarify which teams are responsible for which part of the software product or service. Remember to include how customers interact with the company.

A corporate workflow diagram can benefit a new company: It helps the executive team spot problems and understand how best to support new services and products. The workflow diagram can be used as training material for new staff to help them see how their efforts support the company. Team members will feel empowered by an understanding of how their work contributes to the whole.

Although workflow software and complex diagramming methods are available for capturing corporate workflow, a simple diagram works well for most small companies. Appendix C describes a straightforward approach to diagramming, including a basic example. Even if you have been with your company for a while, you might find it worthwhile to diagram your workflow to gain insight into how the company works and to identify potential areas for improvement.

MAPPING CORPORATE WORKFLOWS

My former company had about 12 different product offerings, and each required a different type of quote. I wrote up the corporate workflow and detailed how the engineering costs tied into each offering. Clarifying the offerings and deciding how we would estimate them was a huge benefit, allowing us to provide faster and more accurate estimates.

A graphical company workflow made it easy for managers to identify ways to improve the process. We also used the material as part of our training for new hires.

—Senior manager

Back to the Big Picture

This chapter has presented a lot of information for you to consider. Here is a big-picture summary to round things out—a checklist of directions that will help you find your way out of the forest.

☑ **Meet the people.** Get to know the people at your company, especially other managers, your boss, and your team.

☑ **Handle problems.** Deal with the immediate issues, but delegate whenever possible. Do not let the immediate demands overwhelm your learning efforts.

☑ **Track issues.** Keep a *prioritized* list of issues. Separate the issues into immediate and long-term ones.

☑ **Collect information and summarize.** Talk to at least a dozen peers and ask about what they do, what is working well, and where the problems are. Create a summary from these discussions. Select some of these items to add to your list of long-term issues.

☑ **Learn.** Spend plenty of time learning about your company's product, customers, culture, industry, technology, and organization.

☑ **Assess workflows.** Diagram the significant corporate workflows and look for opportunities to improve them.

Review this list at least once a week during your first few months on the job. If you are missing information about key areas, consider how you might rearrange your efforts to focus on these areas. No best single approach or formula exists for mapping out your time during the first few months, but if you're constantly in high-stress mode and dealing with one crisis after another, find a quiet space where you won't be interrupted and map out a plan that will allow you to focus on the key areas. If you do not actively plan your efforts, you will likely continue to *react* to bad situations—and the job is considerably more fun when *you* are setting the direction and driving efforts forward.

2

MANAGING A DEVELOPMENT TEAM

As the development manager at a small company, you have a unique role not found in most large companies. Whether your title is *chief technology officer, vice president of engineering,* or *director,* you must connect the CEO and members of the executive team directly to your development team. In a small company, you must be able to stretch in ways that differ from those of a development manager in a large company.

Understanding Your Core Management Values

Before delving into the mechanics of managing a team, let's take an introspective look at what it takes to be an effective manager. Ask yourself how you want to work with your development team and how your core values affect how you interact with others. Your respect for others, ethics, coaching and listening skills, ability to provide feedback, and concern for the success of others all affect how you make decisions.

As a manager, you need a "toolkit" of approaches you can access when working with your team. Your toolkit should include methods for motivating people, making yourself available, choosing the team's tools, organizing the team, setting up the workspace, managing projects, resolving conflict, and communicating with your team. With multiple tools and approaches on hand, you can select the best tools for the job.

In contrast, a rigid manager might have only one tool—the one he used at the last job at the last company. But as the saying goes, *If your only tool is a saw, then the solution to every problem is to cut.*

The following sections consider the key tools and components of a set of core values: trust, flexibility, sincerity, confidentiality, respect, and empowerment.

Trust

Companies with an environment of trust are the most productive, because workers do not waste energy on politics, pointing out others' mistakes, or guarding their backsides. These companies encourage direct communication—employees trust management and each other to pass on correct information and get support for their work. This fosters high worker morale, as workers focus their energies on being productive instead of on being wary.

Employees at small companies must be able to believe what they hear from senior management, because working at a small firm can be riskier than working for a large company. Since small and growing companies often lack significant resources, a high-trust environment drives the efficiencies that are essential to success.

Employees at companies with low-trust cultures waste energy focusing on other people's mistakes and protecting their positions. Workers believe they need to double-check the veracity of all statements from management. In such companies, management perpetuates low-trust cultures by rewarding low-trust behavior, such as political maneuvering, public verbal complaints about others, rumors, power plays to force decisions on other teams, and backstabbing. Low-trust cultures tend to breed in companies at which people are worried about losing their jobs. Management is often authoritative and political. Senior managers spend their energy pulling other people down to pull themselves up. In the absence of focused positive effort by top management, short-term advantages exist for individuals who exhibit low-trust behaviors to advance their position.

Why don't more companies create high-trust environments? Building trust requires that management make a focused effort by discussing company values and core beliefs every day and not just at yearly reviews. A high-trust culture requires that managers hire the right people, train them in company culture, and model the behaviors they expect.

LAST ONE STANDING

Our QA team consisted of six engineers, and we were good at what we did. When our QA manager left the company for another job, the VP in charge appointed a manager without QA experience and without management experience. Our team was willing to give him a chance. However, over the next four months, he managed to alienate all of us by showing no interest in quality. Gradually, the other team members found other jobs and the manager did not replace them.

I was the last QA engineer employed at the firm. I wrote an email to my manager asking him to show more interest in QA. I expressed concern over how the rest of the team had left the firm and how he had not replaced them. He fired me and had me escorted out of the building that day for insubordination. I should not have trusted him to be fair, even in a private communication.

I found out later that this QA manager quit two weeks after I was dismissed to take a management job at another company. He destroyed the QA team and then left the company.

—QA engineer

As a manager, you can build trust by exhibiting high standards of fairness, confidentiality, respect, sincerity, and conflict resolution. You deal effectively with development team members who break your trust. For example, if a team member reports to you that she has completed a task, you expect the task to be completed correctly. If you later discover she did not complete the task, you will no longer trust her. This person will be a drag on your time, as you have to inspect her work carefully to ensure that it's getting done correctly.

In high-trust environments, a development manager looks out for her team. She doesn't view the team as machinery to accomplish a job; nor does she consider her role to be simply a conduit for passing off upper-management's demands and problems to the team. Instead, she acts in the interests of both her team and her company.

Trust can appear to be an abstract concept. The following examples help to illustrate high-trust and low-trust responses to different situations:

- You are attending an executive meeting and a fellow manager mentions that one of your senior developers failed to deliver a project on time. Although marketing contributed to the delay by changing the requirements at the last minute, you and the developer agreed to make the changes.

    - **Low-trust response**   Point out in the executive meeting that the marketing manager made it impossible for the developer to complete the project on time. He changed the definition too many times, running up the costs without your consent.

    - **High-trust response**   Indicate that you agree that the result was unacceptable. You plan to review the project with the goal of improving future performance. You invite the marketing manager to join in the discussion.

- A developer tells you about his interest in getting a master's degree. You know another engineer who would like to join the team if a spot became available.

    - **Low-trust response**   Find an excuse to lay off the engineer who spoke to you because you know he was likely to leave anyway.

- **High-trust response**   Try to determine whether the engineer can attend classes while still working for your firm. Ask him to provide as much notice as possible if he decides to leave the company to pursue an education.

- Your commercial servers went down for four minutes during peak time. Your initial analysis points to an error on the operations team, compounded by a software flaw that prevented the proper system automatic recovery. You do not manage the operations' team.

  - **Low-trust response**   Tell the CEO about the operations team's mistake immediately while pointing out the need for the operations director to improve staff training.

  - **High-trust response**   Spend some time investigating the issue with the director of operations. Then, the two of you meet with the CEO and describe the sequence of events and what steps you plan to work on jointly to prevent this from happening again.

Flexibility

A team of workers who believe they are trusted will act in a trustworthy fashion; being flexible in how you treat your team will help you build a high-trust environment. Treat members of the team as you would like your boss to treat you. Focus on individual successes as well as team successes. Developers are not just hired hands, but people with a career and a life outside of work. If you are fair and honest in your approach with them, they will generally treat you fairly and honestly in return.

You can show flexibility when a team member encounters problems or life situations that make it difficult for her to work in the usual ways. Flexibility in such a situation might mean allowing her to work from home for an extended period or allowing her to take time off. Flexibility can also mean shifting a person's working hours or shifting weekday work to weekend work short-term.

You can also demonstrate flexibility in making work assignments, making adjustments to align required work with the desires of individual team members. Each developer would then be able to focus on particular tasks that are of interest to him or her; this improves team members' morale and usually provides valuable cross-training that does not occur if individuals focus on the same areas repeatedly.

Flexibility does not mean providing the same solutions to all team members, whether or not they have a problem. For example, if one employee has family issues that require him to work from home for a week, everyone on the team should not then be allowed to work at home. When an employee will be working remotely or at hours that differ from those of the team, tell your team about the accommodation to help them understand your decision. Of course, in some circumstances, you should leave the accommodated employee's details vaguely defined, because telling others the details would be inappropriate.

A manager's flexibility has an impact on all the other core management areas. An employee is more likely to trust a manager who shows flexibility when the employee is experiencing a situation that makes it difficult to complete work as usual.

Some employees might take advantage of your flexible approach, but having an employee take advantage of you occasionally is better than being totally inflexible. While a few individuals might be untruthful about their circumstances, most people are honest.

Sincerity

Your team members will appreciate your sincere concern for their success. You can demonstrate your concern in words and actions, but ultimately

---

SINCERITY IS NOT A MANAGEMENT FAD

My manager openly talks about the fact that the job we have now may not be the one we always want to have. She encourages people to explore their interests even if it means they might end up leaving the team. She continues to do this even when the company is not filling vacated positions. She constantly puts our individual best interests first and is committed to working out whatever staffing problems arise as a result. This makes us all want to keep working for her!

—Senior technical writer

WHY NOBODY BELIEVED

The management team held a company meeting to announce layoffs and budget cuts. The CEO indicated that we were forced to freeze hiring and we would have to spend money carefully until business picked up. A week later, all the company managers received Mercedes leased by the company. When asked at the next company meeting why this occurred, the CEO explained that senior executives had previously had a "car allowance" that the accountants said was not tax-deductible. So management leased the cars instead, and they happened to arrive right after the budget cuts. When asked why he did not cut this expense, his response was that this type of incentive was necessary to retain top management talent.

—Hardware engineer

your actions count. If your employees believe you are sincere and trustworthy, they are more likely to follow your direction when you are trying new approaches to solving problems rather than resisting every step of the way.

If your actions show that you are insincere, it doesn't matter how earnest you *appear* while talking to people; you will not be trusted, and you'll be far less effective as a manager, which can lead team members to undermine you. Your team will lose focus on achieving the best results for the company. Consider, for example, the case of an unprofitable company that makes budget cuts. After the manager asks his team to save money and spend only on essentials, he purchases a new computer system for his desk, even though his current system is fairly new; this manager would probably lose his team's respect and ruin his credibility.

Confidentiality

Confidence also builds trust. If an employee confides in a manager, she expects that the information will not be shared with others or used inappropriately. Unless a confiding employee commits a serious ethical breach, violates laws, or puts the company at risk, you should never share this information or use it against the person. By encouraging an environment in which people can confide in you, you can help resolve problems rather than allowing them to grow.

Consider, for example, an employee who tells you that she wants to work on a different type of project. She has spoken with other companies about potential employment. On hearing this information, some managers would immediately lay off the employee or reassign her to unimportant tasks—because she is leaving anyway. However, since the employee has voluntarily revealed this information, it shows that she trusts you, and, in fact, she might not really want to leave—she might be giving you an opportunity to change her project assignment. If she does decide to leave the company, she will likely give you time to transfer her responsibilities to others because she trusts and respects you.

Respect

Individuals on your team must be treated with respect, by you and by other developers and co-workers. Lack of respect can be shown overtly—for example, when someone verbally demeans another person face-to-face or behind the other's back. It can also be shown in a subtle way, such as when someone belittles another person by demeaning his or her qualifications, skills, or abilities to others.

If one member of your team demeans another, pull the abuser aside and talk to him. Don't wait for the situation to "work itself out." Depending on the extent of the problem, you might need to involve human resources.

Build respect by creating a team environment that focuses on solving problems, not pointing out other people as problems. Encourage staff to work out problems individually, and offer assistance only when they prove unwilling or unable to do so themselves.

Empowerment

Successful developers enjoy their work and look forward to the next challenge. They are self directed and empowered because you have defined goals, stepped back, and let them succeed. Empowered workers will succeed.

In contrast, workers who feel micromanaged go through the paces, viewing work as an acceptable task in exchange for pay. They know that the tasks required by management are sometimes inefficient or useless, but they believe they are unable to change the way things are done. Management treats them like plumbers hired to clean out a drain and then go home.

To empower your team members, make sure they understand development goals and boundaries. Boundaries define reasonable limits but are never such sacred cows that they cannot be discussed or changed. Clear boundaries and flexibility to choose a solution will prevent workers from feeling micromanaged.

The following are examples of types of boundaries:

Project constraints Schedules, features, budgets, and resources

Company policies Requiring management approval for spending company funds

Technical boundaries Partner deals that force specific technology on a solution

Business boundaries Choices for specific software components that might require managerial buy-in due to ongoing excessive operational costs

Once you have set up clear boundaries, let team members choose how they will work together to reach the solution. Set the team loose, monitor progress, and coach them to success.

Communicating with Your Team

Successful communication requires that you consider what you want to say and how you want to say it—before you start talking. Your communication should be tailored to fit each situation: Realize that what might work in one environment might not be effective in another.

When communicating with your team, plan to cover project work and people topics. Project work includes development efforts to create revenue, projects to reduce risk, and strategies to improve productivity. People topics include coaching, training, correcting, answering questions, resolving concerns, discussing long-term problems, discussing new ideas, assisting with work needs, and helping with career planning.

Too often, management focuses only on project work, addressing current practical issues that drive the company's short-term success. However, failing to address other issues when communicating can lead to long-term failures that result in decreased productivity, increased staff turnover, quality problems, missed opportunities, and morale problems. Spend at least a fifth of your communication time on efforts not tied to current projects. Consider a communication approach for project topics that differs from the tack you take for people topics; each needs its own venue to ensure that it is properly covered. The following sections discuss approaches to communicating with your team, including one-on-ones, project communication, team meetings, and informal conversations.

One-on-Ones

A weekly one-on-one meeting with individual developers gives managers the best opportunity for covering most people topics. (In contrast, team building requires team meetings to develop relationships and improve interactions.) If your team is larger than six people, you might need to limit one-on-one meetings to every other week because of the time involved.

One-on-one meetings can provide opportunities to build trust and listen to each individual's concerns. Let the employee direct the initial discussion. Try to avoid discussing current tasks and status issues at the beginning of the conversation. Sometimes developers will not be forthcoming with information, so you can help get them started by asking questions such as these:

- Do you have any concerns about your work?

- Have you experienced or noted any problems recently?

- Do you have any ideas for improvement?

- Do you need additional equipment or software?

- What are your long-term career plans?

- Do you have any ideas to share?

One-on-one meetings are ideal for discussing problems, offering advice, agreeing on solutions to problems, and sometimes assigning a task or requesting a solution to a problem. Make assignments clear, but avoid spelling out the exact details of the solution. Instead, establish agreement on what success looks like: Give the employee the authority to solve the problem, and offer advice. In general, don't immediately assign the task of

NOT LISTENING

Early in my career, I had a boss who was a poor listener. When I brought up issues to let him know what was going on, he would interrupt the discussion and start giving me instructions. He would issue orders before I was fully able to describe the problems I was trying to resolve. I stopped discussing problems with him.

—Software manager

problem resolution to the person who brought it up. If you make a habit of doing this, your staff will bring fewer problems to your attention.

If you want to use one-on-one meetings for project status updates, wait to discuss status until after you have covered the other topics. If you start with project status, updates might take up all of your meeting time and other issues will not get attention.

Project Communication

How you handle project communication depends on the size of the project and the release cycle. With short release cycles, *daily stand-up meetings*— 15- to 20-minute meetings in which all participants stand—can be appropriate. The manager structures the meetings at the same time each day, asking participants to offer brief statements that describe what they did during the previous day, what they plan to do today, and any immediate help they require. Stand-up meetings are not intended as problem-solving meetings or topic discussions. Instead, any identified problems can be assigned to individuals for resolution and follow-up.

For projects with long release cycles, *weekly project status meetings* combined with visiting and talking with people at their desks can be helpful. This weekly meeting usually lasts 30 minutes to an hour. Status and schedule meetings usually involve some detailed discussions, along with plans for the next few weeks. The team identifies risks and the project manager assigns individuals to work toward mitigating those risks.

You can communicate project status to the team via intranet/wiki postings, emails, whiteboard messages, or reviews during regular status meetings. Some team members will not know the full project status or will be unaware of recent changes to the project or schedule. Not communicating the overall status to the team can lead to confusion, while clearly communicating this information improves morale and likelihood of project success. If you provide your team with regular status updates, they will be more likely to point out problems and discrepancies early on, and they'll also be more likely to get their status reports to you on time.

When communicating project status to the team, scale the content and frequency of the report to the size of the effort. The status description should include information about projects that have been recently finished, which projects will be tackled next, any product functionality that has changed, projected completion dates as of today, problems encountered, and current identified risks.

On-time project completion depends on accurate status information that allows time for the team to make midcourse corrections.

Team Meetings

Scheduling team meetings at regular intervals will enhance team cohesion and team performance. Team meetings can occur every week or every two weeks, depending on the team size. The meetings can serve as forums for discussing general concerns or as opportunities to provide training on new processes and policies. Team meetings also allow team members to discuss concerns or ask questions.

Meetings should not be ad-lib events, however, so you should prepare an agenda or list of topics in advance. Open a file on your desktop and keep it open, adding items as they come up; this file becomes the basis for the next meeting's agenda. An established agenda will help keep the meeting short and help avoid rambling discussions. Circulate the agenda in advance for an even more effective meeting.

Overly long team meetings drain energy from the team and impact your bottom line, so keep them as short as possible. Long team meetings are expensive, too—for example, a meeting that lasts 2 hours for a team of 12 takes the same amount of time as 3 engineering days (24 hours).

Allow engineers to speak about concerns such as policies and senior management decisions. Keep track of these issues and questions and review them weekly with the team, even if you do not yet have answers. Make sure you provide ongoing status of open items raised at earlier team meetings and work toward closure of issues and questions.

Occasionally, a disgruntled engineer can use a team meeting as a complaint session. If the engineer crosses the line from constructive suggestions to destructive complaining, cut the conversation short and ask him to meet with you individually to discuss his concerns.

Regular development team meetings are not good venues for detailed technical discussions. Set up separate technical meetings, during which you can focus on specific topics, and make most of these meetings discretional, so that people who do not need to attend can opt out. Otherwise, engineers not affected by the specific technical topics will end up spending time listening to discussions that are not helpful to them.

Conflict Resolution

At some point, disagreements will arise between team members. As their manager, you should encourage them to resolve disagreements directly, rather than let disagreements impede cooperation. Typical disagreements concern such issues as technology choices, common resource usage, or inconsiderate behavior. Team members can usually work out technology and resource disagreements directly or sometimes through a moderated discussion, but inconsiderate behavior requires a different approach.

Problems between co-workers can build up to a point at which the people can no longer work together. If one person is angry at another, counsel the aggrieved party to ask the other person to meet in a conference room to discuss the problem so that a solution can be proposed. If they cannot resolve their differences, you can arrange a joint session to talk through the problem. However, if a conflict involves unprofessional behavior, intervening first can work best: Pull the individuals aside at the start and discuss the details of the situation with resolution as the goal.

Occasionally, conflicts occur between members of your team and people in other groups. These conflicts often involve missed deliverables, but poor communication is usually at the core. Encourage the individuals to talk about the issue first. Offer to assist if they cannot resolve the issue or if emotions are running high.

When assisting to resolve a difficult conflict, first speak with each person involved to understand both sides of the issue. Reconstruct the events in a timeline. Then call a review meeting with the participants and their managers, as appropriate. Present the factual events causing the conflict without making judgments. Ask the parties to consider what they can do differently to improve the situation the next time it occurs. Add your recommendations, if necessary.

ACTING TO RESOLVE CONFLICT

A project manager and her boss told me that they were unhappy with one of my engineers. The project was due live on the website at midnight, and work had stretched until after 5 PM. The manager told me that the engineer was supposed to have called when he completed his work. The engineer did not call, so the project manager called another engineer who completed the work just before midnight.

It turns out that the project manager gave the engineer a slip of paper with the person's phone number to call when the work was ready. Unfortunately, the engineer lost the number. Instead, he sent an email when the work was complete. The project manager did not look for the email and thought that the engineer had forgotten.

After talking through all the details of the project, I arranged a joint session with the individuals and the other manager. I stepped through the timeline factually and described the missteps. We discussed as a group how to avoid these issues going forward: For future after-hours work, the project manager would write a one-page plan. The plan would list who is doing what, how completed steps are communicated, and the participants' phone numbers. If a misstep occurred in the future, people agreed that they would call the managers that evening.

After the meeting, the participants indicated that they were pleased with the outcome.

—Web engineering manager

Don't ignore conflicts in the hope that they will go away, though they sometimes do. Instead, pay attention to conflicts, encourage people to resolve them directly, and intervene when necessary. In addition, instead of asking an aggrieved engineer if he would like mediation, coach that engineer on conflict resolution.

Training

Company-sponsored training indicates that the company cares enough about its employees to invest in their futures; most engineers will reciprocate with increased company loyalty. Training, of course, can also improve an engineer's performance, as she learns new approaches to technology, self-management, and work habits.

In general, engineers have based their careers on technical knowledge and respond positively to technical training. Technology changes so rapidly that much of the raw technical details in use today will become obsolete in a few years. Consequently, most engineers try to keep abreast of leading-edge technical knowledge, and this makes training an important aspect of work life. While technology training benefits engineers in the short term, general work skills training can have long-lasting positive effects on their careers. For example, learning time-management skills will make an engineer more productive regardless of what technology he is using. Most engineers will benefit from training on a variety of topics, such as the following:

Time management	Delegation
Project management	Management basics
Making presentations	Conflict resolution
Meeting management	Employee motivation
Systems analysis	Coaching
Negotiation	Interviewing
Marketing basics	Project budget management
Return on investment basics	Customer communication
Process improvement	Understanding emotional intelligence
Defining requirements	Understanding personality styles
Quality improvement	

Unfortunately, training in small companies is often limited by budget constraints. Since training trades short-term costs for long-term benefits, the costs can be difficult to justify when budgets are tight. In addition, many senior managers see little value in providing training to development engineers. This means training budgets are often the first things cut when the CEO tightens the purse strings.

Resist the temptation to ignore training when budgets are tight. Instead, consider various training alternatives such as the following:

- Offer to approve the expense of any reasonable book purchase.

- Select books on a topic and discuss them with the engineers; this can be an excellent way to provide inexpensive training.

- Ask one team member to share information about a topic with the team for an hour.

- Provide the training yourself by setting up a mini-course.

- Investigate online training options.

- Investigate small local training agencies that might be able to provide lower cost training than larger training houses.

- Investigate the possibility of large training firms providing classes to staff from multiple companies to lower the per-person cost.

Unfortunately, management often considers only the short-term costs of training, ignoring the costs of not providing training and the longer term benefits it can provide. Cutting even low-cost training is a strategic mistake for a small and growing company. Training improves employee stability and productivity, and small companies rely on employees and depend on low employee turnover to be successful.

Coaching

One of the most direct and satisfying ways to improve team performance is through individual coaching. Good coaching guides people toward self-improvement, which benefits the company as well as the individual.

CONTINUITY IN THE TRAINING ATTITUDE

When money was available for training at my company, I focused on making a list of training course opportunities and surveyed the development team to determine the highest interest items. I hired a local training company and we received excellent courses on time management, managing meetings, and project management.

The next year, budgets were tight, so the executive team eliminated training expenses. However, the need for training did not disappear. I purchased books on training topics for team members to read. I reviewed the books again and created a course outline, organizing the topic into a flow. After managers had read the books, I gave a two-hour training session on each topic, including a presentation plus a back-and-forth discussion following an outline I prepared.

I found that providing a training course was beneficial to me as a manager. The classes forced me to review the material and thereby refreshed my knowledge of the topics.

—Product development director

Successful coaching requires that the coach understands an individual's goals. Here are some good questions to ask as you coach a member of the development team:

- What motivates you?

- What are your long-term and short-term goals?

- What technologies interest you?

- What training would you like to have?

- What tasks do you enjoy doing most in your job?

- What do you like the least about your job?

Some people find it difficult to vocalize their career goals. As a result, a development engineer might look for a new job to advance her career instead of asking her current employers for more options. Convincing an engineer to stay when she has an employment offer from another company

LISTENING REQUIRES HAVING A CONVERSATION

Early in my career, an excellent engineer left my company because she wanted to do something else technically. Had I known, I could have arranged her work assignments to provide her with the technical challenge she was looking for.

She made the assumption that her current assignments were all that were available and that there was no point in asking for something different. She accepted an offer from another company. Although I told her I could change her work assignments, she did not want to go back on her word. By all indications, if I had known earlier and changed her assignments, she would have stayed.

—Engineering director

is difficult. It's far better to keep employees happy by coaching them and giving them the assignments they want, when possible.

Effective coaching requires a manager's time and an ability to listen. Coaching should be an important part of the weekly one-on-one meetings. You can coach individuals on how to improve their performance in a non-threatening way while encouraging them to improve.

Coaching is not simply cheerleading—it is aligning your team members with what they do best, providing extra training and practice for those who need improvement, and listening to concerns and determining how you can address them. In addition, coaching means pulling people aside and correcting them when they are approaching their tasks in the wrong way.

Motivating Your Team Members

Development teams are motivated in ways that differ from those of other teams—engineers generally do not respond well to "rah-rah" pep talks, emotional appeals, or contests. What motivates individual development engineers varies, but they will usually tell you what they need if you ask them. These are some common motivations for engineers:

- Technical challenge

- Opportunity for career success and advancement

- Opportunity to participate in an outside organization, forum, or technology group

- Financial opportunity such as a stock award or raise

- Chance to go to conferences or seminars

- Flexible work schedule that allows them to schedule their own day and not have to arrive at 8 AM or be marked late

- Recognition from peers

- Recognition from respected managers

- Ability to take on senior-level tasks such as code reviews and new project estimates

- Opportunity to be part of a well-run team—an elite group of engineers paired with great management

- Opportunity to work on a flagship product

- Opportunity to work on a project that has applications in the "real world" outside the company

---

MOTIVATION THROUGH CHANGE

An engineer on my team was unhappy with his assignments. His performance was poor. He was argumentative and often late in delivery. He requested a transfer to another technical area. While my boss advised me to let him go, I gave him a shot at the technology he wanted. Over the next few months, the quality and timeliness of his work improved greatly. He was excited about learning and his attitude improved. The gamble of giving him a chance to do what he wanted paid off.

—Engineering manager

Engineers, like most workers, are usually at their best when they enjoy their work. Adding a little pressure to achieve reasonable goals will add to their overall success. If an engineer participates in establishing and committing to project content and delivery, he or she will feel motivated and enjoy the effort.

If engineers are encouraged and enjoy their work, many will want to put in extra effort. You can encourage them by determining what kind of work they enjoy most and create those assignment opportunities with realistic, attainable goals. Empower team members by involving them in estimating the work effort and delivery dates. Listen to and address your team's concerns. Ensure that the team has the proper tools to get the job done. Then watch them succeed.

In contrast, continually pushing people to commit to excessive overtime will lower team motivation and morale and can lead to people looking for new jobs. Engineers, like everyone else, need balance in their work and lives. You cannot build a high-trust environment or company loyalty if you expect employees to forego a balanced life.

Finally, acknowledge successes publicly. Your direct appreciation of a person's work builds up his or her motivation. You can express appreciation by talking directly to the person. Alternatively, you can show appreciation by personalizing a reward. Reward traditions vary considerably company by company, so consider these traditions when deciding on rewards. If your company does not have a reward tradition, start one. For example, you can set aside a budget to purchase small rewards to celebrate successes—time with a masseuse, extra vacation time, humorous plaques, a bonus or raise, gift cards, and coffee cards, for example.

Coaching Problem Employees

Every manager eventually encounters an employee who behaves inappropriately or who is difficult to work with—a "problem employee." Perhaps you inherited this person from the manager who preceded you, he might be part of a reorganization, or you might have hired him. Even though small companies cannot afford employees who are not good workers, you can and should make a good faith effort to improve an employee's problem behaviors.

You might be tempted to delay dealing with a problem employee because you have so many important tasks to do. However, procrastination just allows more time for the problem to grow and affect other employees. Instead, as soon as a pattern of poor performance emerges, you should deal with the employee's problems.

Two categories of problems are common: employees who perform poorly and employees who disrupt the team with their poor attitude. A poorly performing employee will not deliver work on time or accurately communicate about his or her workload. An employee with a poor attitude has negative or condescending interactions with other employees or continually disparages the company. Like acid, this person will eventually corrode team cohesion and your ability to manage the team.

Start the correction process by talking to the employee about what you observe and try to determine the source of the issue. A number of reasons can exist for the employee's actions, including the following: The employee might need additional training but is afraid to ask; the employee might have a short-term personal problem and needs schedule flexibility to resolve it; the employee might need some coaching on how to be effective; or the employee might be unhappy with his or her work assignment.

Depending on the problem, you can work directly with the employee to offer coaching. However, if the employee insists that no problem exists or behavior explanations appear inadequate, he or she will probably not respond to your coaching. In such a case, you will need to move more rapidly to a formalized performance improvement plan.

When coaching an employee, start by agreeing on specific actions that would improve his or her work; this will provide goals and an impetus to improve. Then monitor progress and offer periodic progress reports. To keep coaching positive and not punitive, encourage the employee to perform well rather than only pointing out mistakes. If you describe what success looks like from your perspective and emphasize the importance of the worker's efforts to the company, he or she will be more likely to take the coaching as a positive opportunity.

If the employee's performance does not improve over the next month or you note a failure to make a reasonable effort to improve, you should consider additional measures, such as a formal improvement plan. The timing for when to formalize an improvement plan varies depending on the situation. Put the employee "on notice" that his or her actions can lead to termination. Although some managers will fire the worker without a plan, you should create a plan to offer a fair opportunity for the employee to change and to provide some protection for your company from legal action.

Requirements for performance plans vary. Talk to your company's human resources group to understand its requirements. A performance improvement plan should define specific problems, spell out the problem behavior as well as what success looks like, and describe the consequences of failure. In general, use no more than a 60-day review period for the plan.

Do not assume that performance plans automatically lead to dismissal. Although some employees will fail or will leave a company on their own, some will make an honest effort to improve and will succeed. Treat employees as though you expect them to succeed.

Reviews and Evaluations

Employee evaluations must be an ongoing effort throughout the year—don't wait until the formal employee review to show appreciation for results or discuss a problem. In fact, an annual review is not the place to bring up problem behavior. Waiting for the annual review to offer an employee negative feedback is a poor but common management practice that usually stems from a manager's desire not to confront the individual about a problem until forced to do so; this contributes to a low-trust environment, however. Though the annual review process usually forces the confrontation, most employees will feel blindsided if the first they hear of an issue is in their annual review. An annual review should reveal no surprises.

Companies handle annual reviews in a variety of ways. Many small companies offer no reviews, offer annual reviews for everyone at the same time, or offer annual reviews based on anniversary hire dates. From the company perspective, the review is driven by human resources (HR) to support corporate needs—perhaps to ensure that a review is on file to avoid potential lawsuits, especially if the person is terminated, or to reward people for good work so that they will stay.

Creating the Review

Do not wait until review time to collect information or offer feedback to team members. Instead, provide feedback all year during your one-on-one meetings. You should also collect data throughout the year by writing notes in a file about each employee's performance, rather than trying to remember this information at the end of the year. Having your notes at hand will make writing the review easier for you and more fair to the employee.

One popular practice is called the *360-degree review.* In this scenario, either HR or the manager collects information for the review from people working with the employee to be reviewed. People in other teams or co-workers can usually offer useful insight into the employee's performance. As part of the 360-degree review, you should also require a self-appraisal from the employee. Self-appraisals are great opportunities for employees to list their achievements for the year and judge their own performance. Often the self-appraisals will remind you of tasks the employee took on months ago that you had forgotten.

A punctual essay review is the best type of review because it covers multiple areas of performance. To write an essay review, start by collecting information. Ask the employee to complete his or her own version of the review and deliver it in advance of your meeting. If the company requires an employee self-appraisal, read it first. If self-appraisals are not required, you can still ask for them. Write your essay review with descriptions of the employee's successes and areas needing improvement. Keep the language straightforward and the text relatively short. On completion, review each sentence to make sure that it fits in the overall picture you want to provide for the employee.

A general format for the review covers results, successes, improvements, and a summary. At the beginning of the review, describe in detail the engineer's projects. The earlier notes and files for the year will make this task easy. Provide a short written discussion of each project, and describe the employee's performance and major efforts. Next, describe areas of strengths and weakness. Suggest techniques that might help him or her improve performance. Propose areas for which the employee would benefit from more training. You should also propose goals for the next year. Finally, provide a summary describing the employee's overall performance.

You might be required to fill out standard forms for the review. This does not preclude you from writing an essay and attaching it to the forms, however.

Delivering the Review

When you deliver the review, discuss each of the different areas reviewed. Avoid the temptation to hand the employee the written review at the start of the meeting, because he or she will quickly read it and not internalize what you are trying to say. Instead, spell out the major points and ask questions to determine whether the employee agrees or disagrees with your assessments. Give the employee time and encourage him or her to ask questions. When reasonable, make the review session a positive, uplifting discussion.

At the end of the meeting, provide a written copy of the review to the employee. You might consider scheduling a follow-up meeting for the day after the review if it seems appropriate. This gives the employee an opportunity to think about the review and convey any thoughts the next day.

Providing Late and Deficient Reviews

Reviews are important to employees for career and financial reasons. Providing regularly scheduled reviews on time is a sign of respect. A late review can be demoralizing for an employee who is asked to wait. Providing late reviews add to employee anxiety and can make the employee believe he or she is neither important nor respected.

The anxiety level is often greater if the review is tied to an annual salary increase. A few companies have the abominable practice of not backdating raises if the manager delivers the review late. In these companies, a manager's delay leads to lost income for the employee, so the review is no longer a positive experience; it has turned into a negative experience that increases the employee's cynicism and destroys his or her trust in the company.

Delayed reviews can cause other problems, as well. Development engineers will let others know of their concerns about the company and management. They might assume management is delaying the reviews so the company can save money and may thus speculate that the company is in financial trouble.

So why do managers deliver late reviews? For most managers, writing a review is a painful process that they avoid by indefinitely delaying the task, not writing anything, or not offering advice during the reviews. Many managers ignore the importance of the review to ongoing employee goodwill.

Poorly written reviews also have a negative impact on employees. Such a review might list only a few bullet points along with the HR-mandated evaluation boxes in a few different categories. The only review worse than a poorly written review is one that the manager did not write at all. If HR requires a review session but nothing else, the review can become a *handshake annual review,* in which the manager offers the employee a few verbal comments along with a raise figure and a handshake.

THE HANDSHAKE ANNUAL REVIEW

I have received a half-dozen handshake annual reviews in my career. I usually find them disappointing, as they offer no guidance for the future. They also indicate that my manager does not want to spend the time thinking about how I really did. The reviews were all positive, so I would have liked a written record. The record is valuable to me, especially when I have a new manager.

My favorite reviews are upbeat discussions with details and ideas for improvement that I can actually act on.

—Engineer

HR departments can make it easy for managers to write poor reviews in several ways. First, the review form can use rating checkboxes that allow a manager to assign a numerical value to each area. In some companies, the sum or average of the numbers on the form constitutes the employee's rating. This approach falsely assumes that all the rating items have equivalent value and will lead to skewed employee evaluations.

Some forms have limited space for including information about an employee's key attributes. Advising an employee is difficult when you are limited to two lines of comments. A reasonable review requires full descriptions.

A minimum standard for quality of the review or feedback is often missing. If a manager can produce an acceptable review by checking boxes and writing "Good work," the standard is too low. A form review can be easy, but it does not serve the company or the employees.

Reviews should be a ceremonial culmination of continuous feedback and coaching. Annual reviews are easy to write by drawing from the outputs of a yearlong coaching system. Employees spend a year of their lives developing software for your company. Condensing a person's effort into a short summary of "Good work" and a checklist is

☑ Unacceptable ☐ Acceptable

on the part of the manager. Instead, use the review to reinforce the coaching you provided throughout the year.

Additional Reading

Here is some additional reading on topics presented in this chapter:

1001 Ways to Reward Employees, by Bob Nelson (Workman Publishing Company, 2005)

Becoming a Coaching Leader: The Proven Strategy for Building Your Own Team of Champions, by Daniel S. Harkavy (Thomas Nelson, 2007)

Love 'em or Lose 'em, by Beverley Kaye and Sharon Jordan-Evans (Berrett-Koehler Publishing, 1999)

Managing Software Maniacs: Finding, Managing, and Rewarding a Winning Development Team, by Ken Whitaker (Wiley, 1994)

Managing Technical People: Innovation, Teamwork, and the Software Process, by Watts S. Humphrey (Addison-Wesley Professional, 1996)

Peopleware: Productive Projects and Teams, by Tom DeMarco and Timothy Lister (Dorsett House Publishing Company, 1999)

Slack: Getting Past Burnout, Busywork, and the Myth of Total Efficiency, by Tom DeMarco (Broadway, 2002)

What Every Manager Should Know About Training: An Insider's Guide to Getting Your Money's Worth from Training, by Robert F. Mager (CEP Press, 1999)

3

CREATING AN EFFECTIVE DEVELOPMENT TEAM

An effective development team creates a strong company foundation with fewer wasted resources. An ineffective team builds a weak foundation that will crumble when stressed.

Company management, across the board, must be supportive of the efforts of the development team to maintain the team's effectiveness. The term *effectiveness* can be interpreted in many ways. At one company, for example, the top executive focuses on engineering costs. But that mentality results with metrics such as *code per dollar*—and teams of low-paid developers spread across the globe. Development engineers are not necessarily effective when they produce the most lines of code in the shortest amount of time. Good solutions based on minimal code are the deliverables of effective engineers.

Let's continue this discussion with a good definition: *An effective team provides the best customer solution per company dollar.* Customer satisfaction, quality, schedule, and budget of project delivery can all be measured over time, and the best customer solutions meet the customers' needs and provide high-quality products delivered on time and on budget. To convince a CEO about effective solutions that require immediate expenses or changes, you need to focus on the long-term corporate goals—a quality product, delivered on time—and meeting these goals requires an effective development team.

Management should consider four aspects: team effectiveness, team member effectiveness, management effectiveness, and effectiveness of team integration within the company. *Team effectiveness* requires an organization that supports the team's efforts and provides solid communication paths. *Team member effectiveness* requires a work environment that allows team members to contribute their ideas and ensures proper communication within the team. *Effective team management* requires a manager who looks out for the team and is willing to encourage some fun along with the work. Finally, *efficient team-company integration* requires a framework for cooperation and communication. These aspects are often overlooked and minimized despite being necessary ingredients for success.

Effective Team Organization

Whether starting a new job or growing a development team, development managers should build team organization based on a planned size rather than letting the team grow "organically." Ideally, three to eight people should report directly to a manager—more than that, and you'll probably not have enough time to spend coaching each developer. In some companies, more than 20 people report directly to a single manager. A manager with 20 reports does not have time to coach each individual properly.

Figure 3-1 illustrates a simple engineering team structure, showing a manager with five direct reports. Each engineer reports directly to the manager for all aspects of his or her work.

As the company grows, the development team grows as well. You can support organized team growth by adding either project or technical leads or managers along with new development staff.

Technical leads deal with the day-to-day technical decisions; they provide the technical leadership and guidance for the team, usually on a product or associated line of products. Technical leads are not responsible for project management or general people management. *Project leads*[1] handle the project management decisions: who to use on

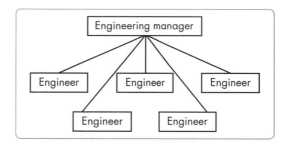

Figure 3-1: Simple engineering team structure

a project, how to plan the project, and how to deal with change during the project. Sometimes a project lead will handle technical leadership, but he or she does not take on people management, such as conducting reviews, hiring, firing, and coaching.

Even if your staff includes a technical or project lead, do not let the number of your direct reports grow much above 12, including leads. Although leads take care of the day-to-day communications on projects and provide help, you, as development manager, are still responsible for conducting reviews, career training, hiring and firing, ensuring regular communication, and coaching.

Figure 3-2 shows a sample team using multiple leads. The solid lines represent the normal management relationship, while the dashed lines represent technical leadership only.

With an engineering team larger than 12 people, keep the

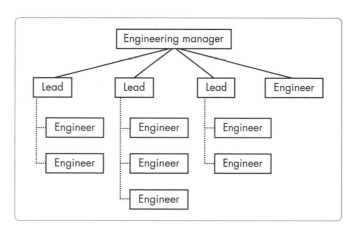

Figure 3-2: Sample team using technical leads

---

[1] The term *project lead* is used here instead of *project manager*, since the latter has become a profession of its own with specific skills and training focused on managing projects of any type.

number of direct reports low by identifying managers who will report to you. These managers can be responsible for all aspects of managing the people reporting to them. A hybrid organization with technical leads and managers can be quite effective, as illustrated in Figure 3-3.

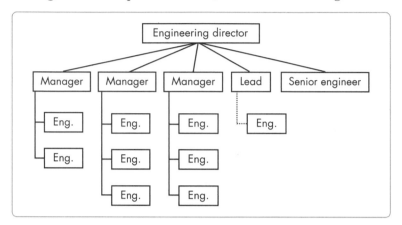

Figure 3-3: Sample team organization with managers

As your development team grows larger, consider alternative approaches to organizing staff. Some companies with many projects adopt a *matrix* management approach in which project managers drive projects and functional managers identify and coach the staff. Appendix A discusses matrix management in more detail and covers how company organizational approaches change as the company grows. As a rule, every time a company grows by 50 percent, you should evaluate whether organizational changes are required, and by the time growth reaches 100 percent, you should already have made changes to accommodate that growth.

For organizations with many projects, a flexible project lead approach can be very effective. *Project leads* coordinate projects using overlapping teams instead of fixed staff assignments. Project leads often have technical leadership authority in addition to project leadership, and they can be *flexible* because each lead usually holds responsibility for only one project. The lead role is not a job title. As projects start and end, leads can be reassigned to other projects as developers or project leads. As project size permits, some leads may share time in different roles between two projects. This requires a team with multiple engineers who also serve as project leads.

The flexible approach empowers teams to accomplish individual goals instead of being part of a single functional hierarchy. It has a large advantage in that the project team assignments can be reconfigured as required. This approach also requires separate *staff managers* who deal with issues unrelated to project work, including staffing, career growth, process definition, and mentoring. A staff manager is a permanently assigned position that does not shift with project changes.

The flexible project lead approach differs from matrix management, as shown in Table 3-1.

Table 3-1: Comparison of Flexible Project Leads with Matrix Management

Flexible project leads	Matrix management
Project leadership is a role, not a permanent staff position.	Project managers hold project leadership as a staff position.
Project leads are chosen from engineering staff and have engineering skills.	Project managers have project management skills and may not possess engineering skills.
Staff managers are assigned to development staff but do not necessarily manage a distinct functional area.	Functional managers manage a functional area, such as database, middleware, or graphics.
The project lead succeeds if the project succeeds.	The project manager succeeds if most of his projects succeed—at least the important ones.

Figure 3-4 illustrates a flexible project-lead approach. The dashed lines represent temporary assignments made for a project and the leadership connection is by project only.

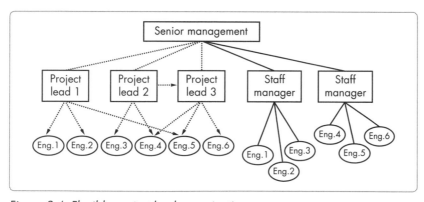

Figure 3-4: Flexible project-lead organization

As you manage a development team in a growing company, think about your vision of the team for the next two years. Consider how you'll build up the team to match your vision. After you have mapped out a team management strategy, decide how you can best use the team's time.

Programmer Efficiency

Software developers need long periods of uninterrupted concentration time. Engineers must solve complex problems and keep many details in mind as they work. Recovering from interruptions can require extra time to "get back into the code" before developers can begin coding again in earnest. An effective development team needs a balance of thinking time and communicating time that doesn't frustrate work efforts.

TIME TO THINK

At my company, noise and interruptions were becoming a big productivity problem for the development staff. As we were all working in cubes, we had no doors to shut, and people would stop by all day.

I purchased several versions of the yellow "Police Line: Do Not Cross" tape for team members. By agreement, a busy developer would put the tape across his or her cube entrance for no more than two hours at a time to indicate that interruptions were unwelcome while focusing on code. We asked people in different groups to respect this time and interrupt only for true emergencies.

—Engineering manager

Although good inter-team development and intra-team cooperation necessitates some communication, good communication does not include at-will interruptions. Interruptions might be normal for other staff, such as sales and marketing workers, who shift efforts constantly during the day. In fact, interruptions may not even be problematic during some programming tasks, but for most development efforts, even short interruptions can cause problems—having to answer the question "Is this a good time?" or "Can I ask a quick question?" will break a developer's concentration. Most questions lead to discussions and resolutions on the spot, as the developer does not want a second interruption.

In some companies, people interrupt engineers continuously throughout the day. Engineers who try to work around and between interruptions find that they are inefficient and prone to making errors. Errors in code lead to more time spent debugging and repairing, which increases development costs. Despite a team's best efforts in testing and debugging, poorly written code ultimately results in poor-quality products released to customers—and this, of course, has big sales and support implications that can create a large impact on the company bottom line.

To accommodate all demands, you and your team can actively negotiate work habits and communication arrangements within the team and with other teams. Consider some systematic approaches to minimize interruptions as part of your effectiveness strategy.

- Use distinct signs that engineers can use to indicate "do not interrupt." In offices, close the door; in cubicles, use a sign or banner. An open space layout encourages interruptions and impromptu conversations. By agreement, an engineer could place a sign on her desk asking for undisturbed time, but this works less well in an open office environment.

- Minimize interruptions by providing other venues for work. Allow engineers to work away from their desks if you can provide no other solutions for uninterrupted work environments. Work venues can include a quiet conference room, a coffee shop, or time at home to spend part of the day designing and writing code. They can use office time for communication, meetings, group discussions, or simple tasks such as reading email.

- Set up a corporate agreement on non-interrupt time that restricts interruptions to specific hours of the day. For example, meetings and engineering team discussions could all occur only in the afternoon hours; this allows the team a period of productive coding time in the morning. This approach works reasonably well if the company culture supports it.

- Allow engineers to occasionally work remotely, if they prefer it to working in the office. Keep in mind, however, that although this is advantageous in that it does not require a company-wide agreement, it can lead to problems. By working remotely, an engineer can become more of an individual contributor and less a part of the team. When engineers are away from their desks, fewer team discussions occur, and this can have a negative impact on the quality of the overall design. It also limits opportunities for team interaction, explanations, impromptu design decisions, and mentoring.

Office Space

Office layout schemes can have huge impacts on development efforts and effectiveness. In an open space layout or a cubicle layout, collaboration and conversation are encouraged, which can both please and annoy busy workers. Team conversations, however, lead to better designs and closer working relationships. Daily informal design discussions can provide a major advantage by encouraging collaboration. Other methods, such as having all team members working remotely and collaborating via email and telephone, are not as effective.

WARNING *Most engineering teams dislike a completely open space layout because of noise and the visual interruptions of people moving about.*

As you plan office spaces, make an effort to stay close to your team; being close by will help you stay informed about progress and problems and will help you build trust with your team. An office close to the team means you can readily coach others in private and conduct confidential conversations. If you are forced to choose between a remote office and a cube, take the cube only if you can arrange for conference rooms to be located nearby where private conversation can occur. You need to be able to close the door while coaching and correcting team members.

In a cube or open space environment, multiple conference rooms should be located near the development area to provide spaces for team collaboration. As you're reviewing space plans, insist on having more than two conference rooms. An insufficient number of rooms shared by everyone in the company will quickly fill up with standing meetings and customer visits.

Arrange the office space so that quality assurance (QA), marketing, technical writing, and engineering teams are located in close proximity. This encourages communication between teams, as most informal conversations occur within a short walk from a worker's desk. Informal conversations among developers and with other teams are generally beneficial and collaborative. If developers' only contact with marketing staff is through formal meetings, the quality of the relationships between members of the two teams will suffer, and so will the product.

Keep in mind, however, that developers need sound isolation from loud neighbors. Since both marketing and sales team members often use the phone and can generate a fair amount of noise, make sure engineering space is set up to reduce noise. Consider several solutions for keeping the work area quiet:

- Rearrange the office space to minimize sound distribution. You can reduce noise by installing dividers between noisy offices and engineering spaces.

- Set up developers' workspaces in an area with little foot traffic. Talk with other managers before moving the team to an isolated spot, however, because the point is to encourage quiet thinking time, not isolating and reducing communication. Avenues of communication must be clear and a cooperative attitude should drive any space decisions you make.

- Create an impromptu conversation area next to the development space. This area can include a large whiteboard and comfortable places to sit. If the space has good lighting (such as a large window) and a welcoming atmosphere, the team will use and appreciate it.

- Ask people to respect others and keep the noise levels down when conversing in hallways, cubicles, or other workspaces.

How Other Teams Communicate with Engineering

Growing companies' development teams create the best products when they communicate successfully with other departments within the company. Good interdepartmental communication keeps the concerns of the customers and the organization aligned with the work being accomplished. The most effective approach for creating successful companies and products is for the entire product team (development, sales, marketing, QA, and operations) to be able to discuss goals, problems, and solutions and then document them together to create working descriptions and a shared understanding of what those descriptions mean.[2]

Contact among company teams improves the product definition and allows developers and others to understand the *whole product* requirements.[3] Appropriate discussions help developers refine solutions before coding begins, saving time. Development, QA, sales, marketing, support, technical writers, trainers, and the customer need to collaborate to define the product efficiently and avoid significant backtracking later.

Open communications between development engineers and QA engineers allows QA to ask questions about the intent of the code, to create better tests, and to provide better coverage for the system, thus improving product quality. It also uplifts QA team morale, as they will be taking part in the development effort. In contrast, some companies limit QA access to engineering so that programmers can be more productive, but QA engineers feel impeded by this situation, finding it more difficult to do good work as the importance of their role is diminished.

TALK TO THE HAND

My current company completely isolates QA from the software engineers. Engineering management told QA that we could not talk directly to the engineers to ask questions, and we sometimes must wait multiple weeks for information we need to do our job. Our QA team is demoralized in general and the quality of our work suffers as a result. This is why I am looking for a new position.

—Unhappy QA engineer

QA team contact benefits engineers as well. QA can provide valuable feedback on the design of the user interface, for example. Close contact between the two groups during testing will allow developers to understand individual defects logged in the tracking tool. Defect clarity reduces

---

[2] See Chapter 5 for more discussion on collaborating on product definitions.

[3] You can read more about the *whole product* concept in Chapter 5.

mistakes in repairing defects, and improved defect repair improves the product schedule, as discussed in Chapter 17.

Consideration and scheduling usually improves collaborative efforts. Dealing with the conflicting needs of access and excess in communications with engineering requires that the manager define a strategy and get the teams to buy into that strategy. For example, to avoid excess interruptions with development engineers, QA engineers could bundle questions to present in an afternoon meeting rather than interrupting developers throughout the day with new questions.

Some managers try to isolate development teams from the other groups in the company by putting the team into a "black box." This forces people outside the engineering box to "throw requests over the wall," while engineering shoves software back out through a slot in the floor (or maybe through a network cable).

A development manager might build a black box around his team with the best of intentions. Usually, he adopts the policy because engineers complain that they cannot get work done because of interruptions from other departments. Engineers complain the loudest when they're behind schedule on a critical project. In response, the development manager tells the rest of the company not to talk to engineers.

On the surface, isolating the development team appears to solve several management problems—the manager no longer worries about other people asking engineers to work on tasks that were not assigned by him, for example. However, this approach leads to long-term failure, because engineers cannot collaborate with others, and it indicates a lack of trust in other managers to manage their teams. The lack of collaboration leads to long schedules, poor product definitions, and low quality.

New Manager, Old Habits

A small company might promote an engineer to development manager because of her technical and product knowledge. This newly minted manager, however, does not instinctively understand her role as a manager, but instead sees herself as an engineer who must now endure more interruptions and more paperwork. This new manager might in fact prefer to continue writing code full time, despite the perceived benefits of a management position. Without training and direction, she won't embrace her less code-oriented role and will believe that her only management responsibility is to answer team questions. The team will almost certainly become disillusioned with this manager.

Delivery pressures compound the new manager's problems. Because she sees that another trained engineer would help her team accomplish its work goals, she will be tempted to take off her manager hat and "be that engineer" for a while. She might assume responsibility for building a section of the code and use this assignment as a reason not to manage the team. When faced with difficult and unfamiliar challenges, new managers often fall back on what they do well—software development.

This problem is more common than it should be. An effective development manager needs to focus her energy on management and not writing code. Her manager should be aware of her needs and arrange for management training and coaching to assist her with the new role. If she is not a good management fit, even after extensive training and coaching, she should perhaps be sent back into full-time programming or another technical leadership role.

An exception to the "do not write code" rule, however, can occur if the new manager can apply her technical expertise to a tiny effort on a rush schedule. Such an effort should last only a few days. After the manager has written the required code, she should immediately train an engineer on the technology involved, so the short-term need should not arise again for that technical problem.

If the development manager with a team of one or two developers is effective at management as well as developing code, she might also be able to do both jobs. This works best for experienced managers who understand how to balance their management time with development effort. However, in most cases, a new manager who also works as an engineer has a fool for a boss.

In the end, a new development manager who likes to write code can spend personal time working on individual projects. Open source projects present great opportunities for working with and staying up to date on new technologies. Working on small projects in new languages or platforms on her own time can also help the new manager keep up with new technology.

Have Fun

One of the great advantages of working at a small firm is that it is easier to blow off steam without running afoul of the "stuffiness police." Make sure that the team atmosphere allows for some fun, especially at the end of the day. The occasional Nerf gun fight can energize the entire team.

Making jokes at work is another great way to keep the workplace congenial. Seeing humor in difficult situations can make the problems of the day seem less stressful. Besides, work is more fun that way.

Additional Reading

Here is some additional reading on topics presented in this chapter:

Managing Software Maniacs: Finding, Managing, and Rewarding a Winning Development Team, by Ken Whitaker (Wiley, 1994)

Managing Technical People: Innovation, Teamwork, and the Software Process, by Watts S. Humphrey (Addison-Wesley Professional, 1996)

Peopleware: Productive Projects and Teams, by Tom DeMarco and Timothy Lister (Dorsett House Publishing Company, 1999)

Slack: Getting Past Burnout, Busywork, and the Myth of Total Efficiency, by Tom DeMarco (Broadway, 2002)

4

GROWING A SOFTWARE TEAM

The human resources department probably defines your company's hiring process, but you, as the development manager, must take charge of the *candidate selection* process to grow your development team and company successfully. A company's hiring process usually consists of defined steps for opening the position, identifying candidates, filling out forms and getting approvals, setting up interviews, checking candidates' credentials, and making and approving an offer. However, this process does not define the candidate *selection* process, in which you decide *who* you want. Creating and following a candidate selection process is essential to finding the right developer for the job.

Because good development teams help small companies succeed and grow, your candidate selection process must be a priority. You define your team's character by your choice of new hires. Hiring the right person at the right time has a positive impact on productivity. Hiring the wrong person is painful and costly. A moderate amount of effort in hiring the best candidates will yield considerable results.

Without a candidate selection process, interviewers will likely focus on the wrong subjects. Engineering interviewers might judge candidates based on only a few issues: knowledge of technologies the company is currently using, projects listed on the candidate's resume, and the candidate's personality. But focusing on only a few traits ignores the importance of other key traits, including the candidate's success history, work habits, industry experience, people skills, and other general (versus specific) technical abilities. A narrow interview focus will result in weaker candidates who possess some technical skills, and although you might like a candidate on a personal level, he or she might not be a good performer on the job.

An organized approach to candidate selection requires that you define desired candidate traits, the handling of prescreening, the approach to the entire interview, and the decision-making process. Keep the big picture in mind as you consider the following areas systematically.

Designing a Selection Process

Start any engineering hiring activity by designing a selection process that outlines the steps you intend to follow as well as your approach to making the selection. Reasonable selection steps for a small company would start by identifying potential candidates from the resumes you have solicited, ideally through your network. Follow this with a phone screening of candidates, selecting the most promising applicants for office interviews. Next, you'll interview the candidates at your facility along with an interview team and convene a post-interview meeting to collect information. After these steps, you should be ready to make a hiring decision.

At each of these stages, select clear criteria for evaluating whether the candidate is a good fit and scale the effort of selection to be reasonable. Use effective methods of screening during the resume review and phone interview so that the few candidates that you interview at your facility are well worth the time spent interviewing them. And, most importantly, decide in advance what you are looking for in potential candidates relative to the position. To encourage this, the next section is devoted to *interview traits* that should help you choose the ideal person.

Interview Traits

Start by thinking about what makes a good development engineer. Using this information, your interview team can evaluate the candidates for these traits during the interview by assigning different interviewers to different traits. For each of the areas, create a list of sample questions that you will provide to members of the interview team. If you evaluate candidates in all of the following areas, you can get a broader picture of the candidate and his or her potential:

Technical skills	Communication skills
Success history	Personality
Cultural fit	Enthusiasm
Work habits and preferences	Problem-solving ability
Industry experience	Sense of humor
People skills	

Each of the traits requires an evaluation method. Direct questions work well for inquiring about the candidate's knowledge of the work. A mix of knowledge and behavioral questions can be useful. Answers to knowledge questions, of course, tell you about the scope of the candidate's knowledge, and answers to behavior questions tell you how the candidate applies that knowledge.

Knowledge questions can be rephrased as behavioral questions that can reveal the candidate's experience. For example, the knowledge question, "How do you prioritize tasks?", can be rephrased as a behavioral question: "Describe a project task that proved difficult to prioritize and the approach you took," or alternatively, "How did you prioritize your tasks on project X?" (where project X is a specific project on the candidate's resume).

Technical Skills

Technical skills include both foundational skills and specific skills. *Foundational* skills include the candidate's ability to program and his or her comprehension of computer science basics, while *specific* technical skills include the languages, programs, and libraries the new engineer will need to use immediately.

Any legitimate candidate must possess the skills required to do the job, and a set of skill-based questions can be useful in evaluating candidates. Unfortunately, interviewers often give too much weight to specific technical knowledge when evaluating potential employees. Instead, focus on the primary technology knowledge required by the engineer and do not over-emphasize secondary technologies. Most good engineers can learn new technologies quickly, so seeking only candidates who match a laundry list of technological expertise will unnecessarily eliminate some strong contenders.

Success History

An engineer's *success history* describes the engineer's successes with past assignments at other jobs. Talk with a trustworthy person who has worked with the candidate in the past, asking the following questions:

- What did the candidate do on the project to ensure that his work was high quality?
- Did the candidate complete his project work on time?
- Did his projects meet their functional goals?
- Did the candidate put in a strong effort to make the project a success?
- Did he ask for help when needed?
- Did the candidate resolve problems well as they arose?

If you cannot find a trustworthy source, or even if you have spoken with someone, you should ask the candidate the following questions during the interview:

- How do you ensure that your work is high quality?
- How often was your project work completed on time? Describe some situations.
- Did your last three projects meet the functional goals planned at the start?
- How did you organize your work on project *X*?
- When is it appropriate to ask for help on a project?
- Describe a problem that occurred during a project. How did you solve it?

Hearing how a candidate functioned in a previous work situation can be a good guide in determining how he will function at your company.

Cultural Fit

Because every company has a unique culture and corporate values, look for candidates who match your company's style and values. A person who is looking for a low-key work environment, for example, would not fare well in a company of hard-driven engineers who work around the clock. An intensively aggressive culture would challenge a quiet and accommodating employee. Candidates who fit within the company culture will be happier, more productive, and more likely to stick around. Candidates who do not fit will be more likely to leave the company for other opportunities when they realize the mismatch.

Evaluating cultural fit can be a challenging task. Most candidates want the job, so even if you ask them directly about their work culture and style, they might tell you what you want to hear—that is, what they know about the culture of your company. It often works better to ask behavioral questions like these:

- Describe the cultures of Company X and Company Y (companies that appear on the candidate's resume).

- How did they differ?

- What did you like about each company?

- What did you dislike about each?

- Of all the companies at which you have worked, which has the culture that suited you best?

After creating a list of cultural fit questions, consider and review your company's culture and the questions with your manager and with other department managers. They will have useful insights and can offer other good questions to ask. Reviewing culture with others can also help to keep the culture in alignment across the company. Chapter 9 discusses corporate culture in more detail.

Work Habits and Preferences

Work habits describe the engineer's habits in a work environment that influence the engineer's productivity. Ask the following questions:

- What is your attitude toward work?

- Where and when do you do your best work?

- What parts of the job do you enjoy the most and the least?

- How much do you work on a problem before you ask for help?

- How do you like to work with other groups—including other engineering teams, marketing, and QA?

- How do you follow up on requests you make of others?

- What motivates you?

- What are your expectations about work schedule and overtime?

- What are your favorite and least favorite types of projects?

- What kind of work environment do you prefer?

- How do you like to be managed?

Here are behavioral questions about project *X* that you noted on a candidate's resume:

- How did you go about organizing your work on project *X*?

- How did you set priorities for project *X*?

- How did you track the details of project *X*?

Industry Experience

Industry experience describes background knowledge of the industry (rather than technology and programming knowledge). For example, if the company supplies medical software, does the candidate understand the medical software field and specific regulations? You can evaluate candidates by asking about industry information relative to the position.

People Skills

People skills describe how the engineer interacts with others, especially when a conflict occurs. When examining a candidate's people skills, consider the candidate's willingness to listen, her openness in sharing information, how she resolves conflicts, her ability to take constructive criticism, and whether she is flexible with assignments. Questions you might ask about people skills include the following:

- Describe a conflict with a co-worker and how you handled it.

- How much information is appropriate to share with co-workers?

- When and why would you hold back information?

- Describe a criticism you received at work that led to your improving your performance.

- Describe a work situation that required flexibility on your part.

Communication Skills

Communication skills describe the candidate's ability to talk, listen, write, and present information. You can assess her talking and listening skills during the interview. To evaluate her writing skills, ask the candidate to submit an example of her technical writing, such as a conference paper (but avoid proprietary information). To demonstrate presentation skills, ask her to present a "chalk talk" on a technical topic. Ask the candidate to draw and describe a software system; this will give you better insight into how well she understands her past work and how well she can communicate her understanding.

Personality

Consider the candidate's *personality* as you judge whether he will work well with the rest of the team. It's easiest to identify red-flag areas, such as these:

- Did the candidate not let you get a word in edgewise during the interview?

- Did he seem a little too chummy, or not friendly enough?

- Did he appear too eager to please and impress?

- Did he have too many negative comments about past situations?

Enthusiasm

People often use candidates' *enthusiasm* to decide which of several quali-
fied candidates to hire. This is generally a good thing. Although engineers
are usually more reserved than sales people, for example, a show of enthusiasm for the job and company is important. Successful employees are
usually enthusiastic about their work.

For young companies, employee enthusiasm can be of particular importance. Young companies need people who are passionately committed to
the business's success and not just their own. Later in the growth phase,
you can hire candidates who are enthusiastic about the technology and
possibilities but don't quite qualify as company "true believers."

Problem-Solving Ability

Problem solving defines the engineer's ability to solve arbitrary dilemmas.
Though some problems can have little to do with the actual software technology, you can and should evaluate the candidate's thought processes
while dealing with problems. As an engineer encounters new problems
outside her current technical knowledge, her ability to think through
approaches to new issues shows her creativity and flexibility.

Ask the engineer about a real and current difficulty your team is facing.
You can extend this to ask the candidate to step through a solution, perhaps including some sample coding for a solution.

Several companies, including Microsoft, have a long history of focusing on
problem-solving tests during the interview process, as William Poundstone
describes in his book, *How Would You Move Mount Fuji?* (see "Additional
Reading" on page 81). As the book title suggests, asking a person how to
move a mountain can get him thinking about how to break down a large
problem into simpler steps. This book offers a good set of general problems and Internet links for finding more.

Giving an engineer an opportunity to address a general problem during
the interview will reveal several aspects of his problem-solving skills. First, it
will show how willing he is to ask questions of the interviewer. This carries
over to how willing he will be to ask for help on tough problems. Second,
it will tell you how he tackles large issues and what skills he uses to resolve

complicated issues. Third, it will tell you how he reacts to a difficult problem that does not have a textbook answer.

Sense of Humor

With all the tasks that engineers are asked to do, do you even need to ask why a sense of humor is important?

Pulling It All Together

With a list of interview topics in mind, you should find it easier to design a selection process based on the most important topics. Consider a good candidate's most important traits as you move through the interview stages—phone screening, interviews, review sessions, and deciding who to hire.

Phone Screening

A full-day interview, as discussed next, gives the interview team an opportunity to evaluate a candidate fully. However, interviews usually consume more than a day's worth of engineering time per candidate if preparations and reviews are considered. Typically, if you're interviewing more than five candidates at your facility, you did insufficient screening earlier. Conducting a preliminary phone screening (or even a face-to-face lunch screening) eliminates overbooking of full-day interviews.

During phone screening, your job is to determine whether the candidate will pass the minimum bar. One approach is to make a list of each category and add a plus, zero (neutral), or minus symbol next to each category based on the quality of the candidate's responses. In the end, invite candidates with the most positives and fewest negatives for a face-to-face interview. It's a simple but effective measurement, and you can use the negative points as follow-up topics during the interview.

The progression of issues to cover during a phone screening session might look something like this:

> **Ask about knowledge of your company.**   A candidate who knows nothing about your company gets a minus.

Discuss relevant industry experience.   Considerable experience is a plus, and very little is a minus.

Ask about a work-related effort.   Focus on efforts for which he was particularly successful or proud of the results. Self-motivated candidates should generally feel proud of work they have done. If the candidate can't point to anything, that should be a warning sign.

Ask about a conflict situation and the resolution.   An engineer who cannot describe a conflict is not a good hire—a minus. One who describes a reasonable conflict and a positive solution is a *big* plus.

Ask about the depth of technical experience.   Focus particularly on the areas that are important to you. Judge the candidate's experience by how it fits your company's needs. An engineer who has worked with many of your technologies can usually learn the others quickly.

Assess the candidate's ability to communicate.   Clear, concise answers during the screening session are a big plus. If the answers are too short or long and rambling, it's a minus.

Ask about salary expectations.   Try to determine whether the candidate is widely out of line with your budget and his background. Many candidates will be coy about presenting a number, but you can usually get a range. If an engineer is looking for a salary way above his experience level, it's a minus.

Ask whether the candidate has any questions.   Any reasonable questions are a plus, while not asking any questions is a minus and shows lack of interest or preparation.

The Office Interview

The office interview provides your best opportunity for evaluating a candidate. Plan in advance not only what information you want to know but how you are going to get it. Discuss this information with the interview team to make sure that each interviewer is prepared and does not cover identical ground.

At least five people, including you, should interview the candidate to provide a broad perspective on his or her fit. When selecting the interview team, choose people with a breadth of experience rather than just depth. Interviewers should represent different interview concerns, have good interviewing skills, make a positive impression on the candidate, and understand the selection criteria. Interviewers should include people from other teams—such as representatives from sales and marketing. Variety in the interviewers' backgrounds and styles will help make the interview process more well rounded.

When planning the interview schedule, think of the day from the candidate's perspective. Keep the interview process from becoming an exhausting marathon lasting longer than eight hours. Allow the candidate to take a breather during lunch by keeping the conversation lighter and less inquisitorial. After all, she needs an opportunity to enjoy her meal. Also, ensure that each interview lasts about an hour. Half-hour interviews are worse than ineffective and can lead to shallow impressions and poor hiring choices.

Coaching Your Interview Team

Interview teams need to be coached prior to the interview. This helps ensure that team members collect the information needed to make a hiring decision. You can also take this opportunity to recommend approaches to selling your company to the candidate. Without coaching or encouragement, interviewers may see the interview as just another peripheral task to get done so they can get back to "real work."

At your interview coaching meeting, start by describing the goals of the interview and the position the company is trying to fill. Make sure team members understand the skill levels and experience expected for the position as well as your view of what an ideal candidate would be like. Without this clarity, interview teams may interview for the wrong set of skills.

Assign specific responsibilities to each interviewer to ensure that they get good coverage of the candidate. Each interviewer should evaluate one to three different candidate traits discussed earlier. So they are prepared to find the information, ask interviewers to carefully review the candidate's resume prior to the interview and prepare a list of questions. To assist, you can recommend questions and interview strategies. You can also ask interviewers to take notes and capture quotes during the interview, which are especially useful during the post-interview review.

Perhaps most importantly, interview team members need to plan how they will determine a candidate's technical competence. Discuss potential approaches to finding this information, such as:

- Ask a candidate to solve a specific code problem using his language of choice

- Discuss details of the programming language your team uses

- Ask for an explanation of a section of code you supply

- Request that the candidate identify defects in a code snippet

- Ask the candidate to suggest improvements to a predefined block of code

Remind your team that the goal is not to "trip up" interviewees, but rather to understand their abilities and approach. The questions a candidate asks and those he does not ask during a technical interview are very revealing about how effective the candidate will be as part of your team.

The interview session provides an opportunity for you and your team to evaluate the candidate, but it's also an opportunity for the candidate to decide whether or not she wants the position. More importantly, it's an opportunity for you to sell your company. Selling your company is vital even if you don't want to hire the candidate, because regardless of the outcome of the interview, the candidate will likely convey her impressions of your company to her colleagues. Consequently, you should always keep the interview positive and professional.

At the end of the day, take the opportunity to gather some feedback from the candidate. Ask for her impressions of your company and the interview process.

Interview Sessions to Avoid

Setting up the interview process is more than scheduling meetings. When arranging interviews, many managers focus on the impact on the interviewers rather than the impact on the interviewee. For a moment, consider the candidate's perspective and reflect on these awkward and intense interview schedules.

If your company specializes in any of the following negative approaches—or "stress interviews" in general—change your approach to focus on more positive tactics that encourage the engineer to want to work at your company. The impact of poor interview strategies is experienced beyond the candidate being interviewed, as he will relay this information to friends and others. Who knows—his stories may even end up in a book!

Marathon or Stress Interview

A *marathon interview* is unusually long, typically lasting more than eight hours. Marathon interviews are a form of *stress interview* designed to stress the candidate to see how he reacts. Stress interviews are especially undesirable for software development work, because programmers do their best work when they are not overly stressed. Their reactions to stress don't produce useful information or useful work; stress simply lowers the apparent performance of the candidate. Stressing a candidate is also a good way to put your company on the candidate's "I won't work for you or let any of my friends work for you either" list.

Keep the length of the interview reasonable, with eight continuous hours being the maximum length. Better to schedule a six-hour process or split a longer interview into two days, since most candidates burn out after six hours and will not represent themselves as well.

A VERY LONG DAY

My longest interview was for a local job reporting to a manager in another city. The company booked me on a flight with the hiring manager, so we talked throughout the flight. The interview was the next day, starting with breakfast at 7 AM. It went straight through to dinner and ended at 8 PM—13 hours. Near the end of the day, I was very tired and having difficulty focusing on the interview.

—Software engineer

Hit-and-Run Interview

In a *hit-and-run interview*, the hiring manager puts a candidate on a five-hour or longer flight to the company locale, interviews the candidate briefly, and then immediately sends her home with no delay. Often, the reason for the strained travel arrangements is to save the company money, at the expense of the interviewee. These interviews occur most often with larger organizations at which human resources (HR) organizes interviews but faces restrictive travel policies and budgets for interview travel. This interview shares all the exhaustive qualities of a marathon interview, but it also indicates little concern for the candidate's time, emphasizes the worst in cost-cutting policies, and leaves the candidate with a bad overall impression.

FLIGHT TO NOWHERE

My remote interview came after I had interviewed successfully with the local team. The next step was to interview with the remote boss. The company gave me an indirect flight to cut costs, but that added four hours each way over the direct flight. In addition, they set it up as a one-day trip to avoid having to pay for a hotel room. The trip would leave a two-hour window in the destination city for the interview.

The trip required me to get up at 4 AM to catch a 6 AM flight. After the stopover, I arrived in the afternoon local time, and the hiring manager delayed the meeting for 40 minutes. He interviewed me for 20 minutes and then had me call another person for a phone interview. I left two hours after I arrived. I took the same double-leg flight home, arriving home after midnight.

This trip told me what I needed to know about the company, and it was not good.

—Engineer

Lunch Committee Interview

The *lunch committee interview* turns a seemingly normal lunch interview into a stress-and-grace test for the candidate. Unlike the other examples, this approach does not take much effort to set up. Four or more people conduct their only interview of the day during lunch with the candidate, loading it with specific goals and a short time limit. Each interviewer proceeds in sequence to ask questions of the candidate that require long answers, ensuring that the candidate cannot eat. (Bonus points are awarded for catching the interviewee trying to take a bite right before the next question is asked.)

With the right intentions, lunch interviews can be useful and positive. A positive lunch interview can uncover the interests and passions of the candidate and also helps you understand more about her personality and cultural fit. It can give the candidate a mental rest so she will not be worn down by the afternoon. Best of all, a friendly lunch shows respect for the candidate rather than a focus on your company's desire to cram as much as possible into a day.

Review Session

After you incorporate the interview team's input, the selection process needs to include a way to get that information back to you, the hiring manager. A *review session* should occur as soon as possible after the interviews take place so that the information is fresh in everyone's minds. If team members are unable to attend the session, you can talk to them directly prior to the review session.

To prevent a few individuals from dominating the conversation, ask people to write down their assessments for each of the focus areas before the discussion starts. Some companies start with a quick "thumbs up/thumbs down" evaluation of each candidate to get the team's assessment quickly before discussing details.

Give every interviewer an opportunity to describe his or her impression of the candidate. Each has a unique perspective based on a particular interview focus. The hiring manager should speak last, as your opinion can unduly bias other interviewers from fully expressing their opinions, especially if they have reservations about the candidate.

Ask each interviewer to describe his results, top-down: Start with the conclusion and work down to more detail. Each interviewer should give at least two supporting reasons for his conclusion; these reasons should be more specific than "I didn't think she would fit in." Then the interviewer can go into details of what he decided, ideally, supported by a quote or two from the candidate himself.

Ask interviewers to answer these questions after they give their thoughts:

- What surprised you about the candidate?

- How has the other interviewers' feedback so far disagreed with your assessment?

- How specific was the candidate in his answers?

When you have finished going around the table, if you find that some information from interviewers is contradictory, continue the discussion, and ask for more supporting information in the area of interest. Before you leave the meeting, you should feel that you have all the information you need to make the hiring decision. If you like the candidate but don't have enough information in some area, make a point of setting up another time to talk to the candidate again to resolve any open issues. If another meeting is not possible, do not hire the candidate.

Making the Choice

As the hiring manager, you decide whom to hire; don't make the decision based on a vote by the interview team. The interview process should have provided you with the information you need to narrow down the candidates and make a good decision. Make offers to candidates about which you have no serious concerns, who meet your selection criteria, and who you really believe will be a great addition to your team.

Even with a good interviewing process, you can have trouble deciding whom to hire. If you are unsure even after completing the process, it might be wise to keep looking for the engineer you really want. Don't hire someone full time who will solve only a short-term problem. Hiring a marginal candidate is rarely a good idea, so be sure you're enthusiastic about the person before you make that offer.

HIRE IN HASTE, REGRET IN LEISURE

Early in my management career, I worked for a company whose profitability varied considerably quarter to quarter. The management strategy was to freeze hiring in bad quarters and open hiring in good quarters. For a two-year period, it seemed that every quarter was alternating between good and bad.

I was trying to hire an engineer. Each quarter, I had to start the approval and justification process, which took weeks. When top management would give the approval to hire, my search for candidates would take several weeks. I would bring in several candidates for interviews and finally select someone. Twice in a row, the whole cycle took longer than a quarter and a new hiring freeze was on by the time the interviews were finished. Frustrated by the process, I made the mistake of hiring an engineer quickly. The ongoing underperformance of this engineer made him a bad choice that I had to live with.

—New engineering manager

Additional Reading

Here is some additional reading on topics presented in this chapter:

101 Great Answers to the Toughest Interview Questions, by Ron Fry (CENGAGE Delmar Learning, 2006)

Dynamics of Software Development, by Jim McCarthy (Microsoft Press, 2006)

How Would You Move Mount Fuji? Microsoft's Cult of the Puzzle: How the World's Smartest Companies Select the Most Creative Thinkers, by William Poundstone (Little, Brown and Company, 2003)

Smart and Gets Things Done: Joel Spolsky's Concise Guide to Finding the Best Technical Talent, by Joel Spolsky (Apress, 2007)

PART II

PRODUCT AND TECHNOLOGY

This section of the book covers product and technology, two areas at the heart of the intellectual property of the company. Superior product definition leads to superior product, and good technical tools and methods enable quicker high-quality results. Understanding how to balance product and technology is one of the secrets of effective development management.

5

DEFINING THE PRODUCT

At its core, a *product definition* is not a knowledge or resource issue; it is a *relationship* issue. When you and your development team build strong relationships with marketing staff and with your customers, defining the product becomes much simpler. Open and regular communication with members of other teams can help you align your development goals with company goals. In addition, developing trust among corporate divisions as well as between the company and its customers can result in a quicker consensus on the most appropriate product definition.

Some of the most difficult relationship strains occur between marketing and development teams. Establishing a positive relationship between these teams can be challenging, because the roles played by marketing and engineering staff are very different. Marketing's function is to understand customer needs and promise the solutions required to meet those needs.

Engineering's role emphasizes the practical aspects of building products efficiently and then supporting them after they are built. With a strong relationship between the two teams, they can work together to devise the best and most balanced solutions to meet the customer's and company's needs.

This chapter covers the basics of defining a product. You'll learn about crucial relationships, study example processes for creating product definitions, read about what goes into a product definition, and learn a bit about prototyping and how to use templates to help define a product. In addition, you'll learn how products are put together and how different partners in the relationship perceive the product.

Product Definition Process

Creating a refined product definition can be a challenge for companies for several reasons: The number of options surpasses the company's ability to build them, information is lacking, and the relationships between marketing and engineering are weak. However, if the marketing and engineering teams' relationship can be improved, they can work together to define the product through a process of high-level reviews and quick cost assessments.

Creating a joint and cooperative definition doesn't necessarily imply that engineering and marketing have completely overlapping responsibilities and authorities in product definition. Some companies give engineering the final word, while others give marketing the lead role. When the marketing team is strong, the marketing-driven approach usually works the best. In either situation, cooperative behavior produces the best results.

During the initial product definition process, short daily discussions between marketing and engineering encourage more rapid closure on choosing the best options to pursue. The daily discussion becomes a *continuous conversation* that allows iterative refinement of the requirements and ultimately the definition. The teams can analyze the feature costs, timeline, and definition in stages—be they quick overviews, intermediate level reviews, or fuller definition reviews. At each stage, the teams work together to select and eliminate options through thoughtful analysis and data collection.

Ideally, the marketing/engineering evaluation works as follows: First, engineering works with marketing to define preliminary quick estimates of product size and scope. Next, both teams agree on how to pare down the list. Remaining items are analyzed with more detail. Then this process is repeated until both teams agree on a final set of product definitions, costs, and timelines. Figure 5-1 illustrates this filtering process.

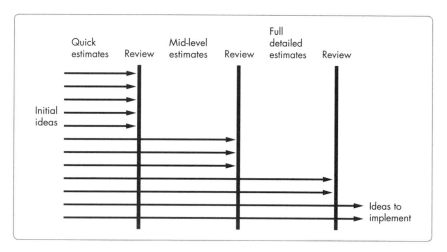

Figure 5-1: Sifting through initial product ideas to produce final choices

If a trusting relationship does not exist between the marketing and engineering teams, the steps in the process will degrade. For example, if marketing treats preliminary quick estimates from engineering as full commitments and pressures engineering to meet those commitments, engineers will probably stop providing quick estimates. Engineers create quick estimates based on limited information; these estimates are unsuitable for accurate budgeting and scheduling, but fine for establishing ballpark costs so that the initial direction can be set. Providing quick estimates as cost ranges emphasizes the uncertainty involved, but the analysis is insufficient to use in creating an accurate project schedule.

Once mistrust has soured the engineering and marketing relationship, the very expensive process shown in Figure 5-2 ensues. In this case, both teams treat conversations as mini-contracts, eliminating speculative discussions. All feature and project ideas require extensive evaluation before engineering will provide any type of estimate, and engineering devotes considerable

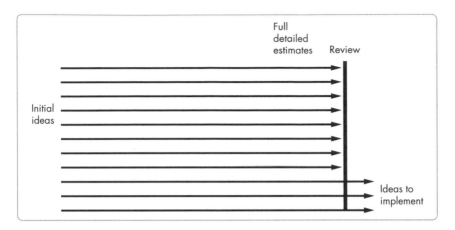

Figure 5-2: Wasteful selection process

time to precise, in-depth estimates. Marketing has to invest substantially more time in fully defining every idea before presenting them to engineering. Worst of all, engineering must create detailed estimates for *all* of the options before presenting them to marketing.

Why do so many companies choose such a wasteful approach to product definition? Past bad behavior usually drives defensive relationships. If in the past, engineering produced quick estimates based on initial ideas, and then marketing insisted that these numbers be treated as final, engineering has little incentive to provide quick estimates in the future.

When operating under a successful approach, however, engineering and marketing can collect more information and refine definitions for the ideas that will be implemented. Figure 5-3 illustrates the pyramid of information associated with refining a definition. Each layer reflects more product information.

A refined definition starts at the *top level* and focuses on the customer's needs. As the definition process continues, marketing and engineering produce a more detailed description of the product: detailed requirements, high-level implementation descriptions, detailed concept models and prototypes, and then the functional specifications. Then engineering considers the product architecture, examines the requirements of the product's construction, and prepares a detailed description of its features and user interface. Finally, engineering and marketing together flesh out the complete definition of the product offering.

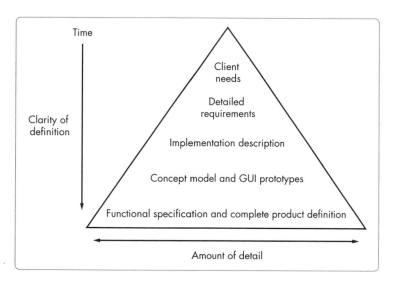

Figure 5-3: Clarity of definition versus amount of detail

The process is challenging because the teams must make product decisions based on incomplete information. Decisions involve trade-offs between features, timelines, resources, and implementation approaches. Making sound *initial* decisions requires not waiting until development is building the product before thoroughly analyzing what needs to be built. If questions about the technical feasibility of specific functions of features arise, a senior engineer should be asked to create simple prototypes for these technical areas before building the software. Prototypes are discussed in detail later on.

Product Definition Contents

As you strive to define your product, create a document that outlines product specifications, and continue to update this document as you work with marketing staff and customers to refine the focus. Sketches and notes might be useful for initial discussions, but they will not provide sufficient background data for the future as you are required to make revisions and improvements.

Small companies benefit from short, concise definitions rather than formal specifications. Instead of creating a complex specification that's time consuming to create and maintain and difficult to read, create your product definition with readability and idea sharing in mind.

Simple definitions improve development agility. Follow these general guidelines:

- Keep the documentation short and readable. Focus on high-level definitions of functionality, and do not elaborate on detailed specifics. Simplicity in definition can sometimes require negotiating with marketing and other teams about the nature of the document. Too much complexity will render the document less readable as reviewers fill in every detail.

- Avoid adding implementation details as part of the definition, because they do not provide clarity to the solution and can limit your options later when you're considering how to supply what the customer needs.

- Keep the document readable in layout. Avoid a formalized template that requires labeling and numbering every statement.

- Include pictures as focal points for written definitions. Reviewers might have a hard time visualizing the top-level system definition if only text is provided. A diagram can be used to clarify difficult concepts and acts as a catalyst for ongoing discussions of the system.

- Layer the discussion by starting with overview information before explaining the lower-level details. Overview information provides context for the product including audience, most important objectives, and problems solved. Engineers often describe systems linearly from start to finish. For nontechnical or even unfamiliar readers, an overview provides context that makes the lower-level details much easier to understand.

- Create user interface prototypes as part of the product definition, and use them selectively in your requirements document. Pages and pages of screen captures don't add context or value.

- Consider employing use cases to define sections of the product. A *use case* describes all the steps a user would take to obtain a specific goal using the product. Use cases supplement and clarify the product definition but should not be considered full specifications in themselves.

- Make requirements testable and nonambiguous. Avoid words that require interpretation or those that QA cannot measure. Requirements outside of functional requirements fall into this category. For example, don't say your product requires *rapid response, high speed,* and *support for large data sets.* It's better to use definitions such as *2 seconds or less response on all screens using our standard hardware, translation data rate minimum of 1.5MB per second,* and *support for data sets of 500 million user records.* Creating nonambiguous and testable requirements doesn't mean that the specification has to be formal and extensive. Just ensure that what you do specify is clear and worthwhile. "Good quality" doesn't cut it.

- Use a requirements definition template to organize your requirements document. A template organizes the information in a consistent way from document to document, which provides an easy context for people in your company who read it. A good template can help you avoid omitting important topics if it properly lists all of the types of information needed. The best templates are accepted by the team as being practical and useful—not just a form to fill out to keep management happy.

A number of good templates for requirement definitions exist. Review multiple templates before selecting one that suits your needs. Figure 5-4 illustrates an example template. (For this template, instructions are written in italics. You should replace all the words in italics with the information required for your project.)

Prioritize requirements as you define the product. If you discuss priorities with marketing early on, product definitions will be smoother and you can avoid having to check back with marketing to clarify issues. Establish priorities for *agile* and *iterative* processes, as they allow you to make trade-offs in the design. They also assist in the project planning, allowing you to organize efforts to focus on highest priority items earlier. Completing the highest priority features first will minimize problems that occur when plans are changed or schedules are shortened as business needs change.

The Whole Product Concept

Customers demand products that offer complete solutions to meet their needs. Software makes a start at solving a customer's problems, but it often falls short in several areas. It must meet the customer's expectations; it

Title Line
Requirements Description
    Author: *Author name*
    Revision: *Revision version*
    Issue Date: *Today's date*

1. Introduction

    1.1 Purpose and Scope
        For software, describe the intent of the project in two or three sentences. Also add a short description of the audience for this document. For example, is it only internal or for external customers as well?

    1.2 Assumptions
        List of assumptions

    1.3 Open Items
        List of items that are incomplete

    1.4 Definitions
        List of definitions used in the document

2. Feature Overview

    This section should provide the reader with an overview of the software, without providing too much detail.

    2.1 System Diagram, Workflow
        Overview of the system, workflow, or site

    2.2 Feature Overview
        List of features in context of the system diagram

    2.3 Other General Overview Items
        Description of items that apply globally to the system

3. Detailed Descriptions

    This section describes the details of the software functionality.

    3.1 Feature 1
        Detailed description of Feature 1

    3.2 Feature 2
        Detailed description of Feature 2

    Continue with 3.*N*

4. General Requirements

    This section includes requirements that are not functional. For example, usability, speed, access, and quality. Quantify all features with numbers.

Figure 5-4: Sample requirements template

should offer flexible options; it should include APIs or other interconnections so that it can integrate with other systems; and it should include supporting services, such as access to trained call center staff, to professional training, and to onsite support. Software that provides solutions in all these areas is called a *whole product* offering.

When defining a product, consider the whole product concept and not just product features. Consider your customers' needs and think about how they make purchasing decisions. Do your product's features *and* supporting infrastructure meet customer needs? If not, adding new features might be only part of the answer; you might also consider adding new interfaces with other systems that make the product easier to deploy in various environments.

NOTE   *You can learn more about the whole product concept by reading* Crossing the Chasm *by Geoffrey A. Moore or* The Marketing Imagination *by Theodore Levitt. (See "Additional Reading" on page 107.) Then discuss your product definition with the marketing team with this concept in mind.*

Define the Product Using Prototypes

The marketing group's first attempt at product definition provides a high-level view of the customer's requirements. This definition does not include enough detail for engineering to build the product, however; several additional layers of information are required to help you build a solution. Engineering must create working definitions of the product's *user interface (UI), application programming interface (API)*, and *business logic*. The most expensive way to create such working-level definitions is for individual engineers to decide how to build the software, build it, and then present the results to marketing. Invariably, this approach leads to several expensive cycles of rework. A better way is to spend the required time up front defining the product in key areas and working with marketing until reaching agreement on a product definition.

After the product has been sufficiently defined, presenting a series of prototypes to marketing and the customer along with new ideas will allow for several quick review cycles and a better final product.

Prototypes in General

Engineers want to deliver software that solves the customer's problems, rather than simply delivering code that's been built based on a marketing requirements document. Generally, marketing and the customer are unable to provide a detailed definition of the best solution. They need to experience a *prototype* to appreciate and understand what they like and dislike about various choices. Prototypes allow customers to "touch and feel" the product to help them make informed decisions. Without a prototype, realizing a clear product definition can require a long process of trial and error.

Prototypes are helpful in obtaining information from the customer and marketing staff. The process only begins with the first prototype developers create—the development team will collect feedback and improve the prototype until marketing and ultimately the customer are pleased with the results. The feedback and prototype improvement cycle enables you to define the product effectively. It also protects you from time wasted traveling too far down the wrong development paths.

You can use a number of techniques to create prototypes. Paper sketches of the interfaces can be presented in different sequences to describe concepts to customers. Better yet, you can use software-based tools to create interfaces that resemble the final software. Many such tools are designed specifically to assist in creating rapid prototypes, allowing you to define a prototype that is both accessible and easy to distribute to others for their feedback. Some example systems are discussed in this chapter.

After you have created a prototype, review it with marketing and the customer, as well as with other teams. Talk with QA, customer service, and operations; they can offer new insights into how the product definition prototype affects other parts of the company and help you define ways to improve the product.

Quick and Nimble Approaches

Limit the time spent creating prototypes to make it easier to consider alternative approaches and changes later on. In addition, avoid creating expensive prototypes, because the high costs can make developers less likely to investigate alternative approaches.

Discourage engineers from spending more than a few days creating each prototype. A developer who has spent many days creating a prototype might be reluctant to make significant changes to it. The developer might also be tempted to turn the prototype into the product itself, which is a bad idea.

Prototypes are usually discarded after you've learned what you need to know from them—another reason to limit resources spent on prototyping. Discarding prototypes will prevent you from being saddled with the flaws inherent in a quick construction. For this reason, you should discourage or prohibit the reuse of prototype code in production code. If the prototype tests the technical feasibility of a concept and the engineer must write it in the language of the final product, ask the engineer not to use the prototype code. Have her build the application from scratch, because building the product on top of prototype code hurts its long-term quality.

WARNING *Always throw prototypes away. Do not use prototype code in products.*

Finally, make it clear to everyone involved that the prototype is *not the product* to avoid unnecessary negative or positive expectations associated with the prototype.

Clickable User Interface Prototypes

With a *clickable prototype*, the user can click through and navigate UI screens. Clickable prototypes should have no features or functions connected to any of the clickable buttons. Their only purpose is to let the customer test the UI. By experimenting with clickable prototypes, customers can get a feel for the navigation and workflow of the planned system.

Many commercial UI prototyping tools are available. These are some examples of popular commercial tools for rapid prototyping.

Microsoft Visual Basic

Visual Basic has a great drag-and-drop interface, and you avoid the temptation of developing the final product atop the prototype since most commercial programs are not written in Visual Basic. *http://msdn2.microsoft.com/en-us/vbasic/default.aspx*

Microsoft Visio

Visio allows you to create pages that can be linked to icons to build a UI prototype that is clickable. *http://office.microsoft.com/en-us/visio/default.aspx*

Adobe Dreamweaver

By using the HTML editor Dreamweaver, you can create a highly portable UI simulation that people can load in any web browser. *http://www.adobe.com/products/dreamweaver/*

Axure RP

Axure RP is a rapid prototyping tool that can create HTML pages or an executable that you can distribute easily to a client for review. *http://www.axure.com/*

You can also create prototypes using systems not normally considered to be prototyping tools, such as Microsoft Word, PowerPoint, Excel, or Adobe Acrobat. Using these tools, you can produce a sequence of screens to represent various workflows.

User Interface Design

Create the UI design early in the product life cycle. By all means, don't wait to improve the UI until after you have shipped the product! It will be too late to make significant changes without incurring significant costs and creating confusion for your customers. Many engineering teams without UI experience design an interface based on ease of implementation rather than ease of use. As the interface is the primary customer contact point, a poor interface can make customers unhappy with a product, even if the rest of the product is superior.

If the product requires a particularly challenging UI design, hire a human factors engineer or usability engineer to help refine the interface. These experts understand how people work with software and can help you make the product easy to use. Their input can greatly improve the product and your customer's satisfaction with it and with your company.

Human factors engineers and usability engineers are not usually employees at small firms, because they typically don't have enough work to justify full-time employment. Hiring a usability consultant can be expensive but is a worthwhile expenditure, and good usability engineers are worth their fees.

The consulting engineer can quickly devise great solutions for new UIs and evaluate existing UIs.

Build a Relationship with Marketing

A cooperative arrangement and good relationship between engineering and marketing can help both teams jointly own the product definition, roadmap, and delivery. In fact, they *should* jointly own these things. A good relationship with marketing will help you do a better job as development manager, improve the quality of your company's product through better definitions, and make it easier to respond to problems that occur during the project tenure.

Reach out to marketing and build a trusting relationship at the start. Behave in a manner that encourages mutual trust and cooperation between the marketing and development teams. Help build the partnership by communicating regularly—daily, or at least several times a week—to build trust and increase your understanding of each other's ways of working and particular needs. Your team's relationship with marketing will be defined by how you handle failures, as much as how you handle successes. Partnership means joint success and failure. When the partnership produces success, you can share the credit. When part of the project fails, you can jointly accept the failure rather than trying to minimize your roles or blame the other party.

To be a strong partner with marketing, you should understand basic marketing concepts, including how product requirements are defined by marketing, how items are packaged, and how various types of customers can be served by a single product offering. Spend time learning about the science and art of marketing by consulting books or signing up for an introductory marketing course.

Although marketing and engineering are the major sources of product definitions in many small companies, other teams also contribute to the product definition. Make sure that you build relationships with operations, sales, quality assurance, and finance. A great relationship with marketing without support from other teams can lead to lack of company support for any plan. Understanding the concerns of and seeking input from other groups will strengthen your team's relationships throughout the company.

Avoid Poor Relationships

You might be surprised to hear this, but the relationship between marketing and engineering teams can be adversarial at times. A natural push-pull tension exists between marketing and engineering over product definition, feature set, cost, and delivery schedules. Marketing teams commonly complain that engineering delivered the product late and that it is missing features. Development teams complain that marketing folks keep changing their minds about what features to include or that they have made feature promises to a client without first discussing them with engineering.

Finger-pointing and defensive behaviors will quickly erode a work environment and slow down product development, because each group will demand a more complete analysis before responding to the other group's concerns, as discussed earlier in the chapter. Marketing and engineering teams that cannot work together cooperatively can make the product development process a nightmare. Game playing, such as "we must have one more feature, but you cannot change the schedule," can frustrate both teams, ruin the product definition process, and wreck morale.

POLITICS VERSUS PRODUCTIVITY

The marketing person I worked with had a long laundry list of things he wanted. To help with initial paring, I did a quick order-of-magnitude sizing on all of the items based on sketchy definitions. We agreed that we would revisit those of interest and figure out the details and then estimate them. Doing a detailed estimate on each item would take too long and required a lot more definition time.

The marketing VP stepped in and selected the items he wanted. He insisted that quick estimates were the final estimates and that he would base the final plans on them. Because of the politics of the company, saying no was not an option. This VP's actions changed the dynamic of engineering-marketing cooperation in the wrong way. Engineering would not do quick estimates for marketing going forward.

—Engineering manager

Keep Marketing and Engineering Teams Together

Marketing and engineering teams should be located in the same facility to encourage cooperation and produce the best product definitions. When team offices are in the same vicinity, the teams can communicate better and build trust. The opportunities for creating a joint product definition are improved when the teams can easily talk and share their ideas on a regular basis.

Conversely, splitting marketing and engineering into two separate facilities can make it difficult to establish the close working relationship that good product definitions require. With remote teams, people miss opportunities for casual communication that helps build trusting relationships. They communicate more often through documents, email, and formal meetings. Whiteboard discussions, which can be valuable during the product definition process, are awkward to set up when teams reside in different locations.

Build a Balanced Relationship

One of the most important requirements for building a good relationship between marketing and engineering is *balance*. You should be able to say no to a marketing request without that decision being considered a rebuff. Disagreements needn't result in the marketing manager asking the CEO to force a decision upon you. If you regularly find yourself in situations in which you cannot say *no*, perhaps you should say *yes* to a new position.

Before saying *no* to a marketing request, consider alternative choices that could be answered with a *maybe* or a *yes*. If you offer options to marketing's requests, you can improve the collaborative relationship and work together to seek the best solutions.

When looking for positive alternatives, consider these options: fit in a new feature or new product later in the product roadmap, swap a planned set of functionality with the new request, or delay a planned release to add the new functionality. In any case, be sure that you can support the alternative solutions that you propose.

Customer Perception of the Product

The customer's perception of a product never really matches reality. For that matter, the perceptions of marketing and sales often do not match reality. Even engineering's perception of the product does not always match reality.

To help you understand this concept, study Figure 5-5, which provides a Venn diagram with some interesting mismatches of perceptions that highlight classic problem areas. The three perception circles show all the different cases that can occur with mismatched expectations. Each case is labeled with a letter. Examine each overlap case separately to see potential problems and solutions for perception mismatch.

A: Alignment

We all perceive the same thing the same way. Perception probably matches reality. For these features, the product works as designed and the customer expectations match. Smile. This is a good thing.

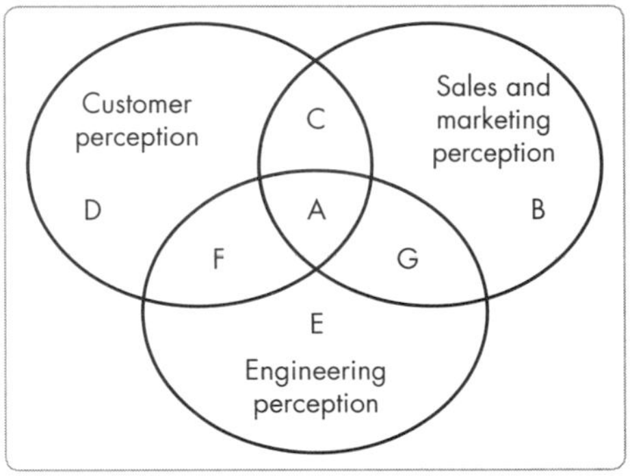

Figure 5-5: Customer perception, internal perception, and engineering perception

B: Fooling Ourselves

Sales and marketing believe the product offers capabilities that do not exist. Fortunately, customers are unaware of these fictional capabilities. The better the communication between engineering, sales, and marketing, the less likely this misperception will happen. If engineering and marketing regularly communicate during development, they should be in alignment about the feature set. Good documentation and good sales training will bring the sales team up to speed. If sales' understanding is incomplete and staff presents the wrong information to the customer, they have created a larger problem, which is case C.

C: Defects, Omissions, or Overselling

In this case, what was sold does not match what engineering built. The cause of this mismatch can be a product defect, problems with the documentation, or sales intentionally overselling the product.

Overselling occurs when sales tells the customer that the product includes a feature that the product does not in fact offer. Some sales people do this to make the sale and then pressure engineers to add the feature quickly to avoid embarrassing the company.

Defect and omission cases are straightforward to correct: Either correct the code or change the documentation to match what is being delivered. If a sales person intentionally oversells the product, marketing and senior management should take corrective action with the person to avoid the situation in the future. Having single sales people define product direction without the active participation of engineering, marketing, and management will derail the longer-term product planning and hurt the company.

D: Great Expectations

The customer thinks the product does something that it doesn't actually do, even if your company did not tell the customer that the feature is supported. This occurs when the customer makes unwarranted assumptions about the product. Good customer-facing documentation, marketing collateral, and proper training for the customer should keep this problem to a minimum.

E: Hidden Capabilities

In this case, the product includes undocumented features that can be unintended artifacts of how the software is constructed. The development team might be unaware of these capabilities. Sometimes an engineer might add such features intentionally without documenting them. Hidden capabilities can be benign unless the customer becomes aware of them and exploits them.

Hidden capabilities should be documented and the cause investigated. If an unintentional side effect of the code creates the capability, it should be either documented as a feature or disabled. If the capability was intentional but added without permission, talk to the engineer who added it to prevent this from happening in the future.

F: Code Artifacts and Unsupported Features

An *artifact* describes a behavior that was unintended and covers some aspect of the system that was an unusual and unexpected case. This behavior or hidden feature was not intended to be included in the product. It does not appear on your test systems and is unknown to you.

When a customer discovers code artifacts or unsupported features, big problems can result. Customers can exploit unintended code artifact effects on their systems, and because your company does not support the artifact, it might not appear in the next new release, leaving the customer without that option in the future.

Understanding the customer-use model helps you identify and avoid such problems. Talk to customers about how they use the product to help identify unusual and unplanned uses. Ideally, map out a customer-use model. Understand how your customers use the product.

Unsupported features can appear when an engineer adds undocumented and unplanned features into a release—perhaps the engineer wanted to experiment with a nifty idea. Some customer service and support technicians will hear of this feature and tell a customer that it is legitimate, because they want to help the customer with a problem. To avoid unplanned features, tell the development team that adding in features without approval is unacceptable. See the next section for more discussion of this case.

G: Missed Opportunities

In this case, the customer is unaware of a feature of the product because the company somehow missed the opportunity to describe the feature and improve the sales potential of the product. You can avoid this situation by fully documenting all features and training sales staff on the most important features. Keep customer-facing documentation up to date to avoid creating missed opportunities in the future.

Surprise! Unplanned Features

Finding features in the product that an engineer added without your knowledge is an unpleasant surprise. Engineers will add unplanned features in the product code for three main reasons, all of which are unacceptable:

- The engineer wants to please someone (a client, a customer service representative, or a senior manager) but knows management will not approve this feature.

- The engineer thinks he knows better than everyone else.

- The engineer wants to experiment with a new feature but does not want to ask permission to add it to the product.

Building unapproved features can delay implementation of required features and can hurt your product. In some cases, these unapproved features can force required features out of a release due to lack of development time. Unplanned features can also create inconsistency in the product, because often an engineer will implement them only in one section of the product. Such features often do not fit an overall product definition or strategy. They also ensure big problems for QA and documentation teams because the hidden feature's behavior differs from the documented behavior. Finally, adding unapproved features to a product shows an engineer's disrespect for everyone else in the company.

A small "back-door" feature might increase immediate customer value and please a client. However, your customers will be upset if they try using this feature in another part of the software suite and find it's unsupported: The surprise feature becomes a major problem for your company. When a customer expresses displeasure, you might be forced to scramble to provide support for the feature. Completing support for a feature after the product is released can be 10 times more expensive than creating the feature at the start and providing support. Suddenly, the small change has disrupted your company's next few releases and potentially its future revenue.

If an engineer adds unapproved features to product code, pull her aside and coach her about her action's impact on the product and the company. When talking to the responsible engineer, remember that your goal is not to stifle innovation, but to encourage team discussion of key features before they are implemented.

BEST INTENTIONS

A customer service employee made a feature request of an engineer working on one piece of our system. The engineer thought it was a neat change, so he implemented it without telling anyone else. When the release came out, the customer service person told key customers about the feature and the customers started using it. A few customers really liked the feature and started using it extensively. Customers built up their own data files tied into this feature.

However, two key customers quickly found out that the product did not support the feature in all areas. This was a huge problem for them and they became vocal about it. As large customers were pushing for the change, they forced us to change our release strategy to support this change. Full feature support was not cheap; we had to implement it as a quickly planned release. This left other customers unhappy and affected our ability to support other critical new features. The unplanned feature really upset the marketing team. Going forward, I instituted clear rules for engineers not to add in any features without approval.

—Product development manager

Improving a Product in an Alpha Release

You can effectively improve a product definition during its *alpha release*— an early version of the software created and released specifically to solicit customer feedback. You can identify cooperative customers who know that the alpha software is not ready for production use but want to contribute to its definition. Choosing existing customers who are enthusiastic about your product will minimize your risks and improve your results.

Success with an alpha release requires that you actively drive the client's evaluation. A *passive* alpha release, in which you send clients the software and then wait for their evaluations, will not produce the feedback you need. Instead, schedule an evaluation time with your alpha reviewers so that you can get direct feedback from them as they are using the product. If the testers are remote, set up regular conferences to discuss their impressions of the product. The goal of the alpha release is not to identify bugs, but to solicit conceptual flaws in the overall product definition, workflow, and features that would lower the value of the product. (Chapter 6 discusses practical aspects of using alpha releases.)

Understanding an Existing Product's Composition

Product definition isn't strictly limited to an initial release. Defining the future of a product requires a clear understanding of the product *as it stands*. Because you might not have been involved at the beginning of the product definition process, you can step back and take a snapshot view of the product and its features to illuminate any problem areas. Understanding an existing product also requires that you check "under the hood" for code and construction particulars.

The customer scrutinizes the product based on its functions and ability to meet requirements. However, under the hood, each product can consist of software packaging (the wrapper around the product executables and libraries that make it easy to unpack, install, set up, and use), multiple code executables, data files, and a database. Small companies often do not properly maintain documentation of a product's "internal engine."

Unraveling which software modules are included in which external product can be difficult if many executables have been built over time and staff changes have occurred during the process. In a few cases, engineers create hierarchies of code components as part of the build or packaging, which makes the product composition difficult to sort out.

For software services with many different components, tracking down which pieces the customer uses and which the administrator uses can be a complex task. Sometimes components are included in the software build but are no longer in use. If the product has a long history in the market, you should talk with multiple engineers, QA, and operations staff to determine the product composition.

In some cases, your company might have heavily customized a product to accommodate particular customers' needs. If the development team did not record these customization details, determining exactly which parts of a product are important to which customers becomes a huge problem when it comes time to maintain or update the product.

Three case histories illustrate the problems with unclear product definitions mapping to code. In all cases, much work was required to reach agreement on defining the product and then documenting the results.

Case 1: Many Compatible Modules

The product offering at Company A had more than 150 different modules that had been developed over a decade. The operations team had built these modules into a hierarchy; the result was a few dozen different product offerings with overlapping modules. Seven levels of grouping hierarchy were required to build some products. The hierarchy and grouping had built up until the people building and packaging the products were unclear about their actual contents.

Unraveling this problem required getting the marketing descriptions, licensing descriptions, and the homemade packaging file. The development manager wrote a program to map components to products and identify overlaps and licensing issues. As it turned out, many conflicts existed, including license duplications. Going through the process simplified reorganization of the licensing and packaging and identified extra software that was being included unintentionally in some packages. This resulted in lost revenue for the company, as a key product was being given away instead of being sold with every shipment.

Case 2: Too Much Custom Code

Company B had created many different products and service offerings. Unfortunately, no one had documented them along with pricing and construction information. Management had no clear vision of the various offerings, and sales treated the offerings as full custom efforts and made no effort to address the process and cost issues associated with this approach.

Marketing, engineering, and management resolved this issue by defining each product's content, construction, and pricing, and then publishing the results. They produced a standard pricing spreadsheet that they required everyone to use. This lowered the need for expensive new development with each new customer. It also streamlined the process of bringing in new customers.

Case 3: Undocumented System with Legacy Code

Company C offered *Software as a Service (SaaS)*, which allowed customers to access the software through an API. The system included multiple modules that talked to each other and resided on different services. To complicate the situation, the company had gone through several different versions of the system, and legacy code still resided in the production code. Various employees offered different answers about the product's composition because few understood the big picture that included all the elements.

After talking to operations and engineering staff, the engineering manager wrote a high-level summary showing the different modules and how they corresponded to the system. The manager created a detailed system diagram that showed the various servers and which modules were deployed to each one, including those used only by operations. The team used this summary for future testing and planning, which allowed for identification of modules to be removed from the system, lowering maintenance costs.

In all these cases, the core problem was that although construction of the product changed over time, nobody in the company drove the choices or documented them. Development management needs to work actively with marketing to define product composition and keep internal documents up to date. Product composition issues might appear to be unlikely problems, but they do occur regularly in small companies.

Additional Reading

Here is some additional reading on topics presented in this chapter:

Crossing the Chasm, by Geoffrey A. Moore (Collins, 2002)

Developing Products in Half the Time: New Rules, New Tools, by Preston G. Smith and Donald G. Reinertsen (Wiley, 1997)

Effective Prototyping for Software Makers, by Jonathan Arnowitz, Michael Arent, and Nevin Berger (Morgan Kaufmann, 2006)

Essentials of Marketing: A Global-managerial Approach, by E. Jerome McCarthy and William Perreault (McGraw-Hill, 2005)

Software Requirements, by Karl E. Wiegers (Microsoft Press, 2003)

The Marketing Imagination, by Theodore M. Levitt (Free Press, 1986)

User Interface Design for Programmers, by Joel Spolsky (Apress, 2001)

Winning at New Products: Accelerating the Process from Idea to Launch, by Robert G. Cooper (Basic Books, 2001)

6

DRIVING RELEASES

A well-defined and well-built release process is vital
to getting your company's software product into your
customers' hands. In fact, the method you use to deliver
the code is not as important as the release process you
use to *prepare* it for delivery. A weak release process can not only add
delays and unpredictability to your product delivery, but it can result
in a low-quality product and a tarnished company image.

Small companies often have weak release processes because management doesn't realize the value of a well-defined plan. A company's release
process isn't considered as important as product development and sales.
Although the release process doesn't affect a company's *short-term* bottom
line, ignoring its importance can lead to ill-advised approaches, such as
emailing the product's executables to customers from a developer's
computer.

An unplanned, "ad hoc" release will negatively affect the company's *long-term* bottom line. The problems created by past ad hoc releases become most apparent as your company starts to grow. Ad hoc releases are *not repeatable*, they are *impossible to support* long term, and they are *error prone*. A release that is not repeatable will lead to problems if and when you need to re-create and repair earlier release code, which typically occurs in supporting a customer using an older version of your product. Second, because of the casual nature of the delivery, ad hoc releases are difficult if not impossible to support. In some cases, engineers will ship a code copy built on a local machine rather than a copy from the source control repository, making it difficult to know which content ended up in which customer's hands. Third, ad hoc releases are error-prone because they do not go through the proper testing, documenting, and labeling necessary to ensure a high-quality, supportable release.

Other problems associated with poor release planning can create nightmares for small companies: Poor release naming can lead to mistakes in the content; releases can ship without plans for resolving customer problems; and customers can become upset because a delivered release was unexpected and they were uninformed of its contents.

Release Planning

Perhaps the most underrated aspect of the release planning process is its ability to reinforce or undermine your company's values and image. Over time, your releases should match your company's long-term vision, whether from the standpoint of strategy or corporate image. For example, if you want your company and its products to be known for their high quality, the release plans should support high-quality releases. If you want to be known for rapid innovation, releases should be innovative and frequent.

Release planning also involves thinking ahead about the type and nature of releases. For example, you might decide that engineering will not plan patch releases in advance because releases will be designed to fix only serious problems. However, engineering can plan for such releases' quick delivery. Mapping out in advance each type of release will better prepare your team for the inevitable changes and surprises that will occur. Planning a release strategy is much better than letting releases just *happen*.

Consider the release timeline and associated early release strategy as part of release planning. Then, with guidelines in place, you can establish release criteria and processes to create more efficient and higher-quality releases.

Release Timeline

Your company's *release timeline* is the most influential part of matching your release strategy to your company's overall strategy and product vision. A clear timeline allows for more realistic release plans and lets your company establish appropriate customer expectations. On the other hand, not planning release timelines means that your results will be variable and unpredictable, and they probably won't convey the image you want your customers to see. Develop a timeline with marketing and review it with the executive team to generate input and support to implement it.

NOTE *This section is intended as an introduction to release timelines and timeline planning. Release planning requires an understanding of several topics covered in Chapters 12, 13, 14, and 15.*

Your strategy for a release timeline will also define the types of releases you will create and guidelines for when they occur. When defining a release timeline, consider your customers' needs and your company's desired market image. For example, if your product is complex and customers want to upgrade versions only once a year, plan for major releases to occur yearly and optional minor releases to occur intermittently. At the other extreme, some product markets are highly competitive and change rapidly; quarterly or more frequent releases might be required.

Consider the practical minimum time for a release. For example, if a release requires four weeks of testing and a two-week approval cycle, more than six weeks must pass between releases. Alternatively, if you are building a web-hosted product that can be tested in a single day, fewer timeline restrictions apply to your strategy.

In addition, if your main product can be customized for individual customers, you could release customized versions more often than general releases. Another consideration is how far in advance your customers need to be informed of imminent releases. If, for example, customers require four weeks' notice before new software is released and available, having less than a four-week development cycle does not make sense.

After you have created an overall release strategy, consider your short-term plans for the next 6 to 12 months. During this period, you can map out your expectations for the following:

- Number of major releases
- Number of minor releases
- Customized releases
- Expectations for patches
- Expectations of work not included on the normal release cycle

With these expectations in mind, you can plan and number the near-term releases. When you are assigning approximate timelines, allow gaps in your schedule to accommodate unexpected issues and patch creation. If you do not include time for surprises, you will be habitually late in releasing your product. Make sure you have an up-front agreement with marketing and other teams about the flexibility of timelines. If product release dates require rigid, unmovable dates, increase the buffer time to allow for unknown events and opportunities that will occur.

As you plan the next few releases, consider both start and end dates for each release cycle. Releases that consider only end dates can suffer from overlapping resource use if separate parallel release efforts are planned. By mapping out start and end times for each planned release, you can determine where and when resource conflicts might occur.

Finally, for your next major release, consider the milestones for that release before finalizing your plan. If you plan a release date without considering testing, approvals, customer checkpoints, alpha releases, or beta releases, you will have to backpedal later.

Next, we'll look into the early release strategy and its impact on release timelines in more detail.

Early Release Strategy

The *early release strategy* is an approach that provides customers with prerelease versions of the product to improve the product definition and minimize the risks of uncovering problems in production or post-production. Companies use many different prerelease approaches, but this book uses the following definitions:

Alpha release

An *alpha release* is early product code delivered to a few customers who can test the product's features and concepts and offer feedback. This code has typically undergone limited testing by either engineering or QA, and it might not yet be feature-complete. Customers should anticipate lower quality since alpha code is not production ready.

Beta release

A *beta release* is early product code delivered to a few customers with intended final product features usually completed but not fully tested. As with the alpha release, the hope is that customers will provide feedback on product features and concepts. In addition, because the code has undergone more testing, customers can often use it for practical applications, which can help them provide early feedback about implementation problems or omissions. Customer expectation of quality varies depending on your company's history in delivering beta releases.

Limited release

A *limited release* is a complete, production-ready product release delivered to a few friendly customers before widespread release with the goal of identifying serious problems.

Figure 6-1 illustrates how a company might use these different release strategies at different points in the release cycle. Although the figure shows a milestone diagram, it does not imply any particular process.

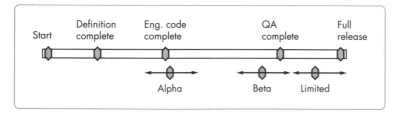

Figure 6-1: Release types: alpha, beta, and limited

Each of these approaches poses different risks and rewards. Review all three release approaches with marketing, and decide together which risks are appropriate for your company. All early releases impose costs on marketing and development that will slow delivery of the full releases.

Alpha Release

Alpha releases allow customers to offer useful feedback early in the production cycle while it is still relatively easy to make changes to the product code. In addition, customers can help you find problems that can be corrected well before QA has invested considerable time reviewing the code.

Two notable problems occur with alpha releases, however: First, customers often have inappropriately high expectations for the release. When reality does not meet those expectations, the customer can get a negative impression of the software and might not want to use the production version. To minimize such problems, you should properly describe the state of the alpha code to the customer along with the alpha release. Also consider adding a startup screen that highlights the fact that this is an alpha release with alpha code. This can help minimize problems that might occur, for example, if a primary customer contact passes the code to others in his company without passing them the disclaimers.

A second problem occurs when customers use alpha releases in a production environment. Sometimes impatient customers will run their production data against alpha or beta code despite their having agreed not to do so. Then, when a serious problem occurs with alpha or beta code, these customers will argue for immediate repair and data recovery. The common justification? "The new feature was so critical that we needed it immediately." You can avoid this problem by disabling or limiting the capabilities of the alpha release to prevent a customer from using it in a production setting. Unfortunately, this might not always be possible, as some alpha testing requires that the product be used on large data sets.

WARNING   *If a customer has a history of misusing alpha releases, consider giving them only beta or limited releases or not using that customer for an early release program.*

Overall, alpha releases are useful, but consider the risks and work to minimize them before shipping alpha code.

Beta Release

The goals of a beta release are to get advance notice of problems when the customer uses the code and to get feedback on new features. However, making changes to the code in response to beta feedback can require production schedule changes, because beta code versions are typically sent to customers near the end of the release cycle—before QA has completed testing.

A beta release faces the same risks faced by an alpha release, but the quality risk is lower than an alpha because QA has completed more product testing. In a beta release, that extra QA testing lessens the chance of a code malfunction disillusioning the customer. It also provides a more appropriate opportunity to test the code in actual customer situations to determine whether customers can uncover any prerelease problems. Make sure your customers have a clear understanding about the valid uses and risks associated with beta code. To improve your beta results, engineering should let the customer know the true status of the code and set the proper expectations.

Limited Release

A limited release differs from alpha and beta releases because the code is ready to ship. The goal of a limited release is to reduce the risk of widespread visibility in the event of problems. As a result, limited releases are sent only to *friendly* customers. This approach works well if errors or problems found post-release are costly to repair, especially if customer safety or data is at risk.

Because problems in the code haven't reached all your customers and the code is production-ready, the limited release is a risk-reduction technique. If someone discovers a large problem, a few users will be unhappy, but not your entire user base. The situation is better than a full release because the team can focus directly on fewer customers. If a customer finds problems, the release team can create a patch as quickly as possible.

The biggest disadvantage of this approach is that only a few customers review the code; most customers get the new final software a few weeks later. Limited releases also add to the overall cost of software development, as the development team does not fully focus on the next release during a limited release.

Planning Product End of Life

Small companies can benefit from creating an *end-of-life* process—that is, a process for retiring products. Planning for this stage might seem odd at first. Most software managers in small companies think, "We just created our product line, so why would we think about killing parts of it? End of life is something that large companies worry about. Not us." However, end of life issues can arrive *earlier* in small companies that tend to attempt several different solutions to a problem. And every software product has an ongoing cost that small companies can least afford. The real benefits of a good product retirement plan are improved customer satisfaction, reduced internal costs of supporting your customer base, and improved profits if your company can remove unprofitable products from production.

When and how do you actually realize those benefits? When you're planning for your next release, review your products and consider candidates for end of life. From an engineering perspective, a good candidate could be software whose platform is old or obsolete. *Platform* in this case includes the hardware, operating system, or even a third-party software package. From a marketing point of view, the key factors for end of life are customer use and revenue. Products with small customer followings, significant technology issues, and little future potential might be good candidates for retirement.

It's true that retiring a product can annoy some customers who still use it, but sometimes the cost of supporting that product exceeds the value to the customer and the company. You and your team are in the best position to identify the costs associated with ongoing builds, testing, support, and maintenance. You're also best equipped to identify technical failings, which raises another important point: Sometimes development needs to take the initiative and raise the issue of retiring products. However, the engineers' assessment must recognize and balance technical dislikes and costs to the business of product end of life.

When you reach internal consensus to retire a product, create an end-of-life process. This process keeps you from missing important steps that can cause problems for your customers, cost your company money, cost your customers money, and hurt your image with your customers. Major steps to consider for this process include the following:

Understanding customer impact

Marketing and sales can do the footwork to establish whether retiring the product will impact current customers. Consider providing an alternative solution for these customers among supported products.

Reviewing contractual and legal obligations

Establish whether contractual or legal issues affect product retirement. Legal issues might exist that govern how long you need to maintain customer data after you have retired the product.

Creating a plan and timeline

When you identify products for end of life, work out a timeline and plan the process with input from the marketing team. This plan should describe the steps and schedule required for removing the product from production.

Communicating with your customers

Inform customers of your decision as soon as you decide to retire a product. When possible, talk to customers directly and follow up in writing.

Planning the steps

Your end of life plan should align with the release schedule so that you remove the product during a normal release. It should also include release-related steps, such as the following, for removing it as a supported product:

- Removing the product from the engineering software build
- Removing the code from the release media or platform
- Removing the code from the packaging and release software
- Communicating the product end of life event in release notes

Returning customer data

Many systems have customer data associated with them. Naturally, you need a method for returning the data to the customers. Engineering should identify a migration path for current customers to another available product to improve and sustain customer goodwill.

Deleting or storing customer data

After you have retired the product and shipped the customer data, the plan needs to describe whether the customer data is permanently stored or deleted.

PRODUCT END OF LIFE

My company had a customer-customizable reporting interface to our production server. When I joined the company, I discovered that this product had no specification and had not been properly tested, and large customer reports could slow down the system for everyone.

I first looked at testing and repair, but discovered that the estimated costs would be high. With marketing, we looked next at how it was being used and anecdotally heard that the usage was low.

By agreement with product marketing, we made this product a candidate for end of life. Marketing surveyed our customers. They found that customers occasionally used it. Unfortunately, one customer liked it. We decided to end of life the product and worked to create standard reports to meet the one customer's most common use.

Because we were a small company, the end of life for the offering occurred three months after the initial discussions. This decision reduced the testing burden, which was high for that product. It also prevented the future quality issues that would have occurred if more customers had started to use it, as the product had significant quality problems. Overall, it proved to be a good company decision.

—Director of engineering

Overall, planning for product end of life solves many potential problems and improves customer attitudes toward your company, even if they are unhappy with the end of life decision.

The Release Process

The *release process* describes the steps required to release the product once development has built and tested it. It is a single step in the overall product development process. To develop a release process, first consider the process goals. Internal releases need to be named clearly and consistently. The process needs to support customer communication about critical issues such as timing and features. It also needs to be repeatable, must minimize release errors, and must have a review and improvement mechanism in place.

Let's look first at criteria for release, followed by advice for defining a release process.

Release Criteria

Release criteria define what a successful release should look like. It answers the age-old question, "Are we there yet?" Knowing in advance what you expect in a release—when it comes to features, timing, process steps, and quality—will allow you to guide your team toward success while monitoring progress. If the criteria have gained consensus within your team, it can also minimize pressure to release the product prematurely.

The problem that often arises without release criteria is "tunnel vision." Without a definition of what a *completed* release means, engineering will focus only on delivery date. The release will consist of what is available near the delivery date, with less attention paid to functionality and quality.

Release criteria can and should be unique to each company. For example, a company whose product and image require high quality will produce release criteria of high minimum quality standards; a company that emphasizes customer satisfaction should produce release criteria that require proper customer communication prior to the release; and a company that emphasizes ease of use should produce release criteria that require specific approval ratings from customers before the product is shipped.

It is wise to work with marketing and consider your business needs before setting the release standards. Ensuring that you have corporate buy-in on those standards will help the team make good decisions when the pressure is on near release time.

To set release criteria, consider the following questions:

- What is the minimum quality acceptable for a release?

- What is the minimum testing required for each type of release? (For example, patch releases might have different testing standards.)

- What kind of customer communication is required before and after a release?

- What is the minimum that should be done in an emergency release? (An *emergency release* is a release that must be created immediately to prevent significant harm to the customer or your business.)

- What is the minimum level of customer data compatibility that's acceptable for a release?

- What is the maximum delay for the release that does not significantly harm the customer?

- What is the earliest that your company can release the software? (For some businesses, releasing server-based software early will be disruptive to customers who might be planning for changes on a specific day.)

- How extensively do features need to be described to customers well before the release? Is there room for making late feature set modifications without being disruptive?

When considering all of these criteria, be careful not to overdefine the minimum standards for a release. Sure, management wants the best in all categories, but from a practical standpoint, that cannot happen. It is better to emphasize one aspect of the release criteria with higher standards and set more generous lower standards for other aspects of the release to provide some flexibility in decisions.

With release criteria in place, defining a release process will simplify the mechanics of pulling a release together and make it easier to estimate and automate releases.

Process Steps

With these major goals in mind, consider several important steps when designing the *release process*. Integrate these steps into the major development process.

Final release naming and numbering
> Engineering and marketing jointly define the final release name and release contents. Typically, marketing and engineering agree on release naming before the product is developed, but finalizing the names and numbers occurs near the end of the cycle, as changes might be required.

Early customer release notification
> Marketing should provide customers with advanced notice of the release so they can plan for implementing the new product and not be surprised when it arrives. As early as possible, provide customers with release notification for any platform changes intended as part of the release. Customers might need to change usage or hardware to support your release and will be upset if they're notified too late to make a pain-free transition. This can also affect the customers' budgeting process.

Customer release information
> Engineering and marketing should create customer documentation as appropriate for the release—typically an update to existing documentation. This documentation can include release notes, marketing release communications, product brochures, press releases, and any pricing or service level changes. Engineering should review with marketing the final set of release changes and check marketing material to see the impact of late changes.

Release notes
> The documentation team should produce release notes describing what is present in the release in a high-level overview. These notes describe changes in the release relative to the current version.

Informing customers of the status of their reported defects

Customers want to know whether defects they reported will be included in a release for their internal planning. A release process should require that customer service provide individual customers with the status of their reported issues relative to the release. Many software companies avoid doing this because of the time involved, but providing defect resolution notes can greatly improve customer goodwill. Customers will appreciate that you are being responsive to their needs. When the customer base is large, an acceptable alternative approach is to include a selected list of defect resolutions as part of the release notes. However, with a small customer base common to small growing companies, consider the individualized approach.

Internal training

Engineering, customer support, and marketing need to ensure that any staff working directly with customers are properly trained on the new release.

Product release

At this point, the release engineer makes the software available to the customer. The physical release of the software can be through a CD, via a new download setup, or by switching the server software to the new version. Be sure to document and automate the release steps. The release process documentation should specifically describe the locations of the source files, configuration files, and releasable files. It should also provide enough detail so that anyone on the team could perform the product release.

Release acknowledgment

Marketing should inform customers of the product's release in an email right after the release ships.

Post-release review

After the release, host a review meeting to discuss issues that occurred during the release cycle and ways to improve the next one.

Post-release tracking

QA should track the defect count and the customer call count after a release. Learning about customer concerns will lead to improvements in the code or documentation.

Post-release Review

The *post-release review* is an opportunity to review the last release, suggest changes to improve future performance, and boost team morale. The review meeting should include development teams as well as other teams involved in the release cycle: marketing, customer service, and QA, for example. Informal one-hour sessions will probably be sufficient. The session should cover these points:

- What went well in the release that we should continue doing?

- What were the problems, and what could we do differently?

- What risks should we have identified earlier, and how can we spot them next time?

- How would we prioritize the problems we encountered?

- What solutions can we identify?

For a long release cycle that lasted more than nine months, a few post-release review meetings of one to two hours each can be helpful. These meetings require much preparation, and everyone should be aware of that. Create an agenda for each meeting, and ask all participants to come prepared with their thoughts on the agenda. Also, arrange for a conference room with a whiteboard and mark out general categories of problems that are relevant to the release to help people generate ideas during the meeting.

To get ideas flowing at the start of the meeting, pass out large sticky notes and ask participants to write down issues or problems, one issue per note. Each person can post one problem at a time and say a few lines about it. This is not the time for detailed discussion, however—it's about collecting thoughts and ideas. Move around the room from person to person to assure that everyone, even quiet team members, can have his or her say.

Depending on the length of the session, attendees can prioritize the issues and problems at the end of the meeting or in a second meeting. After you've grouped similar issues together, ask the team to set priorities for important outstanding issues. At the end of the prioritization, write up the results to highlight the issues and priorities and send this to everyone who participated. Then ask the group to be prepared to talk about potential solutions for the highest ranking problems at the next meeting. At a follow-up meeting, each person can present solutions to the highest priority issues, using sticky notes to summarize ideas in a single sentence. Avoid lengthy discussions on single topics until everyone has had a chance to present his or her ideas. In-depth discussions can occur later.

After the solutions meeting, write up the top problems and their solutions. Then ask team members to review the results and provide additional ideas. Select the problems you can address, and let the team know the plan for making improvements. Any problems you cannot address directly can be discussed with the executive team. Larger, expensive solutions might require that you write a business case to justify the costs and efforts. Large or small, make a good faith effort to address the important issues, and inform people about which issues you aren't addressing and why.

Be thorough and follow through with the ideas and solutions generated in post-release reviews. Conducting an abbreviated review with no follow-up can be worse than having no review at all, because a lack of attention to issues can result in staff cynicism and a belief that the problems will never improve.

Release Version Identification

Software naming and version numbering might seem inconsequential, but small companies often run into difficulties by not properly identifying their releases. Poorly identified releases lead to wasted time and effort due to the following possible consequences:

- Engineers add code to the wrong release.

- Marketing sends the wrong information to customers about what is included in a release.

- QA and engineers find bugs difficult to track down because of improper release identification.

- Nobody knows which customer has which release.

NOTE *This issue is so common in small companies that this chapter provides an extended discussion of product numbering issues and practices.*

While large firms usually apply a well-defined version numbering sequence, small firms often use inconsistent version identifiers. Frequently, the first identifiers are release names based on feature sets. Examples would be the *Database Throughput Release* or the *Customer ABC Support Release.*

As your company gets a few releases under its belt, the need to identify each release in a unique and informative way increases for several reasons. Customers reporting issues need a clear version number to reference when reporting problems. Development needs to know which of the upcoming releases will get which critical feature. And both engineering and QA need to know which errors were found in which version to resolve each issue properly.

Clear release identifiers also make defect-repair planning easier, since you can assign individual defects to specific future releases. They also aid the documentation team in pulling together release notes. All of these reasons should push you toward an effective release naming method as early as possible in your company's growth.

Three-Number Release IDs

There is a lot of psychology in how people react to numbers—a version number of 17 might imply that the developers never got it right and had to keep putting out major releases, while when a major new version comes out, the company renames it something new, like *version 2.0.* Most software goes through quick cycles of initial growth and sustained use, and a common and simple numbering approach uses three numbers separated by periods, followed by a build number. This is referred to here as *three-number release identification* (or *release IDs*). With this method, an example release number could look something like *3.5.2 build 13* or *3.5.2 B13* (see Figure 6-2).

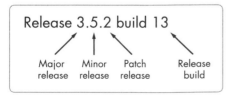

Figure 6-2: Release numbers illustrated

The first number is the *major release number*, sometimes known as the *marketing number*. This number is incremented no more than once a year, and it rarely gets far into the teens for most projects, because customers perceive version numbers such as *17.0.1* to be too old and outdated for their purposes—they expect a new major release instead of an updated old one. For long-lived products with many releases, marketing typically renames the product with a major rollout instead of issuing a new release number. Mature products do not undergo future major releases, only minor ones, limiting the first number.

The second number defines the *minor release number*, which represents feature changes rather than substantial changes to the system. A minor release occurs regularly during the year. Either *0* or *1* works for a starting value, but it should be consistent.

The third number, the *patch release number*, changes when a small defect is repaired (with a patch) in an existing release. This number can start with either *0* or *1* but should be consistent.

A *build number* tracks the software executable version during the release cycle. For convenience purposes, most build systems auto-increment the build number with each new executable. A development cycle for a release requires the creation of multiple builds, which engineering and QA then evaluate and test. With such an iterative process, the build number uniquely identifies the final build from earlier builds of the release.

These examples help illustrate how to apply numbers to a sequence of releases:

- 1.0.0 B104: Initial release

- 1.1.0 B99: A minor release with notable changes

- 1.2.0 B57: Another minor release with notable changes

- 1.2.1 B12: Patch release to 1.2.0

- 1.2.2 B9: Patch release to 1.2.1

- 2.0.0 B89: Major upgrade to first release

- 2.0.1 B14: Patch release to 2.0.0.

Patch Releases

Although the release numbering system allows for patch releases, it should not *encourage* them. That's an important distinction. Treat patch releases as an admission of a mistake, not as a quick opportunity to drop in another feature. Marketing might put pressure on engineering to add a critical feature to a patch release, but resisting this temptation will allow the required patch to be released quickly and with properly focused testing. Adding new features should always move the release into the minor release category, which requires more testing and time to ensure proper quality.

Patch releases do require full regression testing to ensure that the patch does not make the product fail. Hence, patch releases have a high cost per benefit compared to a regular release.

Some companies avoid patch releases and bundle many patch issues into a quickly created minor release. This approach can be effective, but only if the minor releases go out often enough that your customers aren't suffering from the lingering problems.

Component Numbers vs. Release Numbers

Software releases commonly include more than one component or product that a customer uses. In a multi-component release, some components interact with other components, thus requiring a simultaneous release. The choice on how to label release components is both a marketing and engineering decision, because it has implications on customer perception, customer service, defect tracking, and engineering defect investigations. Consider the issues related to different component naming strategies while your company is in the startup stage, rather than waiting until your company is in the growth stage.[1] A thoughtful component naming convention allows you to track the dependent pieces and use these names in discussions internally and with customers.

Each customer-viewable component in a release requires a unique identifier. One approach is to allow the components to keep individual numbers that change when the component changes and then bundle them together into the release. Another approach is to assign all the

---

[1] See the book's introduction for definitions of various company stages.

components in the release the same release number regardless of whether they have changed.

Figure 6-3 illustrates two common approaches—independent component numbers and dependent component numbers matching the release.

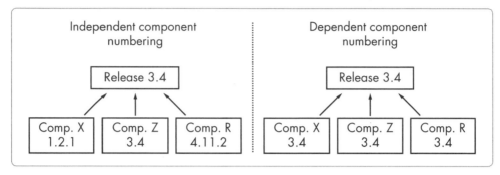

Figure 6-3: Two approaches to component numbering

Independent component numbering allows different numbers to be used for each component. In this approach, the numbers advance only when the component is changed. Tracking down components for a past release can be difficult down the road, however. A table showing the mapping must be publicly available and kept up to date so that teams working on the code can easily identify the source version of particular user-reported problems. Relying only on the source control system to track this is a poor strategy and is prone to operator error—plus, it's time consuming.

Dependent component numbering matches the components to the release number. The modules all get their numbers advanced to the release number even if no code changes. This approach makes it much easier to track what changes are included in which modules in each release. Determining the history of defects in each release is much easier with common release numbering.

Numbering Across Releases

Numbering across releases has several different driving concerns. Most software consumers expect release numbers to be sequential. Development organizations assign release numbers early, often before development has a clear idea of what will go in each release.

Early release numbering can cause problems with sequential release numbering. Early release numbering reflects the *future* planned release order. The original intent for the release numbers was to release them in sequence, but this does not always work out.

Figure 6-4 illustrates an example of out-of-sequence release numbers. At the start of release 2.3.4, the plan was to release 2.3.4 first and then 2.3.5. In this case, development delayed release 2.3.4, while 2.3.5 shipped as planned. Following release 2.3.5, development released number 2.3.4, and now the numbering is out of order.

A company can live with an out-of-order release sequence; however, an alternative approach is to renumber future releases so that numbers are always sequential. Sequential numbering avoids confusion months or years later when, inevitably, problems occur in a past release. Referring to Figure 6-4, when the planned 2.3.4 release does not release before 2.3.5, you should retire the number 2.3.4 as a non-release and rename it with the next incremental number, 2.3.6. Do not increment the number until it is clear where final delivery will fall relative to other releases. For this example, the timeline would look like that shown in Figure 6-5. One caution when you renumber a release: Make certain that the documentation and the source code identifiers use the new number.

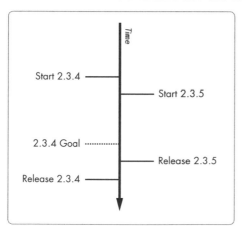 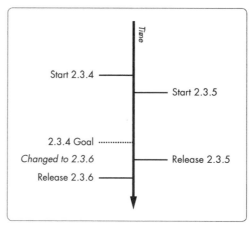

Figure 6-4: Release numbers fixed at project start

Figure 6-5: Release numbers always sequential at release

Software for the Gentleman Farmer

For a humorous cross-section of component numbering frustrations, read the following example.

DISCLAIMER   *All names are intended to be fictitious. Any resemblance to real names or companies is coincidental.*

You own a software company, Givemeabreakfarming Software, Inc., that writes software for people who want to run small, part-time hobby farms but don't have much farming experience. You produce a suite of products. The main product is FarmingBreak, and you also provide add-on programs to help with specific activities and crops: CowBreak, CornBreak, and WheatBreak. Customers must buy the main program, FarmingBreak, to use any of the add-on programs. After the first release, your products were all numbered 1.0. The version number of each product is visible on the product's user screen.

The CowBreak product was rushed to release and had a weak feature set, so you provide an upgraded version four months after your first release. As you map out the next release, you realize that you have a numbering choice. You can do one of the following:

- Increment all items to version 1.1 and recompile all the modules to match.

- Increment only CowBreak to 1.1 and leave the other products numbered at 1.0.

You decide to take the easy way out and modify only CowBreak. This avoids having to increment the number for all products to 1.1 and then explain to customers that nothing has changed.

Later you reach another decision point for the WheatBreak upgrade release. Should you call it 1.1 or go to 1.2? You elect to call it 1.1. Immediately after the release, a major problem is found, so you have to send out a patch. After the patch, WheatBreak is numbered 1.1.1.

You again modify CowBreak and name it 1.2 to add major dairy functionality.

As your business progresses, you map out a release to FarmingBreak, which you decided to call version 1.1. However, you have to change the database, and all of the products need to be recompiled to new versions, so you up their numbers. Now you have FarmingBreak at 1.1, WheatBreak at 1.2, CowBreak at 1.3, and CornBreak at 1.1. For new customers, this doesn't pose a huge problem—you just send them the latest versions of your software regardless of the number.

A few years down the road, your products are at the following version numbers: FarmingBreak 1.8, WheatBreak 1.9.2, CowBreak 1.4, CornBreak 1.5.3, and SoyBreak 1.1.3. During this time, you make one more database change that is incompatible with past versions. A customer calls with a problem in FarmingBreak 1.5 that you recall fixing a while back in FarmingBreak 1.6. The customer also has CornBreak 1.3.1 and SoyBreak 1.1. You agree to ship him an updated FarmingBreak copy, but you can't remember whether his other products are compatible or not. Furthermore, he doesn't want to upgrade to your latest versions, as he heard they were slow—so that eliminates the easy solution. At this point, you don't have version compatibility at hand and can't easily tell what is compatible, since you didn't keep all the products synchronized in version number. To resolve this situation, you stay up all night and read your notes until you can figure out which version numbers go with the customer's release. You then re-create those versions to ship to the customer, since you didn't save compiled copies, only the source.

Vowing to clean up some of your mistakes, when you make some major upgrades to FarmingBreak, you increment all your products to 2.0 and archive copies of the code. From now on, you will keep your product numbers synchronized so you won't have to keep capability notes. Version 2.0 is a success.

With success in hand, you announce to the press that version 2.1 is due out in six months. Two months after the announcement, your marketing team (yes, your company has grown) insists that CucumberBreak must have an immediate release in one month to deal with a strong competitor. Now you have a problem: If you call CucumberBreak version 2.1, then your main release will have to become 2.2, but you already announced it as 2.1 and have done all of your internal planning using that number. Hmm . . . maybe you jumped too quickly to synchronized numbering. You decide to keep the *main release* name as 2.1, but you allow release components to have numbers out of synchronization with the release. Going forward, you will keep careful records of component capability.

Additional Reading

Here is some additional reading on topics presented in this chapter:

The Build Master: Microsoft's Software Configuration Management Best Practices, by Vincent Maraia (Addison-Wesley Professional, 2005)

Manage It!: Your Guide to Modern, Pragmatic Project Management, by Johanna Rothman (Pragmatic Bookshelf, 2007)

"Software release life cycle," from Wikipedia, *http://en.wikipedia.org/wiki/Software_release_life_cycle*

Software Release Methodology, by Michael E. Bays (Prentice Hall, 1999)

7

EVALUATING YOUR TOOLS AND METHODS

Modern software development requires that a set of key tools and methods be used to protect intellectual property, produce quality code, and manage operations efficiently. Although large companies can afford a large support staff to maintain tools and enforce the use of specific approaches, small companies do not often have that luxury.

Failing to protect your company's *intellectual property* is gambling with your company's assets and shareholder value. *Intellectual property* doesn't just refer to your company's code, it also includes how you build and release your product, your ideas and data, how you track defects (bugs) and the defect data, and what technical documentation you create. A large component of a small company's value consists of intellectual property. If your company is being sold, the purchasing company considers the intellectual property as part of the offer price. If you have poorly maintained your company's intellectual property, then the buyer will see less value and make a lower offer for your company.

To protect your intellectual property, and ultimately your company's value, review your tools and the methods you use in at least the following areas:

Data backup   Have a systematic and automatic approach to creating secure secondary backup copies of data on a regular basis.

Document availability   Provide an easy method for making available all technical and product documentation for internal use.

Source code control and configuration management   Track and archive source code files during and after development, and identify sets of files into defined releases.

Software builds   Control how the software source creates the executable code that clients can use.

Bug tracking   Use appropriate technology to track defects (bugs) and their repair.

Release method   Employ the appropriate methods and technology to release your software.

Consider *tools and methods* in terms of your overall software development processes and practices throughout software development and support. Figure 7-1 illustrates this interaction. *Backup* and *document communication* cover the entire software release cycle. *Source code control* and *software builds* apply during code development until development releases the product. *Bug tracking* tracks problems discovered at any time. The *release method* describes the process of making the product available to your customers.

This chapter describes the different tools and methods used across the software release cycle, individually and in detail. Although some considerations might seem routine, digging deeper can help you uncover hidden risks and opportunities for improvement.

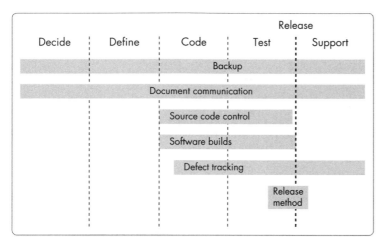

Figure 7-1: Tools and methods used across the software release cycle

Backing Up Intellectual Property

A *backup mechanism* provides the first level of protection for your company's intellectual property. Without a backup mechanism in place, all intellectual property can disappear instantly if it resides on your server's disk drives, because disk drives can and do fail for a number of reasons. In addition, without having secure backups, you can lose intellectual property due to a fire, a malicious hacker, or a malevolent employee. A development manager must either ensure that a backup mechanism exists or immediately direct its creation. If a separate IT organization backs up your intellectual property, you should review the organization's backup strategy. Often you will be surprised to find that your important data is not a part of their backup strategy.

Several best practices are recommended for file backup. You can customize these to your company's needs based on costs and staffing requirements:

- Full copies of files are stored on permanent media (tape or CD, for example) and are not overwritten.

- Full copies are stored on a regular basis in an offsite location.

- Users are notified about which parts of the file system are backed up so that they can appropriately store their critical data.

- Backup copies are made daily. A company usually can't afford to lose more than a day's data.

- Source control and configuration management tools are used and the repository is backed up. To be effective, this requires team discipline, as the team needs to check files into the repository often.

- Restoration of files from the backups is tested periodically. Otherwise, system administrators can discover backups that are incomplete or unusable after disaster has struck. Common causes of backup problems are ignored error messages in the backup logs, unexpected mechanical device failures, and the omission of needed files from the backup list. Test your backups at least once a quarter.

WARNING   *Backup failures discovered after disaster strikes are a common occurrence, so the remedy bears repeating: Regularly test your backups by restoring backed up files to test their viability.*

A number of different backup approaches can be used, with different trade-offs for complexity, cost, risk, time to implement, and time to recover data. Your choice will depend on how you determine the relative balance of these needs for your company. Common backup approach considerations include the following:

- Amount of disk space to include in the backup

- Choice of backup media

- Amount of automation in the backup process

- Ease of use of the equipment versus associated costs to purchase and staff time

- Regularity of the backups

- Storage location of backup media

- Choice of complete backups or partial backups on a regular basis

Backup Frequency

Three common approaches to frequency of backup are used:

- Daily full backups

- Weekly full backups, with daily differential backups from the last full backup

- Monthly full backups, with weekly differential backups and daily incremental backups

Companies also use variations on these approaches. Figure 7-2 illustrates these approaches.

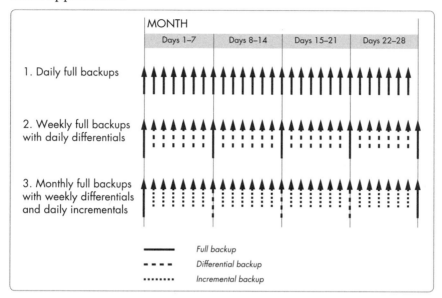

Figure 7-2: Three backup approaches

These approaches trade off administrator time and backup media space for ease and availability of data recovery. *Daily full backups* require the most backup media and potentially the most operator time, depending on the equipment used to perform the backup. However, a full backup approach allows you to restore files using a single day's stored backup, while other approaches do not permit this. You should start with this approach. When the backup time starts taking too long, try differential backups.

Weekly full backups plus daily differential backups from the last full backup takes less time during the week than full backups. However, in some cases you might need two sources of backup media to recover multiple files. The extra effort in recovery and the time to recover creates an effort "hill" you'll need to climb to recover files. This extra effort can make the backup administrator slow or reluctant to locate file versions that have been inadvertently lost. This approach works well for companies in the growth stage.

Monthly full backups with weekly differential and daily incremental backups require the fewest number of backup media and administrator efforts over a given month. However, a series of tapes can be required to recover a set of files. Set up each weekly differential to cover all files that changed since the weekly backup (and not the last weekly). Avoid this approach unless you must back up large amounts of data and you have limited backup capabilities, or you are not concerned with time involved for file recovery during normal business operations.

If full or full-plus-incremental backups don't seem right for your situation, you can use other strategies regarding frequency and amount of data for your backups. For example, the backup administrator could modify the approach to conduct full backups every *other* day. This would save backup time, but it increases the loss risk to two days' work instead of one day's work. Alternatively, the administrator could perform the incremental backups to cover only a single day's changes. An example would be setting Friday's incremental backup to cover only Friday's changed files instead of all the changes that occurred since the last full backup. Recovering the system to Friday's state would require the last full backup media plus all the incremental backups created that week. However, with this approach, the daily backups will take less time during the week. This modification trades administrator time for decreased cost to recover files.

In general, you should choose the simplest backup and recovery approach when you're starting out—probably one of the first two options. As the data grows, look at other strategies and consider changing your backup equipment to minimize administrator effort. However, don't skimp on performing proper backups on important information because the backups take too much time.

Offsite Copies

Regardless of the backup approach you choose, you should move your backup copies offsite to another location on a regular basis. Your choice of backup schedule reflects the trade-off of effort and risk. On the risk side, consider how many days of development work your company could afford to lose as part of disaster recovery. On the effort side, consider how much time your company can afford to spend making additional copies and moving them offsite.

As tapes can be required to recover lost files, consider the time hit spent creating tapes for shipment offsite. An expensive and time-consuming approach is to create duplicate copies for onsite and offsite copies every night. Most small companies use a simple approach of alternating onsite and offsite storage of their full backup copies. This approach is not very expensive, but it makes file recovery more difficult when you need to recover a file that is stored in an offsite backup.

Some customers might compel you to keep offsite copies of product code. Additionally, some customer contracts can require *software escrow* (periodic archiving of your source code with a third party). Customers ask for software escrow to minimize their risk; if your company fails, the customer receives a copy of the source code. This requirement forces periodic full backups of parts of your source code in addition to the regular backups.

Most small companies look for simple solutions to offsite backups. If you start with the assumption that a disaster will damage only your physical facility, then moving copies out of the facility will be sufficient. The media should be stored in a commercial backup storage facility or a second building in the same town—not at the administrator's home. Storing backup media in a person's home can be a problem if the person leaves the company (or the country).

To create your offsite backups, you could create an additional copy of each backup daily, but this would double your daily backup time. Instead, take full backups from your regular process offsite. If you need quick access to backup files in your facility, consider making duplicate copies of offsite backup media.

Disk-Only Backup

Some system administrators use a dangerous backup practice of making periodic image copies of disk files to another disk, overwriting the last copy. When used as the sole backup mechanism, this method suffers from many weaknesses:

- Corrupt source files might corrupt the backup copy and permanent records do not exist.

- A disgruntled employee can alter the data. The backup files will store a copy of the problem code as the administrator creates these periodically but does not create a permanent record.

- Occasionally, hardware does fail. Although unlikely, both disks could fail, obliterating all your files.

- Users can delete files by accident. If you discover a lost file after the administrator makes the backup image, you cannot recover the file.

- Disk-to-disk backups are usually done with onsite disks. Consequently, if disaster strikes your building, you will have lost everything.

In general, avoid disk-only backup approaches in which you image your data and then overwrite the image. It will not help if you need to restore a file that was deleted weeks ago. Instead, back up to a permanent or stable medium. A disk-to-disk backup can be cost and time effective only if different images are made and saved regularly and a complete backup is kept on permanent media.

Creating and Managing Development Documentation

You can improve your development team's productivity by making development documentation easy to create and access through wikis, intranets, or content management systems. This will encourage the creation and use of documentation. Not having a system will lead to minimal documentation being created and shared.

Unfortunately, many managers ignore documentation during the company startup phase because of lack of interest and because its absence does not appear to be an immediate problem. A small team can track internal documents easily, but as the team and product line grows, tracking all the internal documentation becomes difficult because of the number of documents and versions that can exist. Locating the most current version of a file for a six-month-old project requires an archeologist's skill and patience when a documentation repository does not exist or the document creator is no longer with the company.

With no development documentation, the task of training new people is difficult. The lack of documentation also wastes the time of the current team as they try to locate information that doesn't exist. As individual engineers store pieces of essential information, lack of diversified information creates a bottleneck when a key engineer is not available—development can get stuck.

Small company development environments often release many projects in rapid succession; you can't expect developers to remember the details of projects from more than a few months back. The cost of poor documentation can be realized months or years later when developers badly need the information. Trying to understand someone else's code can be difficult enough; trying to understand the motivations of specific design decisions can be nearly impossible.

Development documentation covers many topics in addition to functional specifications. Here is a sample list of categories to consider:

- Product definition documents and specifications
- Technical background information
- Internal design documentation
- Customer system architecture
- Data file format information
- Database design schemas
- Process definitions
- Application programming interface (API) description
- Schedules

You can use various methods to make internal documentation available in small firms. Simple methods include keeping the main copy on local directories of work machines, emailing copies of documents to those who need them, creating copies in shared directories, and creating intranet pages and links.

All of the simple approaches have drawbacks, however. Document submitters can find many categories in which to place a file, and the team can find it difficult to track down the desired information. In addition, when a developer locates the information, she might not be able to determine whether she found the current version. With some approaches, opening the documents requires many mouse clicks. Simple approaches limit the file or text formats that are acceptable and do not block simultaneous edits. Finally, simple approaches do not provide levels of restricted access, so everyone has full access to every document.

One reasonable solution is to set up a wiki with a tool such as MediaWiki (*http://www.mediawiki.org/*). Wikis are simple to use, but creating and editing wiki pages is not always "what you see is what you get," or WYSIWYG—it can involve a multi-step process of cutting, pasting, and formatting information into the wiki from other documents. Wikis also require an administrator who can set up and maintain the site.

A *content management system* provides a method for everyone to access and edit documentation. A number of great open source systems are available, with Plone (*http://plone.org/*) being one good example. Excellent commercial systems exist as well, such as Microsoft Project Server.

The benefits generally exceed the costs, however, as a good system will:

- Allow easy searches for files
- Allow different levels of access for different account groups
- Make file uploads simple for all file types
- Make reading documentation easy, requiring a single click to open and instantly view documents

Multiple commercial and open source tools are available for use in creating collaboration sites. Selecting the proper content management tool, setting it up, and maintaining it constitutes a major project. In addition, the content system administrator will require time to set up the system and organize the data. You will need to assign a person to drive the process.

All data storage systems need a *gardener* to keep them organized. Without constant maintenance, the data in the systems quickly becomes "weedy" and out of date. As the data grows, the administrator will reorganize the layout as needed and manage or archive data that has become too old.

Source Control Versioning

Source control versioning (SCV) software allows you to save and retrieve multiple versions of different files, tag groups of files, and retrieve desired versions of files in a straightforward way. SCV software allows a team of development engineers to work on a product collaboratively, effectively sharing the use of a common set of source files. SCV software acts as a traffic cop to avoid file collisions and an archivist to track which files correspond with which product version.

SCV software supports the definition of *named versions* of sets of the source code files. With SCV software, you can re-create a named version of the code later. SCV software also helps manage conflicts when two developers want to use the same file at the same time. An engineer can reserve, or *lock,* a file for editing, preventing other engineers from modifying that file while it is locked. Without SCV locks, an engineer working on a file could find her changes overwritten by another engineer who modifies the same particular source file.

WARNING *Review the default behavior of your system for file checkout and locking. A common problem for engineers is assuming they have a lock on a file when they check out the file from the repository, but the default behavior for many systems is to lock files only when specifically requested to do so. Choose and configure your tools carefully to achieve the desired behavior, and then train your team to use the tools properly.*

Alternatively, a second engineer can make his changes on a duplicate copy of the source file and use the SCV *merge* feature to merge his changes in with the first engineer's changes after the lock is released. Newer SCV systems have effective merge systems that allow for two sets of changes to the same file to be correctly combined under the review of the last engineer checking in the code.

WARNING *Unfortunately, file merge can be flawed or can get confused on some SCV systems, effectively corrupting the resulting file. In some cases, sections of code or bug fixes are inadvertently removed from the source file without clear detection by the merging engineer. Engineers need to check the source file carefully to ensure that the merge was handled properly.*

Although SCV systems are well entrenched in software companies, management rarely defines best practices for their use. It is a good idea to set up best practices for the development team to minimize errors and potential team friction. These include the following practices.

For single-repository systems: Allow single-person checkout of files.
    This method implies that only a single engineer can check out a file for modification at one time and avoids the potential for code merging. Automatic code merging causes problems that you might

not see until after a release, because it can accidentally and silently remove earlier repairs from the system. An alternative is to require manual merging of files for cases in which multiple engineers need to work together. If a developer must perform a manual merge of files, he can carefully inspect the merged code sections. If they overlap, the developer can create a new version of the code to incorporate both sets of changes as appropriate. Even with a careful merge, the merged code often has unexpected behavior because each engineer built his code from what was previously there, not accounting for the others' changes.

When planning work, ask developers to examine the sections of the code with which they need to work in advance and set up a process that avoids coding collisions. Developers can work around each other, communicating clearly about where in the code they are working and being considerate about how long they check out common files.

NOTE *This recommendation does not apply to systems designed to work without a single main repository, such as Git.*

For single-repository systems: Lock-breaking should be rare.

Breaking locks on other engineers' files is a bad practice. An engineer who needs a locked file should first ask the lock holder to check in her work. Breaking another engineer's file lock forces her to merge her changes into your file. Merging is time consuming if done by hand and error prone if done automatically. Both types of merges often lead to hard-to-find errors and create the potential for bug repairs to be accidentally dropped.

NOTE *This recommendation does not apply to systems designed to work without a single main repository, such as Git.*

Comment file check-in notes should be descriptive and useful.

Comments should always be required for all code check-ins. The comment should be descriptive—simply adding "fixed bugs" is not useful to anyone. Describe the defect number as well as the section of the code that is changed to make the comment useful for other team members and QA. Descriptive comments are especially useful for tracking down defects as regression behavior changes.

Use macro variables to simplify build identification.

Key names and numbers in the code are changed as new builds are created and files are checked in. Most source control systems have macro languages that allow for easy substitution of text into the file during check-in. Examples of common macro items are product names, release versions, build dates, build numbers, copyright years, legal disclaimers, and version numbers. The development team should be required to use the macro feature.

Using macro names makes it much simpler to keep source files up to date when global information changes. For example, the user interface can display the product version numbers to the client, enabling them to associate problems with specific code versions. Macros eliminate the need to check the version number manually in the code.

NOTE *Other approaches to automatically labeling code versions exist, including using build-and-release systems to update the numbering.*

Companies in the very early stages of development do not always use a source control system, especially if only one to three engineers are on staff and they communicate frequently and maintain separate files. As these companies add developers to the team, they might resist using a SCV system because of the extra effort involved in setting them up and using them. Startup engineers can resist SCV systems on cultural grounds, as they like the idea of working "fast and loose." In this environment, you'll need to provide careful preparation and introduction of the system. Involve the engineers in the discussion and point out the costs of "fast and loose" when new engineers end up inadvertently stomping on others' work and the difficulty of recovering an older version of the code.

SCV packages vary considerably in quality, complexity, and scope. Some tools are tightly integrated with information reporting, bug tracking, and build systems. Investigate at least three packages before settling on one to use.

Software Build Method and Timing

A *software build method* is the approach you use for extracting the desired versions of source files, creating one or more executable versions of the code, and then storing it in the appropriate location for use. A standardized software build method ensures that one set of source files compiles into the same program, thereby avoiding the potential errors of manual program creation. Usually, the build method interacts with the source control tool.

In small companies, software build methods often start out being ad hoc designs. Different programs have different build methods because the methods were created by different engineers, probably at different times. Ad hoc designs are often problematic, and few people know how to use them. One engineer might be the only person who knows how to build certain program executables.

You must ensure that the build process for each product is *written down* and *tested successfully by a second engineer.* Having a second engineer go through the steps of building the code usually ensures that the instructions are correct. Often the creator of the instructions will leave out details or make mistakes because she knows the process too well. Ask the engineer in charge of the build to include a list of common problems that could occur and potential solutions to these problems.

When builds are done regularly, productivity is affected as well. Most small companies start out creating builds as needed. As the team grows larger, build collisions occur, with two engineers trying to build the code set at the same time, but using different files. At this point, regular builds become essential.

Daily builds work best, although development can build the software less often. At some companies the daily builds are really *nightly builds* that occur every evening. With daily builds, the build administrator finds file check-in mistakes daily, instead of later in the development cycle. In addition, the team will not push to delay a build so they can add more features or code—with weekly or less regular builds, the team might be tempted to delay weekly builds to accommodate last-minute changes. The team will also discover code integration problems after a while, making the debugging and repair considerably more difficult.

Building software during working hours has advantages over nightly builds. Daytime builds allow the team to see problems immediately so that the developer who created the problem can fix it quickly. With a nighttime build, the developer who created the problem might not return to work until later in the morning, leaving other developers with the task of cleaning up the problem or sitting idle, waiting for the developer's return.

With either nightly or daily builds, the developer who creates the problem should be held responsible for fixing it promptly. Breaking the build breaks the team's momentum and adds delays to the project. As developers can perform trial compiles and tests in their own local accounts, they have few excuses for breaking the build.

NOTE *The best approach is for the build administrator to configure development sandboxes at the start of the project to ensure consistency of layout and versions. Mismatched sandboxes can lead to broken builds after check-in of code.*

As the code becomes more complex and the team grows larger, you should hire a single person to control and monitor daily software builds: a *build engineer*. The build engineer builds the software, maintains the build tools, and reviews build problems from the previous night. Require the build engineer to pursue build problems until they have been resolved.

In summary, you should move from an ad hoc build system to a repeatable system that runs regularly. Do not wait until your company is in growth mode to set up the system. Document this system and have an alternative engineer trained to understand how it works. Finally, treat your build system as an important part of your development infrastructure.

Software Release Process

The software release process describes the tools and methods required to get the software into the customer's hands. A release process moves the executable and supporting files into the release location. The process can include automatic changes to the database, creation of multiple image copies of files for multiple servers, and changing of file attributes so they correctly run on the production machine.

As software distribution models vary considerably, release processes vary as well. The mechanisms of the process include customer downloads from a website, CD distributions, or files copied to customer-acceptable servers.

Like many processes, the software release process in small companies is usually ad hoc. As the software and product line become more complex, the frequency of release mistakes will increase, as each release is often a slight variation on a basic theme, providing opportunities for typing mistakes or mistaken assumptions about what is required to use the release.

At many small companies, only one person knows how to release the product—releasing software is a thankless task and not interesting to many engineers. If the engineer releases the code properly, nobody notices; if the engineer makes a mistake, everyone complains. Making the release effort more appealing to engineers is difficult, but showing appreciation for the engineer's effort is always worthwhile. In general, spread the release knowledge around the team and make it as simple as possible. Ensure that the release engineer writes down the process clearly and that at least two other people know the release process.

You should automate the release process as much as possible. Release automation can be as simple as shell scripts, or you can include more complex scripts or commercial programs. In all cases, automation not only shortens release time, but it reduces release errors. Serious release mistakes can take days of engineering work and recovery time.

As the company grows, teams other than engineering can take over the release process, such as members of the IT or operations groups. Not

---

RIGHT INSTRUCTIONS, WRONG ORDER

Our company had a separate release engineer who released the software during the nighttime when the server was not heavily used. The engineering team would create a set of release instructions, which QA would test, and the release engineer would execute to release the software.

On one release, the release engineer executed the release instructions in the wrong order. This led to product data being improperly updated. Several engineers worked for three days to fix the problem, as they had to write custom SQL scripts to correct it.

—Director of engineering

having releases assigned to your team does not mean that you can ignore associated problems, however. Work with the managers of the other teams to improve the release workflow. Some additional engineering effort can lead to savings for the company overall.

Bug-Tracking System

Bug-tracking software records problems and enhancement requests for your company's software products. Many different commercial and open source tools are available with different feature sets. Given the significant capabilities of this software, you should select an available tool rather than creating an ad hoc tool of your own.

Bug-tracking programs are a necessary part of a quality assurance process. Note that tracking of defects is only a part of the total QA process, which includes unit testing, test planning, traceability of test coverage, and recording, evaluation, repair, and validation of defects. Spend time considering your choice of tools based on how well they support the QA process you want to put in place. Some common issues that arise when considering bug systems that might affect your choice are as follows:

Cost   If the bug-tracking system is expensive on a per-person basis, deploying it to everyone in the company may not seem cost effective.

Configurability of workflow   Some systems have very limited ability to change their built-in defect workflow, which would force you to match their flow.

Data collection   Some systems will not allow you to change the data collected at each step or put entry restrictions on the data users enter during each step.

Remote access   Systems have variable abilities to permit access and bug entry remotely. If you have development teams working on the same product internationally, this could be a big problem.

Reporting   A manager's ability to see what is going on depends on flexibility in getting reports of the data in the system. Reporting capabilities vary considerably.

SVC integration   Integration with source control systems can simplify associating bugs with code.

Small companies tend to use bug-tracking tools in sloppy and changeable ways, leading to wasted efforts and quality problems. Here is a humorous top ten list of abuses of a defect-tracking tool. Avoid these strategies at all costs:

10. Submitters do not review and "close" defect reports when development makes the repair and assigns the defect ticket back to submitters for review.

9. Reported problems are ignored by the assigned engineer because no process for nagging the engineer exists.

8. Submitters enter a defect so badly worded that nobody can figure out the problem or whether a problem even exists. When asked, the submitter does not remember what he was concerned about.

7. Defect submissions describe ten different problems in one defect report so engineering finds it nearly impossible to close the ticket out or track any of the problems individually.

6. A defect submitter assigns the problem an incorrect and unusual status state, making the defect untracked.

5. A submitter enters a core-dump error message into the defect system but does not include an explanation.

4. A submitter's full defect report says "the software is broken."

3. The system administrator turns on the email feature of the defect system so that email replies automatically log into the defect system—along with all of the reply messages in the email chain. Defects become massive in size and nearly impossible to read after a few exchanges.

2. A support team member pastes in a 50-page customer email chain into a defect ticket with no explanation: "This customer is unhappy about something, but dang if I can figure it out."

   (Drum roll, please....)

1. A submitter writes schedule reminder notes into the defect system, because she thinks that someone will actually read the defect reports.

With all the potential ways to abuse a defect-reporting system, having some human intervention is usually necessary. Without enforcement and review of data in a bug-tracking system, so much junk data gets stored that people ignore older defects. Ensure that the defect tool has a clear process associated with it and enforce the process. A great way to enforce the process is to have a gatekeeper or gardener for the bug system who is responsible for the health of the bug data, not the system per se.

As part of the defect system process, define and enforce standards for *resolution notes*. Resolution notes describe how the defect was resolved and are useful to the submitter, but they are also helpful in defect analysis and end-of-project reviews. Train other teams that use the bug-tracking system in proper system use, including customer service, sales, marketing, technical writing, and any consultants. Failure to train people will lead to extra effort in development dealing with the defects that people improperly submit.

In summary, first make sure that your team has a useable defect-reporting system, and then ensure that your team has a proper process for using it. Monitor the usage and refer offenders to the proper correction institution. Finally, refer to Chapter 17 for more information on bug tracking and entry.

Selecting the Right Development Tools

After you have reviewed all the basics of tools and methods, you can select at least one replacement system. Fortunately, in many small companies, the development manager can direct the choice of development tools. Having this choice gives you the flexibility to change and reconfigure systems as your needs change. This is not necessarily the case in large companies.

Managers in startup companies often base their tool selection on two criteria: familiarity and price (preferably, free). A thoughtful choice, however, will prevent future problems when the company grows and the product takes off.

Don't let price alone drive you toward selecting only from free, open source tools. Establish your long-term needs before ruling out buying a commercial tool. Since the cost of changing to a different tool later is

Many large companies do not give engineering management the choice of tools. They have multiple layers of management and many different projects. A senior technology manager removed from individual developers will choose the tools. Choice of tools will usually reflect several factors: price, technology features, ability to handle the largest and most complex project in the company, and what is commonly being used in different divisions.

However, if your group isn't currently using one of the newly chosen tools, libraries, or databases, then you will be forced to convert your software to the new tools whether it makes business sense or not.

usually very high, picking a tool based just on short-term finances will sometimes lead to painful development issues a few years later. If price must be an overriding factor (that is, if there literally is no money to spend), plan in advance for a transition strategy to your ideal tool when money is available.

Tool vendors can push hard during the selection process. Vendors may offer low introductory prices, free first-year licenses, bundled software, or promises of special future features. When considering these incentives, ask for a longer-term price guarantee for future purchases—ideally, five years. Do not include promises of future features in your decision process unless the feature description (along with a delivery date) is included in the purchase contract alongside a penalty clause. Once the sale is made, you may see your vendor's priorities change.

Smaller vendors may take special interest in making the sale to you because they can use your company as a reference account, get a sale, and have the potential for future sales automatically as your company grows. In contrast, larger vendors will likely press less hard, as their sales focus is likely to be larger companies willing to buy larger numbers of tools at once. As the selector, you may feel camaraderie and empathy for another small company trying to reach success; however, recognize this influence when making your decision. Do not make the wrong choice simply to help out another small company.

Once a development organization uses a tool, it can be expensive to replace, because of the costs associated with migrating the data and retraining the team. To make the best choice, create a table comparing tool options covering these areas:

Initial cost   Consider initial sale price and installation costs.

Impact on productivity   Weigh the savings in salary time due to more efficiency of the system and fewer errors.

Recurring costs   As you add more users, consider what happens to the cost per person. Some products have low introductory rates for small teams but can get expensive per person as your company grows. Nailing down the recurring costs as part of the original deal gives you perspective on the future.

Maintenance costs   Consider how much labor and maintenance the tool will require. A few tools require half- or full-time staff to maintain them for a good-sized team.

Integration with other tools   Know whether the tool integrates well with other tools—for example, consider whether a defect tool integrates with source control and whether the source control program integrates with the integrated development environments (IDEs) being used.

System performance after growth   Consider what the system performance will be when the team size grows.

Remote development   Know whether the system can handle users who are working remotely. Consider its effectiveness with different development centers overseas, if necessary.

Ease of use   Consider how easy the tool is to learn and use.

Data security   Does the tool manage your data securely so it won't be lost or revealed inadvertently?

Data access   Know whether data can be reasonably imported and exported, which allows for future migration and integration with other tools.

Tool familiarity can be another trap in the selection process. Many people will choose a tool one of the team members is already familiar with instead of taking a risk with something new. A familiar tool has the benefit of less training time—at least for the person selecting it. However, choosing an inferior tool based on one person's familiarity can lead to team resentment, as other team members will have to live with the tool's problems. Tools are changing so rapidly that choosing a known tool can result in choosing an obsolete tool. Instead, spend the time to investigate other options rather than simply choosing what's familiar to you.

Time pressures often force managers to make decisions before they can fully assess a product. Delegating the investigation and recommendation of tool choices to an interested senior engineer can improve the selection process. Delegation of the investigation benefits you and the team because it helps build trust: You will have shown the team that you trust them with the company's interests as well as their own. In contrast, engineers can react negatively if you select a tool without their involvement.

Ask the engineer to deeply investigate at least three tools before making the recommendation. A deep investigation requires trying the tool with realistic data on real problems your team faces. This will ensure that the tool meets the team's needs not only on the surface, but also in practice.

Once the tool is chosen, make the selecting engineer the tool's champion. He should help other engineers with the transition, answer questions, and monitor the tool's use. Having the selecting engineer actively use the tool will let him understand its problems and investigate potential solutions. More of his credibility will be at stake for making the tool a success, and he will be more likely to ensure that his peers are satisfied with the choice, because he has to work with them daily.

Additional Reading

Here is some additional reading on topics presented in this chapter:

The Build Master: Microsoft's Software Configuration Management Best Practices, by Vincent Maraia (Addison-Wesley, 2005)

"Defect Tracking Tools," *http://www.testingfaqs.org/t-track.html*

DMOZ Open Directory Project website, *http://www.dmoz.org/*

Software Release Methodology, by Michael E. Bays (Prentice Hall, 1999)

8

ASSESSING YOUR TECHNOLOGY

Evaluating your technology base *early* helps you avoid problems that create crises *later.* As development manager, you are entrusted and expected to keep the technology in working order at all times. If you fail to do this, any serious problems that are encountered can lead to you making poor decisions while under duress. Better to learn your technology early and well, before you face major problems.

To understand your company's technology, you must evaluate a number of key areas. Unfortunately, a thorough technology assessment is not always a top priority in small companies. The following list covers some of the most common technical areas that management does not fully scrutinize:

System documentation	System API
System scalability	Security
Failure modes	Data reporting and analysis
Error handling and messages	International support
Software system flexibility	Test harness
Third-party packages	

As you assess your technology, consider the completeness, quality, and long-term impact of choices made to date: Regarding completeness, consider all the key technologies in place; regarding quality, consider whether the technologies being used are reliable and implemented with current best practices. This chapter provides an expanded discussion of considerations for each technology area.

System Documentation

Many small and growing companies do not sufficiently document their software or systems for many reasons, including lack of interest in doing the job, pressure to achieve short-term goals, changing definitions, and perceived lack of need. Most engineers want to write code, not technical documents. Time pressures can be considerable in small firms because the next delivery is always around the corner. Changing definitions make it difficult to keep documentation up to date. And the need is not perceived: The senior architect understands the system in detail, so why document it for others, when he can explain it?

Good system overview documentation is critical. Without it, your company faces long-term problems and lost opportunities. New engineers need a technical overview of the system as part of their initial training. In addition, as the development team makes changes to the system, they might not see the far-reaching effects of their changes without access to proper overview drawings and descriptions. Documentation is also important because your growing company might eventually face audits by customers or certification agencies (for example, Cardholder Information Security Program, or CISP, in the financial world). Audits usually require system documentation. Finally, if another company wants to buy your firm, it will review your technical documents as part of the due diligence.

Your first step in documenting your system is to create a *system overview diagram.* You can obtain the information you need by interviewing development team members and possibly by gleaning data from any partial documentation that exists. Create the diagram as a useful working document, not just fluff for sales presentations. Summarize the software and system correctly and in detail. Organize the diagram for easy understanding by rearranging the layout to minimize the number of crossing or overlapping lines. Make it visually consistent by using only a few box sizes and a few types of symbols. Finally, label paths and contents clearly and consistently.

After creating the overview diagram, examine the system documentation for the amount of detail. Too little detail provides little utility, while too much detail makes the document difficult to use and maintain. Review the documentation to ensure that you have included enough information by asking these questions:

Is the documentation sufficiently complete to support training a new engineer if two individuals on your team left their jobs?

Multiple people leaving a company at the same time is a common occurrence. People who enjoy working in startup situations might look for the next opportunity and invite co-workers to join them.

Is documentation sufficiently complete that removing a team member will not disrupt operations?

Nobody on the team should be so critical that losing him or her would mean that production would fall apart. You should be able to deal with a personnel change without losing too much ground.

Would the documentation satisfy a company that might be interested in buying your company? Will your documentation support a reasonable valuation?

Scrambling to create documentation when someone is interested in acquiring your company does not result in good work. From a buyer's perspective, a large part of the corporate value of a software firm is its intellectual property. Failing to build detailed documentation can have an impact on company purchase price.

Does documentation provide accurate, up-to-date technical documentation so a customer can understand how to integrate his system with your software?

> A poorly defined application program interface (API) or poor integration documents will frustrate customers and consume valuable development time.

Do not stop at a high-level system diagram when considering your system documentation. Consider all of the interface directions, including control files, APIs, and error messages. Consider descriptions of how your system fits together, as well as inclusion of customer usage models. Consider risk when thinking about the documentation. If only one engineer is an expert on important aspects of the product, that engineer needs to document these features.

A minimum list of recommended system documentation includes the following:

- System overview
- Outstanding issues[1]
- Detailed system architecture description
- API description and usage
- Error handling, including cases and messages
- Control file formats
- Internationalization support description
- Database schemas
- List of technologies and libraries used
- Build instructions for all product parts
- Packaging and release instructions for all modules
- Workflow required to support the system

System Scalability

System scalability describes the ability of the program or system to maintain acceptable performance as the volume of users and data increases significantly. Scalability means that the usability and speed of the system do

---

[1] To qualify as an outstanding issue, the issue should have the potential of creating a noticeable impact on the product. The description should explain the impact and why the issue is unresolved.

not degrade significantly as usage increases. Obviously, at some level, all systems will fail, but setting a reasonable maximum expected usage size and knowing that the software can handle that size is what scalability is all about.

When a young company starts developing a new project, development focuses first on creating core functionality, and scalability is often an afterthought. The team might consider scalability of the system at times, but this objective is not analyzed, monitored, or properly tested because of the expense and time involved. Few companies run enough tests to generate an accurate scaling model for what happens at different volumes of usage.

Ignoring scalability creates a huge risk factor for the company, however. (Are you noticing a theme here?) Scalability problems can sink a company if its system fails or slows down when the volume reaches the peak. For example, without proper scalability design and testing, systems with high uptime requirements can fail at high load, sometimes in unexpected ways. These failures can result in the loss of customers or even a direct financial loss if your company has guaranteed system availability.

A detailed *system diagram* provides a great starting point for examining system scalability. The diagram should show hardware, applications, and software for the entire system—a whole system overview in enough detail to analyze it. You can create a scaling model from a detailed diagram if you have reliable test data. If you do not yet have the test data, the diagram can direct you to the tests you need to run and help you identify potential failure points.

Various methods and tools can be used to evaluate systems, including commercial packages used by IT shops, modeling programs, and even Excel spreadsheets. Your choice of approach depends on the complexity of the system. You can use a spreadsheet successfully to build up scalability models for simple systems with the proper data. For complex systems, system-modeling tools are better choices.

Analysis alone does not ensure system scalability; you must also create a test lab to experience in practice how the system performs. As most modern systems find the biggest delays in the data layer, senior database engineers usually run the labs and perform the analyses.

Scalability presents an ongoing problem to the development team, requiring vigilance as the team develops new code. Engineers not trained in database scaling can easily create queries that slow down the system. The engineer most experienced with database queries can review all database queries as part of the code review process. Finding and fixing a problem in the design phase is far less expensive than discovering the problem in a test lab.

Failure Modes

A *failure mode* occurs when your software or system fails in ways that you did not expect and from which your software does not directly recover. *Failure mode analysis* involves a systematic analysis of general ways the program or system can fail. Small company development teams often do not systematically examine how their product or service can break. Instead, most wait for a failure to occur and patch the system to fix it.

Small company developers usually focus on making the product work, rather than looking for what will cause it to fail. Breaking the product is a job for quality assurance. However, the QA team does not have the insight into the internals of the code that are required to perform a proper risk analysis. Engineers themselves need to analyze the risks and failure modes of every product or system.

A failure mode review must examine the system as a whole and in parts. Failures can occur in components or in the interactions of several components; some single components might show no obvious failure issues, but their interactions with other components can cause the system to break. In addition, a review must consider how unexpected customer data or usage can affect the system, including the effects of unusual data, overload of data streams, data size issues, data rate issues, and timing issues.

External abnormal occurrences can also cause problems to the system and should be studied. Using a system diagram as your reference point, ask a series of questions about what could happen, such as the following:

- What happens if third-party vendors do not provide the bandwidth needed?

- What happens if someone cuts a cable or a machine goes down?

- If a system loses data, how does its recovery mechanism work?

- What synchronization problems can be identified?

- What happens when the wrong data enters the system?

- How does the system respond to data provided in the wrong order?

- How will the system detect unauthorized access?

FAILURE MODE

The company I joined had a complex system that synchronized data between two different data sets. The system had a synchronization problem that would occur a few times each month. When this occurred, an engineer would repair the problems directly in the database.

While reviewing risk factors for the system, I starting asking questions about this failure mode and became concerned. Under certain conditions, the failure rate could be high—it would require a system problem and a failure in the monitoring of the system by the operations team. The architect believed they would never see this problem, as it required that a system problem would have to go unmonitored by the operations team for many hours. The system had real-time monitoring in place, so he believed it would not happen. As the company planned for increased system traffic volume over the next year, I insisted that we plug this failure mode in the next release.

A few months after the release, the meltdown system failure occurred, causing a key system component to stop. The operations team had turned off the monitoring of this server six months earlier without engineering's knowledge, because the monitoring code gave too many false warnings. By the time we discovered the problem, the improperly synchronized data far exceeded what we could have repaired manually. Fortunately, the automatic repair mechanism did the corrections and kept the system running. We were one system redundancy away from a complete meltdown of our business.

—Software manager

Scale the analysis based on the potential problems a failure would create. Although intense failure mode analysis approaches can be used, most products require a less intensive examination, except for cases in which failure could have an extreme adverse effect on the customer.

Requiring a systematic analysis of failure modes will improve the reliability of your product or system. As a manager, require an analysis for every major release of a system. Perform this analysis early in the development cycle and act on any issues uncovered.

Error Handling and Messages

Error handling and *messaging* concern how you process your system's reasonably expected usage problems. Error handling occurs within normal operation of the system and allows for continued usage. It differs from failure modes, as failure modes represent system or product failure cases in which the system operation *breaks*. With a failure mode, manual intervention is often required for recovery. With error handling, the processing is routine and part of normal product usage. Error messaging describes the message sent to the user when the error is detected and is sometimes used to describe all of error handling.

Error handling is designed as the product is created. When an engineer sees a use case that results in a detectable error, she creates an exception case in the code to handle it while informing the user about the problem. However, development teams often do not examine the messages after the initial creation, causing many error messages to go untested and ignored.

Development teams in young companies rarely document error conditions because the lack of error documentation does not block sales and does not cause short-term problems. However, not documenting error conditions opens testing holes and opportunities for failure modes to occur as part of the error processing. For example, an untested warning message, when activated, can cause the program to fail or cause database corruption. In addition to identifying problems earlier, documenting error conditions helps QA test efforts and simplifies internationalization of your software. Knowing the error conditions will also support risk analysis. With all of these benefits, it is best to create error documentation before your company enters its growth phase.

NOTE *A good standard practice is for QA to test all error handling and be able to run unit tests during development. QA's careful checking of error conditions can assist in documenting the conditions as well as finding critical failures that can occur in the error resolution code.*

To create the error documentation, request a list of all the error phrases in the system from your development team. Ask the team to identify error conditions that are not currently associated with a textual message. Use this information to improve the product's error handling by creating log file records. This can improve your testing because you can create targeted test cases to activate those error conditions. Documentation should cover the general error modes, error display, and error recovery. In addition, document error conditions that only a system administrator of your product would see. These conditions are often neglected in testing.

It's also useful to review error messages for reasonable practices. Since developers focus first on the successful workflow, they might not spend much time thinking about the unsuccessful workflows. For unsuccessful workflows, developers should consider the following:

Does a recovery path exist to resolve the issue for the customer?

A good recovery path puts the user back to the location where the problem occurs, retaining as much of the entered data as possible, so that the customer can attempt his task again in a different way or at least save his data.

Does the error message provide information that hackers could use to break into the system?

For example, does the message provide a list of data elements when a fatal flaw occurs?

If multiple errors occur, does the system separately list messages for each? Does each message provide useful information?

A useful message should clearly describe the problem; provide data that would assist development in resolving the problem if the customer cannot do so; and provide a location of the problem in the code, rather than a generic "it broke."

Software System Flexibility and Maintainability

System flexibility describes the ease of expanding the product with new feature sets and capabilities. *System maintainability,* on the other hand, describes the ease of coding bug repairs and adding minor features. Both are determined by the architecture and techniques used to create the code and resulting quality of the code.

When engineering builds product code with flexibility and maintainability in mind, the company gains a long-term corporate advantage. Flexible code can be a decisive factor in product success, because cost and time to market is critical for small companies. With maintainable code, the lower overall cost of working on the code, especially when someone other than the author is doing the work, can mean the difference between success and failure for a growing company in a competitive market. Understanding the state of the code will allow you to make much better predictions about the costs of making major changes to your product.

As head of engineering, you need to know the flexibility aspects of your company's code as well as its maintainability. These things affect both short-term and long-term planning: In the short term, maintainability and flexibility affect the cost of repairs. In the long term, maintainability and flexibility affect your decision of when to overhaul or replace the current code.

Many small companies lack foresight about how code will be reused across the system. With few customers on board, receiving the proper input to plan for the future can be challenging. If the team focuses on quick delivery, programmers will often reinvent similar code rather than ensure that the code offers maximum reuse. This approach creates a maintenance nightmare, however, because the code now contains many different versions of similar functions. As the product changes and grows, changes to functionality will require far more effort, as each different version of the function will need to be modified. Because developers implement functions in different ways, the cost of modifying two similar functions with one change can be more than twice the cost of merging the function code from the start.

Software maintenance problems build up over time and are sometimes unnoticed because they amount to small increments in a total effort.

However, when they become more important because of significantly slower development efforts and more quality issues, the difficulty in recovering can be too large to be easily resolved.

Consider the following two cases, observed "in the wild" and related to flexibility and maintainability of code:

Engineering builds the software to minimize costs, but intends to replace the software at a specific time.
> Engineering should test this assumption with the executive team before building the system in this way. Don't surprise your company with a quickly built system that cannot be modified easily. Instead, let the executive team know and get their buy-in before opting for this choice.

New customers are supported by engineering copying old code and customizing it to meet the customer's needs.
> This provides a short-term boost but a long-term disaster. The problems associated with copy-and-customize do not justify the quick support provided for new customers. The maintenance cost of the application multiplies with each copy. Changes development makes to improve one customer's code base are not portable to another customer's code base; this situation stalls out your product development and turns your efforts into custom coding.

Regarding both flexibility and maintainability, you need to make conscious choices and get buy-in from the executive team, and you should continue to be aware of your product's status. There is no "one-size-fits-all" solution to flexibility and maintainability problems. Different product roadmaps have different requirements and expectations as to when the software will be overhauled or replaced.

Third-Party Packages Integrated into the System

In most small software companies, the development team integrates third-party code into the product because it shortens development time. You need to identify and document these packages for a number of reasons:

- Potential investors will request this information as part of due diligence.

- External security audits will require a list of third-party packages used.

- Third-party packages can increase your product costs if the vendor raises its rates.

- Third-party package vendors can change licensing requirements, making it difficult to meet your goals and the license requirements.

- Third-party packages can affect the quality of your product.

- A third-party package that you have modified can increase ongoing costs, because the vendor might deliver later versions of the package, which means you will have to modify your code again.

- Third-party vendors can go out of business or drop support for the package, leaving you with a major problem.

To determine what packages have been included in a system, ask the system architect to create a list. (Do not be surprised if no documentation exists.) Turn the list into a one-page summary and make it available to the development team for review. Then, ask the team to identify potential risks, including those that might appear as the product usage grows. Example risks include scalability issues, quality concerns, and overall utility.

Once you have documented a list of third-party packages, assign a senior engineer to maintain this list and make it easily available. This will help avoid a crisis when trying to pull the information together at the last minute and will keep the team thinking about the impact of integrating new packages into the product.

Analyzing the third-party code in the existing system does bring to light the process of "make versus buy" decisions. With all of the potential problems that third-party code can present, why use it at all? For most small companies, cash is limited, so getting a product to market quickly is a key goal. The best strategy for achieving this goal is to create only the sections of the product that are not currently available as third-party packages and buy the rest, but only when the business case makes sense. When reviewing the business case, you should consider all the issues raised in this section as well as cost and time to build compared to cost and time to buy and integrate. A good rule of thumb is this: Buy when the cost and time are less than or nearly equal to the build option.

System Application Programming Interface

Small company development teams commonly underdocument system application programming interfaces (APIs). The API allows customers and other companies to communicate with your product or system through a data or software interface. Most modern programs use an API because it provides huge flexibility and speed advantages.

Customers often complain because incomplete documentation forces them to make assumptions about how the product API works. This can lead to wasted customer efforts and demands to change the implementation. Incomplete documentation also forces costs back onto your company, as your development and support teams have to answer questions about proper usage. A poorly documented API probably has not been completely tested either, leaving your customers to find problems, especially with lesser-used features.

Review the current API specification to ensure that it clearly states legal data values, interaction of data elements, error conditions, and error handling. If the documentation requires more information, ask an engineer and a documentation writer to fill in the gaps. If you create a solid API definition before your company hits its growth phase, your company will avoid serious problems with unhappy partners and customers (as well as the costs of supporting them).

API documentation needs more than just an interface description—it needs well-chosen use case examples. Providing an API description without use case examples is like handing someone a foreign language dictionary and expecting them to learn the language. Use cases should illustrate common usages that you expect your customers to integrate with their product to solve their problems. If you continue to update the descriptions as more customers use your product, the API document can be a positive asset in technical sales.

Security

Although many engineers consider product-usage security an IT or operations team task, the engineering team should play the major role in creating a secure product. Consequently, you must make security an integral part of your development process. The most effective way to do this is to review security elements as programmers develop the code and as QA tests it.

Security often becomes a high-priority development issue when some driving event occurs—a customer asks questions about security before buying the product, a certifying organization requires a security audit, or a hacker breaks into the system. Don't wait until a driving event occurs. Instead, secure your product before being asked to do so, either by hiring an outside consultant or assigning the project to a team member. Whatever your choice, select one member from engineering and QA as the security gurus for their respective teams. Then ask them to spend time learning about security practices and testing methodologies.

Software security requires continuous focus during every development cycle. By assigning a software engineer to review the code for security flaws before QA tests the code, you can find problems earlier and improve security with less impact on cost and time. Security flaws found late in the development process can be very costly to fix.

Making security a priority in your system requires that you take extra measures. Consider acquiring security analysis tools appropriate for your product or system, and use them for every release. In critical systems, use a security consultant to review your system and identify problems. The additional costs are always justifiable by the results—problems identified before the product is released.

When determining how much to budget for the security effort, consider the types of security failures, the costs of each, and the probabilities of each. These costs will vary considerably based on the type of industry the product supports and the nature of the product. Devise a development plan in which sufficient money is spent on security to bring the failure probability multiplied by the cost down to a reasonable level.

Most companies do not spend enough time and effort building secure products or systems. More important, the effort spent is often at the wrong time in the development cycle—during testing or post-release recovery. But testing and repairing security in a built system is very expensive and sometimes impossible. As a practice, establish security requirements at the beginning, and then ensure they are considered and reviewed during the design.

Do not wait until an audit or hacker forces you into action, because your team will have a much greater problem improving security after the software has been built. Take software security seriously, because the damage done by poor security can be impossible to repair later.

Data Reporting and Analysis

Many companies' products store customer data, especially if the company offers a web-hosted service. Small company systems commonly store customer data in a database from which the team designs SQL queries that allow the program code to access data. In addition to allowing programmers to enter and modify the data in the database, many products include a data-reporting functionality that is often added through separate modules or through a purchased reporting software package.

A simple database approach can work well to get the initial product off the ground. As your customer base grows or the volume of queries grows significantly, however, the system will slow down. If this happens rapidly, your product's release cycle might not occur often enough to correct the problem before it becomes a huge issue.

Investigate the query speed of your product and estimate where speed problems might occur. Also, estimate likely customer volume increases and timing. If you do this in advance, you will be prepared when speed might become an issue. Typically, query speed becomes an issue when your company enters a growth phase. You can minimize speed problems by carefully reviewing and testing SQL queries in a lab, but this will only get you so far. Large reports covering months or years of data will slow down over time. As a rule of thumb, when a report takes more than 10 seconds to display, customers become dissatisfied with the wait.

Database information displayed in reports can change over time. Customers find it disconcerting to see their data from two months ago change from what your system reported two months earlier. Changes happen because the algorithm for displaying the report changed or because parts of the underlying data changed. An example of underlying data change might be the removal of an account that the customer created in error and you closed. These inconsistencies can be handled in several ways: by letting the customer know about the volatility of past data and getting their acceptance; by restricting any changes to past data even if the data contains errors; by modifying the database or business logic so that reports don't appear to change; or by using a data warehouse. A data warehouse, although expensive, can be a great solution in terms of both data consistency and speed.

Data Warehouse

A *data warehouse* stores snapshots summarizing the data at regular intervals with the goal of providing rapid access and consistency in responses. Common snapshot intervals are daily, weekly, or monthly, depending on the data and the customer need. Data warehouses are an expensive, albeit effective, approach to improving data reporting.

Creating a data warehouse requires that you decide, in advance, what data to accumulate, how it's accumulated, and how it will be reported. While you can add reports to the data warehouse after it has been built, it should be initially designed to meet your long-term needs. Any changes added after the warehouse has been built do not become useful immediately, because data must accumulate before it can be of enough significance to measure in a report. Because creating a data warehouse has many pitfalls, you should hire someone with experience in data warehouse creation before taking this approach. Both database and IT experience are required to set up the warehouse properly.

A data warehouse solves the data change problem as well. Because the warehouse takes snapshots of data used to generate a report, the displayed data will not change even if the underlying data has changed. So, for example, monthly historical data will not change unless you run that month's generation routine again. This can be especially useful when the formula for calculating some of the presented data necessarily had to change over time, but the new formula isn't appropriate for the older data. On the other hand, for customers who want to propagate changes back in time, the data warehouse provides a means for doing this in a controlled manner. Such changes can be analyzed and proper business logic applied before running the program to update the warehouse, so that the changes are verified as correct and made when appropriate for the business needs.

Warning: Data warehouses are an order of magnitude more expensive than a pure database approach and are time consuming to set up and maintain.

Make sure that the need for a warehouse is justified from a business perspective before building it. For the following reasons, creating a data warehouse is an expensive and lengthy task:

- A data warehouse often requires that you acquire additional hardware.

- A data warehouse requires rewriting all of your reports and creating a program to generate the summary data.

- A data warehouse requires ongoing maintenance.

Because of the costs and time delays, plan for a data warehouse *before* your company hits its growth phase to minimize the disruption. Waiting until data access becomes a problem will not allow your company enough time to solve the problem, as building a data warehouse can easily take six months or more.

International Support

Many web applications and some desktop applications require *international support*, and that means much more than just translating English text into another language. It often requires rethinking and reworking parts of your software. In addition to language support, other issues include changes in user interfaces, changes to workflow because customers or business practices differ, legal issues related to site usage or guarantees, and currency issues if you are selling the product or the product deals with money.

In most American startups, development builds the first product to support English-only for the US market. The introduction of support for other countries and languages often follows from sales opportunities rather than a technology plan. Ad hoc internationalization can lead to major surprises for development and the entire company due to the unexpected costs, lack of required expertise, and development delays.

Treat international support as a major release. Recognize that internationalizing your product will increase your operating costs and add release delay going into the future. You can implement internationalization during the company growth phase, but planning for it in advance can save you headaches later.

NOTE   *Assessing the internationalization costs requires a detailed review. Appendix B covers internationalization issues by providing questions to ask your company management regarding internationalization along with options to consider during development. It also includes an overview of best practices when implementing internationalization on a site.*

Looking at the Big Picture

This chapter covered many technological areas that require adequate review. Trying to make all of the areas ideal may not be practical. In fact, for most business, the different areas vary in importance. A good approach is to review of all of the technological areas and assess which are terrible, which are tolerable, and which are great. Then, bring the terrible areas up to at least tolerable. This will minimize your technological risks with the least investment.

Additional Reading

Here is some additional reading on topics presented in this chapter:

Documentation

Developing Software with UML: Object-Oriented Analysis and Design in Practice, by Bernd Oestereich (Addison-Wesley Professional, 2002)

The Fine Art of Technical Writing, by Carol Rosenblum Perry (Blue Heron Publishing, 1991)

"Software Documentation," from Wikipedia, *http://en.wikipedia.org/wiki/Software_documentation*

Scalability

"Scalability," from Wikipedia, *http://en.wikipedia.org/wiki/Scalability*

Risk Factors

Manage It!: Your Guide to Modern, Pragmatic Project Management, by Johanna Rothman (Pragmatic Bookshelf, 2007)

Waltzing with Bears: Managing Risk on Software Projects, by Tom DeMarco and Timothy Lister (Dorset House Publishing, 2003)

System API

http://lcsd05.cs.tamu.edu/slides/keynote.pdf, "How to Design a Good API and Why It Matters," by Joshua Bloch, provides a good summary discussion of APIs

Error Handling

Code Complete: A Practical Handbook of Software Construction, by Steve McConnell (Microsoft Press, 2004)

The Pragmatic Programmer: From Journeyman to Master, by Andrew Hunt and David Thomas (Addison-Wesley Professional, 1999)

Security

Secure Coding: Principles and Practices, by Mark G. Graff and Kenneth R. Van Wyk (O'Reilly, 2003)

Securing Java: Getting Down to Business with Mobile Code, by Gary McGraw and Edward W. Felten (Wiley, 1999)

Security Engineering: A Guide to Building Dependable Distributed Systems, by Ross J. Anderson (Wiley, 2008)

https://www.pcisecuritystandards.org/, PCI Security Standards Council website focuses on account data protection

http://www.cert.org/cert/information/developers.html, CERT Information for Developers, provides information for developers on coding standards

Data Reporting

The Data Warehouse Lifecycle Toolkit, by Ralph Kimball, Margy Ross, Warren Thornthwaite, and Joy Mundy (Wiley, 2008)

Internationalization

Developing International Software, by Dr. International (Microsoft Press, 2002)

Maximizing ROI on Software Development, by Vijay Sikka (Auerbach, 2004)

PART III

OUTSIDE OF ENGINEERING

While your relationship with the development team is crucial, you should not ignore your relationship with teams outside of engineering. Even if you have the best engineering team working with you, you will not succeed if you have poor relationships with marketing, sales, your boss, or your peers. Building these relationships helps ensure your success—and it can be a lot of fun, as well.

9

WORKING WITH YOUR COMPANY

Since a company's practices, culture, and values set the tone for interactions within the organization, a development manager's success depends on her ability to work effectively within the company's culture and also her ability to influence it. Conversely, a manager whose style is contrary to company culture and practices will encounter friction with other managers and other employees.

To understand a company's culture and practices, the new manager must first inquire about it and then observe what behaviors actually occur in the workplace. If you focus on the following five areas, you can develop a good sense of your company's culture and practices:

- Ask how decisions are made.
- Observe how people reach agreements.

- Understand how meetings are conducted.

- Know how people problems are resolved.

- See what behaviors get rewarded.

As a manager, you can also influence your company's culture and practices by actively promoting new practices among fellow managers and modeling appropriate examples. Cultures and practices can shift in small companies as they grow and develop, providing opportunities for change and improvement. If your CEO wants to improve corporate culture, your influence can motivate changes as the company grows.

Company Culture and Practices

Company *culture* and *practices* refer to the shared understanding of how employees behave in a company and how they interact with one another and with management. A growing company's culture helps define the company and makes it unique. If a culture is easily identifiable and projects itself in a positive light, prospective employees will be attracted to the company and current employees will be more likely to stay with the firm. From a purely financial standpoint, a positive culture adds value to a company. From a people standpoint, a positive culture makes working for the company an enjoyable experience.

In a small growing company, a culture can form on its own, without any particular guidance from employees or management. However, this often results in a culture that reflects the values and practices of top management, whether explicit or not. Company culture reflects what management rewards and encourages in employee behavior, and employees usually follow management's lead or decide to leave.

You want first and foremost to promote a culture of trust and collaboration, in which individuals are encouraged to share information and perform at a high level with the expectation that management will support them in their endeavors. If employees know that they will be treated fairly and they feel secure about their jobs, a culture of trust grows. Employees don't worry about losing their jobs for political reasons. When conflicts occur, employees handle their problems first with the individuals involved and not through email blasts to management.

More important, in a healthy culture, the overall focus is on company success, rather than individual success. Employees are willing to take reasonable risks and stretch their abilities on a project because doing so is in everyone's best interest. Also of benefit is a focus on long-term as well as short-term efforts. A long-term investment in productivity at the expense of short-term results might make sense, but that approach won't work in an environment that lacks trust.

Contrast a culture of trust with a culture of *distrust*: Employees greet mistakes and failures by blaming others, politics are prevalent, and management fires people for reasons other than performance and finances. Employees work to pull themselves up by pushing others down. Their behaviors are driven by the fear of losing their jobs because they have seen it happen to others. They focus their efforts on never failing, and they don't take reasonable risks if those risks could lead to failure. In a culture of distrust, management punishes people for making mistakes.

Knowing a company's culture before accepting a job there will protect you from a major mismatch down the line. Unfortunately, companies do not always characterize themselves clearly during interviews. Getting an accurate picture of a company's culture can require that you work there for a while if you aren't able to get details from a person you trust.

To encourage a positive culture in your team and your company, think about how you interact with members of your team, and make sure you are building positive relationships with them. If you support a culture based on trust and collaboration, your team will be stronger and will benefit from higher productivity, your company will retain the best employees, and everyone will be happier.

Corporate Style

Corporate style concerns the general manner in which employees interact with one another. Interaction styles vary across companies and sometimes across departments in larger companies. Styles of interactions you might experience include highly confrontational, highly political, low confrontational but aggressive (passive-aggressive), and highly collaborative. Some companies encourage confrontation for all issues and have resolution methods or processes in place. Others encourage collaboration and almost no confrontation.

Management Style

Management style is a subset of corporate culture. Management styles vary considerably from company to company, not to mention from boss to boss. It usually boils down to how management fewer makes decisions and who in management makes the decisions. Some managers focus on details, while others focus on the big picture. *Detail managers* focus on knowing every detail of the staff members' activities. In contrast, *big picture managers* keep their eye on the overview and do not want to know details. It's also common to see strict hierarchical management and diffused decision-making management. A *strict hierarchical manager* focuses on giving directions to people and making most decisions higher in the management chain. With *diffused decision-making management*, managers allow team members to make most of the decisions.

CEOs often hire managers and staff whose styles and values are similar to their own. This does not necessarily result in uniformity of management style, but a CEO can effectively create a consensus-type management style. That style tends to propagate down in a growing organization because of the continuous hiring requirements in a small company.

Knowing the management style will allow you to understand how best to drive forward your ideas and important efforts. Matching your interaction style with that of the company will lead to greater success. However, if you are not comfortable with your company's style, do not try to emulate it. A significant mismatch in style can be a good reason to look elsewhere for a new position. As you consider a new employer, look carefully at the corporate culture and management style before accepting a position.

Meeting Style

Meeting style refers to the way teams of people organize their discussions and decision processes. Small company management typically does not define meeting style, which tends to evolve as the company grows.

When a company is tiny, with 12 or fewer employees, all of the employees communicate continually and most are up to date with events, agendas, and important decisions made by the company. Conversations are *informal* with few preset meeting times, agendas, or lists of invitees, while *formal meetings* are usually rare or nonexistent.

As a company grows to about 50 employees, it transitions to a point at which formal meetings seem to develop a life of their own. The number of potential two-way conversations increases exponentially—so, for example, a company of 5 people has 10 different two-way conversations possible, but a company of 50 people has more than 1,000 different two-way conversations possible. As a company grows, it becomes impossible for every employee to know every other employee well—which was possible when the company was still tiny in size.

Company management usually responds to growth by *compartmentalizing* functions. This ensures that not everyone needs to talk to everyone else in the company. Most employees communicate with people who work in their functional area and in some restricted way to people in other teams.

Invariably, the transition from a tiny company to a small growing company results in an explosion of meetings. Many small companies develop a culture of too many formal meetings: Management sets up regularly scheduled status meetings, one-on-one meetings, company meetings, technology meetings, and team meetings. With so many meetings to attend, a manager has little time to do his work or interact with his teams. If more than half of each day is devoted to meetings, the only way a manager can interact with his team members is to . . . *set up a meeting*.

Formal meetings are not a bad thing, unless too many meetings are scheduled. They are not always an effective use of people's time and can slow down progress in a growing company. Many bad practices are brought into meetings by people who missed meeting training. Many formal meetings are a waste of people's time because too many participants attend, no agenda is offered, no conclusions are reached, no action items are recorded, meeting members are allowed to pontificate, and meetings are scheduled when an email or hallway conversation would be more effective.

A management day chock-full of formal meetings leaves little time for other activities such as getting your work done, talking with team members at their desks, impromptu hallway conversations, and problem solving. Spending the day running from meeting to meeting also drains your enthusiasm. You might respond to excessive formal meetings by spending your nights getting your own work done, not getting key work done, skipping meetings without explanation, pushing back on meetings, and

MEETINGS ALL DAY LONG

As a mid-level manager at a large software company, my time is not my own. We use Microsoft Outlook and Exchange so that anyone can set up a meeting and send you a request. Every day, my schedule gets booked solid with meetings. Many meetings are regularly scheduled. The other irregular meetings fill in the gaps. If people see a break in my schedule, they fill it in.

I get frustrated, as I do not have time to think or do my own work except in the evening after 5 PM. Sometimes people insist on meetings from 5 to 6 PM as that time is the only slot available on my calendar. I am frustrated that my time is not under my control.

—Manager at a large company

blocking out time on your schedule so that you can't be added to another meeting roster.

To reduce excessive company meetings, you will need to discuss and advocate for the changes to gain the support of your boss and peers. The CEO and other managers might have open ears to suggestions about improving efficiency, because, like you, they probably have too many meetings crammed into too little time. You can also collaborate and share ideas with peer managers about how to make meetings more efficient. Actively define best practices for meetings to keep them from becoming the dominant time-waster of everyone's day. Illustrating best practices in the meetings you chair can influence others as well. In all cases, avoid lecturing others about poor practices.

Solving the "too many formal meetings" problem requires collective cultural action. An "all-day meeting" culture might survive in a large company, but in a small growing company, this culture saps employee vitality.

Effective Meetings

Creating an effective meeting culture can require a shift in company practices as the company grows. Your company should provide annual training for employees on running effective meetings. A good course will cover how to run an efficient and useful meeting, how to choose attendees, and when to use other means of communication instead of calling a meeting. If management properly calibrates employees' attitudes, employees will respond honestly if you ask whether a meeting is necessary.

Several general principles can be followed in setting up a meeting:

Define a clear purpose.   Define a purpose and the desired results before calling the meeting. In the purpose definition, include your thoughts about the results of the meeting and define the type of meeting you seek. Common meeting types are information presentation, data-collection, and decision-making. At an *information presentation meeting*, you present information you want the attendees to know. At a *data-collection meeting*, you try to collect information about a problem as a group. At a *decision-making meeting*, you discuss a problem and come to a decision about how to handle it.

Choose attendees.   Choose the minimum number of attendees, limiting the list only to those who can contribute. You can inform others later of information they need to know in an email or in meeting minutes.

Create an agenda.   Before the meeting, define and distribute an agenda that describes the main points you want to discuss so that people come prepared.

Distribute clear invitations.   Define a location, date, and time for the meeting and let people know these details well in advance. Make sure that they consent to their participation, and do not assume their availability.

Start on time.   Encourage a culture of starting meetings on time or no more than five minutes late, even if some of the participants are not present when the meeting starts. This will avoid wasting time waiting for tardy participants. If meetings always seem to start late, attendees will show up late.

Leave gaps in the schedule.   It is difficult to start a meeting on time when it is scheduled back-to-back with other meetings. Leave a 15- or 30-minute gap between your meeting and the last meeting on each participant's calendar whenever possible. This will allow everyone a short but much-needed break and avoid delays in starting your meeting.

Follow these general principles for running an effective meeting:

- Designate a moderator to run the meeting.

- Designate someone to capture information and keep minutes as needed.

- Stick to the agenda. If meeting members stray to other topics, stop the discussion for a moment. Agree on a place in the agenda to discuss new items or whether attendees should discuss new items in another meeting.

- Manage the meeting time as you discuss topics. Large meetings are expensive for small firms. Consider the cost of the meeting time, preparation time, and the inefficiencies of breaking up people's days with another meeting.

- The meeting can cover the statuses of earlier action items. For ad hoc meetings, assign a "customer" for the action item who will follow the item and judge its success. This will often be you by default, but it doesn't need to be.

- At the end of the meeting, review action items and ensure that they are recorded in an identified location. A standard location can be used for distributing meeting minutes.

- After the meeting, ask participants about the value of the meeting so that you can make improvements for the next meeting. Do not take suggestions personally.

Learning how to be effective at meetings takes repeated training and effort. Time spent on this effort will pay off in improved productivity and morale. Employees do not find work rewarding when they can't do their jobs because they must attend too many meetings.

Handling Interteam Problems

As a small company grows, the CEO forms functional teams headed by different managers. As the teams grow larger, the feeling of camaraderie can shrink and competition and conflict can grow, making interteam problem-solving more difficult. If a problem-handling strategy is not in place, people will push problems up to the executive team, who will push them back down again after making a decision.

As the company grows, problem resolution can consume huge amounts of executive time. In the process, executives can become micromanagers who are constantly resolving conflicts. A corporate approach to problem resolution can help.

When workers are reluctant to tackle issues with fellow employees in other functional areas, they will try resolving issues through email exchanges. For difficult issues, some find it easier to offer long responses to emails rather than talking through the problem with another individual. They believe the problem is off radar once they have sent their email responses, so they can go on working. Here's a good rule of thumb regarding this type of conversation: If you are on the third email in an inconclusive problem discussion chain, talk to the person face to face or call him or her on the telephone instead of continuing the email correspondence.

One rapidly growing company, for example, had a prevalent tendency to bounce problems to the top and back down, and it was getting worse as the company grew. Fortunately, the executive team recognized the problem and took action by training people on a new approach that looked like this:

1. Work directly with people in other groups to resolve the problem. Ask for their help in solving the problem rather than demanding a specific resolution.

2. If the problem cannot be resolved, meet with the other team member's boss and invite the other team member to join.

3. If the issue still cannot be resolved, you can meet with the boss's manager and invite your own manager.

The goal of this approach is to encourage employees to resolve the problems as close to the source of knowledge without involving top management, and it's effective if management regularly trains employees in how to do it. It does require a shift in thinking on the part of staff about dealing with problems cooperatively and not treating other employees as the problem.

Advise your staff that when trying to resolve a difficult problem with another person, the focus should be shifted from the other person to the actual problem itself. One way to do this is to shift physical positions, from each party directly facing each other to both facing a whiteboard with the problem written on it. The change can shift the relationship from confrontational to the two parties viewing the problem as something about which they can brainstorm and jointly solve.

As your company grows, actively encourage your team and others to work through problems directly with other teams. If your company has developed a culture of trust, workers will come to discussions not trying to enforce demands, but rather looking for the best joint solutions to any problem. Talking one-on-one with difficult co-workers can be a trying experience short term, but it will improve everyone's work environment in the longer term.

Growing Peer Relationships

Build relationships with your peers and you build influence within your company as it grows. You should develop a *peer relationship* with co-workers who are not your direct boss or your direct subordinates, such as other managers on the executive team and staff workers in different departments such as human resources, finance, marketing, QA, and customer service.

You can benefit from getting to know people you do not normally see daily. Workers from other departments can offer insights into problems faced in their teams, which can help you better understand how to modify your work to improve the quality of the overall effort. It can also lead to your helping other teams with their problems. Understanding others' problems can yield better insights into selling, serving, supporting, and upgrading your customers, and it could provide opportunities for you to suggest solutions for internal improvements that increase the bonus pool or even keep the company (and your job) alive. Delivering value to internal departments outside of your primary responsibilities also builds trust and respect within the company.

Strong peer relationships also benefit your team, because your relationships with other managers will encourage cooperative behavior between the teams. For example, say you have created a good relationship with the marketing team manager and the two teams are aware of this; if a technical writer on the marketing team needs information from an engineer, the engineer will likely provide the information directly to the writer instead of claiming he's too busy and forcing the task on you, his manager.

Good peer relationships can also decrease the political maneuvering in a company. Political mischief increases in companies whose employees build walls between groups. One team can find it easier to criticize another team if the two teams have not developed a working and trusting relationship. When more direct relationships are established, politics are reduced.

You can encourage peer relationships by staying behind after meetings and initiating conversations with others about the meeting or about other topics, if you or they don't feel pressed for time. Post-meeting discussions can be informal chats about work problems, an opportunity to share opinions on important work topics, or even a chance to converse about non-work–related issues.

Another approach that can improve peer relationships is asking for help with general management or personnel problems—both good topics to discuss with another manager, as long as they do not involve confidential information about an employee. Asking a peer manager for advice shows that you respect his or her abilities and trust his or her discretion, and it can lead to good discussions and valuable advice. But don't invent a problem or ask for advice if you have already decided on a solution.

If you are not in the habit of talking to a wide range of peers, it can take some directed effort to reach out to people you don't know and talk to daily. Spending time walking around and talking with people, as opportunity permits, or inviting peers out for lunch or coffee provides a less formal setting for conversation. Less formal settings allow you to get to know your peers as people, not just as corporate entities.

In addition to the benefits it provides to your team and company, getting to know others is fun. Talking to people in different areas can provide a broad perspective on how your company works. If you are sincere in your desire to get to know your peers as people, it will show. Make an effort to talk with others, and do not treat interactions as a work obligation. Focus on the positive attitude that can come from getting to know new people.

Engineering Team Respect

One remaining aspect of company culture is identifying which team's efforts are particularly emphasized and respected. Each small company holds a unique view of its software development team. Some departments view development as a key company resource and give the team commensurate respect, authority, equipment, space, and flexibility. Management usually treats engineers in startups as heroes, while their development efforts produce the initial products for the marketplace.

As the company grows, a management shift in attitude toward engineering can occur. This shift happens because sales or marketing teams become key drivers of new revenue after development has created the product. When this happens, management does not view the development team as the most important source of innovation and value. Instead, management views development as part of a production organization and as a corporate cost. This shift can lead to team dissatisfaction as engineers see their status diminished.

Management sometimes even considers development engineers as the *cause* of company problems, such as poor quality products, dissatisfied customers, and slow software releases. These issues can be the result of improperly built software during the startup phase, however.

If senior management treats engineering as merely another corporate expense, you need to advocate for your team. Base the advocacy on real team successes and potential for the future. As you advocate, acknowledge past problems and explain improvements that will prevent them from being repeated. Development teams can be drivers of innovation and profitability, not just sources of order fulfillment.

Spend time at senior staff meetings describing ideas collected from your team to demonstrate the value of developers to the company. Describing team accomplishments at a company meeting is another great approach. Keep up to date on changing company needs, including those driven by the market, because you can use this information to propose revisions to your product roadmap. You can also promote your team by asking developers to help solve problems for other departments—sometimes small efforts by development can be of tremendous help to another group.

Additional Reading

Here is some additional reading on topics presented in this chapter:

Behind Closed Doors: Secrets of Great Management, by Johanna Rothman and Esther Derby (Pragmatic Bookshelf, 2005)

Death by Meeting: A Leadership Fable...About Solving the Most Painful Problem in Business, by Patrick M. Lencioni (Jossey-Bass, 2004)

Essential Manager's Manual, by Robert Heller and Tim Hindle (DK Adult, 1998)

The Five Dysfunctions of a Team: A Leadership Fable, by Patrick M. Lencioni (Jossey-Bass, 2002)

Joy At Work: A Revolutionary Approach to Fun on the Job, by Dennis W. Bakke (PVG, 2005)

Managing Technical People: Innovation, Teamwork, and the Software Process, by Watts S. Humphrey (Addison-Wesley Professional, 1996)

Overcoming the Five Dysfunctions of a Team: A Field Guide for Leaders, Managers, and Facilitators, by Patrick M. Lencioni (Jossey-Bass, 2005)

Peopleware: Productive Projects and Teams, by Tom DeMarco and Timothy Lister (Dorset House Publishing Company, Inc., 1999)

Slack: Getting Past Burnout, Busywork, and the Myth of Total Efficiency, by Tom DeMarco (Broadway, 2002)

To Do, Doing, Done: A Creative Approach to Managing Projects & Effectively Finishing What Matters Most, by G. Lynne Snead and Joyce Wycoff (Fireside, 1997)

What Management Is: How It Works and Why It Is Everyone's Business, by Joan Magretta (Profile Business, 2003)

10

WORKING WITH THE CEO AND THE EXECUTIVE TEAM

When you're asked to lead a development team in a small company, your new relationship with the CEO and other members of the executive team can be one of your largest and most unsettling adjustments. The CEO is your boss, your peers are the executive team, and you aren't in Kansas anymore. You are accountable for the entire company's technical practices and how the development team's software affects business. You no longer define success based on your technical capabilities alone. You need good people skills and the proper attitude to be successful in your new role.

Decisions made at the executive level differ from many of those made at lower levels in a company. They are based on the company's business needs and focus on a management perspective, not on superiority of one technology over another. Consequently, you will need to understand the business aspects of your decisions and incorporate the opinions and knowledge of other executive team members as you make those decisions.

The information in this chapter will be helpful for a senior technologist who is serving on an executive team for the first time.

Supporting Your Boss

Your job as the development manager in a small company differs from a management position in a large company, because you are probably kept accountable by the CEO and other executives in the company. You are in charge of software engineers who report to you, but you must also report to your boss at the top.

Knowing your boss's background will provide some insight into his or her management style and priorities. In any business, CEOs and presidents tend to focus on areas in which they have the most expertise. CEOs with a sales background, for example, may focus on company sales and have a shorter-term focus. CEOs with a technology background may dig into the technology, sometimes overemphasizing its importance over market and customers. CEOs with a marketing background may value the product and market, not always pulling together the operational pieces. By understanding your boss's background, you can determine the best ways to provide him or her with information as well as how to make a winning business case for efforts you want to undertake. So, for example, with a finance-focused CEO, you could make the case for the revenue benefits of your efforts; with an operations-focused CEO, you could emphasize productivity; and with a marketing-focused CEO, you could spotlight the market penetration benefits.

Your relationship with your boss can also define how the company perceives your efforts and those of your team. When your team does good work, you need to promote these successes. Your boss's perception of your performance influences how she directs you and how successful you will be as a leader. A little self-promotion can help you and your team gain respect, improve your boss's confidence and trust in you and your abilities, and help your boss and the company be confident of your team's contributions. Remember that a little self-promotion goes a long way: Avoid excessively promoting or bragging about your accomplishments.

A strong relationship with your boss based on mutual trust will also improve your effectiveness: When your boss trusts you, your recommendations will carry more weight and your decisions will be met with fewer roadblocks. On the other hand, when you trust your boss, you are better able to support her decisions, because she will have considered your input along with the needs of the company as a whole.

You earn the trust of your CEO by supporting her leadership. You act in the interest of the company and not just yourself; you support the rest of the executive team; you don't reveal confidences to make a convenient point; and you follow through with your commitments. If you gain your boss's trust, she will give you more responsibility and share more information with you.

Act professionally and responsibly with your boss, as you would want your direct reports to act toward you. Avoid the pitfalls of not being responsive, thinking you know better, not fully supporting or criticizing her efforts, and not providing information she needs. A positive approach can build a strong foundation of trust with your CEO.

Let's consider several areas of interaction in more detail: clarity of goals, timely information, communication, and decision making.

Ensuring Clarity of Goals

Your boss undoubtedly has goals in mind for the development team and probably made these known to you when you began your position in management. You may think you understand each of these goals, but you can make sure by repeating them back to her in your own words. It's critical that you understand her perspectives from the beginning and that you meet with her periodically to determine whether goals have changed.

Ask your boss to describe her expectations of you and your team as well as broad and specific long- and short-term goals. Goals should not be viewed merely as a to-do list, but as a vision of success that can help you create a mental picture of what you need to achieve and why. As you discuss these goals, work with your boss to define them in a way that is both sensible and achievable. After you have spent some time reviewing the goals, discuss problems or questions to be sure you understand each completely—blindly charging ahead without fully understanding what is expected of you can lead to many wrong turns and will ultimately hurt your team and the company. Work with your boss to ensure that each goal will benefit the company and your team in the long term.

Goals should be set up and reviewed regularly—ideally, every quarter. Reviewing quarterly goals with your boss allows for larger tasks to be divided into short-term goals that can be achieved by the end of each quarter. Yearly goals, on the other hand, are often too broad and can miss the mark, because the needs of a business often change throughout the year. What was crucial at the beginning of the year may seem unimportant by the end of the year. If your boss doesn't require that you set quarterly goals, take the initiative and propose them.

Providing Useful Information

Provide your boss with the right information at the right time. Consider what types and the amounts of information are most appropriate to provide as you discuss results, status, outstanding issues, risks, and staff. Instead of providing too many unnecessary details, summarize information regarding schedules, technology, and staff issues. Regularly provide a summary document showing project status. Summarize technology issues using business terms—cost, time, trade-offs, and risks—rather than complex technological terms, unless she asks for those details. A high-level summary of staff issues works best. Avoid discussing details of individual workers' personal issues unless they could seriously affect the company.

When reporting information, consider your boss's background, style, and priorities. If your boss has an analytical bent, she may prefer more data as well as the source of data. If she's a big-picture person, she may want to see only a high-level summary of project progress. Your reporting should focus first on your boss's priorities; then you can cover your topics. If, for example, your boss's top priority is releasing a particular feature, she will want to hear about that first.

Your boss needs to be presented regularly with useful information, but she doesn't want to wait to be surprised by big issues that can affect business. Don't wait to inform your boss about large, important issues. No manager likes to hear about a significant problem late in the game, when there is little time to correct the situation.

Communicating

If you do not make a point of communicating regularly with your boss, you will miss opportunities to provide and receive critical information. Do not assume that your boss always knows exactly what you do.

To communicate effectively with your boss, learn her communication style—every boss has a unique one. Some will set up regular meetings and encourage drop-by sessions. Others will stay in their offices and talk with you only at assigned one-on-one meetings. Others will walk around to see firsthand how work is going.

WHEN IS A ONE-ON-ONE NOT A ONE-ON-ONE?

My boss held all of his one-on-one conversations in a group meeting. He required all staff to attend the meeting one afternoon each week. At the meeting, he would talk with each person individually for 20 to 30 minutes and expect everyone to listen. This meeting would go on for 4 hours every week.

This approach was not popular with his staff. It had all of the disadvantages of a group meeting and none of the advantages of a one-on-one meeting. People did not talk about confidential situations or issues they did not want to discuss with the team. In addition, when it was not your time to talk, you had to spend time listening to conversations that were not relevant. It felt to all like a wasted afternoon once a week.

—Engineering and IT manager

It's a good idea to talk with your boss in informal as well as in regular, formal meetings. Catch your boss late in the day for an impromptu conversation—this can be a great time to find out what your boss is thinking about key issues and to discuss problems as they occur.

As the head of engineering, you are tasked with communicating information from your boss to your team and vice versa. Being a megaphone for your boss is not effective—being an effective communicator requires filtering information so that it is most useful to the team. It requires that you interpret your boss's and executive team's goals in ways that the development team can understand and use and that you present appropriate information to your boss and other managers regarding your developers' needs.

Influencing Decisions

When an issue arises that requires the input or approval of your boss, describe each problem and outline what you believe to be the best particular approach to solve it. She may have questions, solution suggestions, and issues of her own to contribute. The best decisions can be made together after a thorough discussion.

Do not assume that your boss understands issues exactly as you do or that her decisions and conclusions will necessarily be the same as yours. Your boss will sometimes disagree with your approaches to solving problems as well as which problems need to be solved. When this happens, ask questions to try to clarify your understanding of your boss's perspectives to learn about outside factors that affect her opinion. If you and your boss still disagree after a discussion, suggest even more alternative approaches. A good boss will listen to other options and sometimes change her decision. More input on problems and solutions usually yields better results. If your boss decides to stick with her original decision, support her.

Never criticize your boss or her decisions to your team. Managing a team is a difficult task; managing a staff that does not support its leader's decisions can be impossible. Supporting your boss and her decisions will make you an effective part of an effective company. Not lending support to your boss will lead to major problems for your company, for you, and for your team. However, if your boss's approach goes against your core management or ethical convictions, you'd be wise to look for a new position. You'll be better off if you recognize the mismatch and move on rather than stay in the position.

Collaborating with the Executive Team

Many development managers at small companies were once excellent senior developers who were promoted to senior management roles. Being the senior technical person who reports to the CEO puts you on the executive team, whether your title is chief technology officer, vice president of engineering, director, or manager. Consequently, you need to be prepared to handle that level of responsibility.

When facing an unfamiliar role as a member of the executive team, a new manager should concentrate on four areas:

- Conflict
- Confidence
- Communication
- Collaboration

Resolving Conflict

Working with other senior managers requires that you be able to work through conflicts; however, conflicts you encounter with the executive team will differ from conflicts that occurred with the engineering team. While engineering conflicts usually focus on technical details and personality differences, executive team conflicts will be driven by executives' varying priorities, backgrounds, and styles. Each executive's priorities are based on his or her experiences and job function.

Compare, for example, the priorities of the vice presidents of sales, finance, marketing, and engineering. The VP of sales will focus on the short-term sales funnel; he may aggressively push for getting the next best sale, which might require that developers build custom features to land a prized client, even if development is a bit understaffed or underequipped. The VP of finance will focus on financial regulations, accounting, longer-term financial health, and keeping the cash flow positive; he may oppose the purchase of extra equipment, even if it will help with development. The VP of marketing, on the other hand, may prefer to drive the product toward general solutions that strengthen its position in the marketplace;

development tools are the least of her worries. And *you* want your team to be able to purchase extra equipment to ease the development burden and focus on rapidly creating technically great solutions.

It can be difficult to navigate through perfectly valid but competing interests; however, considering the requirements of other departments within the company will serve you and your team well. If you meet with other executives to discuss their priorities and views of the development process, you will build rapport and make conflict resolution easier. Building solid relationships among other executives will help each of you appreciate the pros and cons of proposals from each functional area.

On the other hand, if a fellow executive points out a problem with you or your team during an executive meeting, you must avoid becoming defensive in your response and avoid finger-pointing or personal attacks that force the CEO to referee. Instead, suggest that the two of you meet later to discuss the situation and work toward a solution, perhaps even proposing a specific time and place to meet. If a positive corporate culture exists and trust has been established among members of the executive team, resolving problems brought up in meetings can be a constructive and professional process.

In general, don't treat conflict as a personal affront, and don't keep score by counting "wins" and "losses." If a conflict remains unresolved or is poorly resolved, everyone loses. Treat each challenge as an opportunity to understand other professional priorities, backgrounds, and styles. Set a collaborative tone so that you can work out conflicts quickly and effectively.

Taking up Your Mantle with Confidence

As the head of software development, you won't need to look for conflict; it will find you. Even a cooperative team will encounter conflicting goals, limited resources, unfortunate events, misunderstandings, and individual mistakes. People react differently to stressful situations: Some may shift blame to another person; others may become angry and argue relentlessly; still others may become quiet and withdrawn. If you are the victim of blame or an angry tirade, resist the temptation to fire back and escalate a conflict or waffle about what can be done. Instead, treat other team members with respect and actively reach out to work cooperatively with them.

Some executive meetings can be intense, especially when key decisions are being considered that can directly affect the success or failure of a company or its product. It is important that you show confidence in your ability to manage yourself and your team while working with others in executive meetings. Sometimes other executives or your boss will suggest technical solutions that make little sense to you. Rather than meekly accepting such tasks without discussion, consider and offer alternatives that may help solve core problems. A development manager needs to be honest and be able to say *no* when the best answer is *no*. It's better to ask for more conversations about a request after the meeting than to acquiesce or argue during the meeting. On the other hand, confidence does not equal bravado or avoidance of responsibility. Accept responsibility for areas and developers under your control, and take measures to resolve issues that fall within your realm.

Most of all, don't mislead others by providing information that is inappropriate, incomplete, or untrue. If you are unsure about how to answer a question from another executive, don't make a bad impression by waffling or avoiding the question. Indicate that you will provide the information and specify a deadline—one to five days is usually appropriate for answering most information requests.

Opening Communication

Regular communication with members of the executive team improves company success as well as others' perception of your efforts. Communication allows for coordination of efforts and discussion of overall company challenges. A lack of communication results in executives making assumptions about what others are doing, which leads to wasted and duplicated efforts. For example, sales should not be looking for customers for a new technical innovation if development already abandoned the idea without informing sales.

Communication is especially important when mistakes occur. You may be tempted to avoid advertising mistakes that originate in engineering, but exposing them early and working with other executives to resolve problems can yield the best results for you and the company. For example, if a software defect leads to a major problem with a client, the sales VP needs to know so he can talk to the client and help mitigate any damages. This approach works best when a culture of trust has already been established.

How you communicate is just as important as *what* is being communicated. Consider three common communication venues: executive team meetings, special status reports, and individual conversations.

Most small companies have weekly executive team meetings that tend to reflect the CEO's objectives and interests but usually provide opportunities for each team member to speak. Although the format and content vary considerably depending on the company and its current goals, you typically will be given the opportunity to summarize your team's activities. Use this time to highlight delivery changes, problem areas, and successes.

A brief summary in an executive meeting often isn't enough to provide thorough status information in a rapidly changing business. You may want to consider providing weekly one-page status summaries to members of the executive team. Each summary should describe recent results, project status information, expected delivery dates, and problems encountered and resolved. More important, it needs to be quick and easy to read and understand—both are critical for busy executives. Avoid low-level technical details. The report could include information on the following:

- Projects in progress and completed since the previous report
- Next priority efforts with estimated delivery schedules
- Unplanned work that has arisen
- Hiring and staffing update
- Risks identified
- Positives (new ideas, happy customers, successful efforts)

While a good communication approach during executive team meetings is important, talking with other executives individually will lay the foundation for more positive working relationships. You can also walk around the office and talk with other executive team members individually—not just about work items, but also about hobbies and/or other interests. Get to know their backgrounds and their work objectives to help you understand their perspectives. Look for opportunities to collaborate on joint problems, offer assistance, or ask for advice. Informal conversations are great for team building and discussions that are more detailed.

Collaborating Effectively

Once you're engaging in strong, positive communication with other managers, you can improve your relationships further by focusing on collaboration. Collaboration at the executive team level is essential for solving the larger problems your company will face, such as how to stretch finances during tough times, major product failures at a customer's site, or how to deal with an unhappy customer. Don't wait for the CEO to ask you to work with another team member to resolve a problem. Build the relationships first so that when a problem occurs, you are already working collaboratively with the appropriate manager.

To solve some problems, a team or manager may be required to change an approach. For example, if improving the *request for quote* (see Chapter 11) process requires that sales supply engineering with more information up front, your team gets the immediate benefit of time savings while the sales team incurs additional costs. However, the company as a whole will benefit from the changes. If you have a good working relationship with the sales manager, such changes will be easier to support and endure.

11

LISTENING TO YOUR CUSTOMERS

The development team's relationship with sales and customers can be a source of inspiration—and a source of frustration. It can be inspiring because great ideas come out of customer and sales interactions; it can be frustrating when communication problems lead to unnecessary work and when sales promises features or products before consulting with development about the reality of those promises. As development manager, you must always remember that the company's success depends on pleasing your customers—even if that means dealing with frustrating situations.

Although many software engineers at small companies have some customer exposure, most engineers do not see customer communication as a primary strength or personal work goal. If you are new to the head of engineering position, you will need to appreciate the importance of customer-engineering communications.

This chapter covers several considerations that can be important when working with sales and customers: customer satisfaction, meetings, sales promises, requests for quotes, and client requests.

Customer Satisfaction

Keeping customers satisfied is a necessity for a small company that hopes to be successful. Simply creating a great product will not guarantee ample sales if you and your company fail to focus on customer problems and requirements. Remember that buyers always have other options: They don't have to spend their money on your product.

Customer satisfaction is not just a sales and account management goal; it requires the efforts of the entire company, including members of the development team. As development manager, you are responsible for delivering a reliable product on time, but you also need to provide service to company customers during and after development.

By providing clients with updates of work in progress, seeking their opinions, and listening to their concerns, engineers can help instill confidence in the company and its products. Speaking with clients after product delivery to listen to their concerns can help you catch problems early before they get out of hand.

Of course, customers expect you and your company to deliver a working product on time, but if you know you can't meet a delivery commitment, you need to be honest and straightforward about the situation. If delivery will be late, the client needs to be informed of the delay as soon as possible. Early communication allows customers to adjust their plans and schedules for rolling out the release when it is easier and less expensive for them to make such adjustments.

Before contacting any customer directly, discuss your concerns with your boss and the marketing, sales, and customer support teams to determine the best communication approach. Marketing, sales, and customer support teams might believe you are undermining their efforts if you communicate with a client without including them in the discussion. Since sales and customer support are responsible for each specific customer relationship, let managers know what you plan to communicate and work out the best approach—the interaction can be a joint phone call, an email, a meeting, or a direct call in which you or another manager summarizes product problems or concerns.

REALLY LISTENING TO AN ANGRY CUSTOMER

A former boss did a great job handling a product failure. An older product experienced a significant failure. The customer was really upset and ready to stop using our product and take his business elsewhere.

In response, my boss listened to the customer and then acknowledged his concerns and our failure. He then proposed that it was time to get the customer off this older system and on to something more current, as the product had aged with all of the custom changes made to it. The customer responded positively and was pleased when they received the new version of the software at a significantly discounted price.

—Engineering manager

When a product or service disappoints a customer, listen carefully to the customer's concerns. Acknowledge the concerns and provide accurate information about the problem along with an explanation of what went wrong and how you will improve it now and in the future. If you can, find and present alternative solutions to the problem.

If a serious quality or reliability issue is discovered, a more in-depth response is necessary. Investigate the problem, provide an explanation of what happened, and outline the steps that will prevent the problem from reoccurring. Learn about the specific client's needs before preparing this information. Some prefer a cursory explanation, but others want to be presented with considerable detail to help them fully understand what happened. In some cases, you may need to discuss what you hope to say with company legal counsel before you contact a client so that you can be informed of any legal issues related to providing detailed explanations of problems.

Customer Meetings

A great way to understand your customers is to meet with them. Seek out opportunities to listen to their concerns firsthand and to learn how they are using the software. Understanding common problems and requirements is a crucial part of setting long-term product direction and making short-term improvements. Avoid the temptation to meet with clients only when specifically asked to do so.

When a client requests a meeting with engineering, a specific technical goal is usually the focus. As engineering manager, you may be expected to discuss the product from a high-level technological perspective, but avoid providing too much technical detail to those who require only a summary. Also, always show enthusiasm for the product and technology, because it helps build the customer relationship. An enthusiastic development manager builds customers' confidence in the company.

Before the meeting, learn about the client's concerns and what he or she hopes to gain from the meeting. Work with the sales team to determine which topics to cover and what the company's goals for the meeting are. Get an agreement from sales about engineering commitments regarding deliverables, and be prepared to respond if you are asked to make a commitment during the meeting. If your answer is not an obvious *yes*, set a specific day by which you will be able to provide the answer—better to take some time to think through your answers to requests than to disappoint an important client. During this time, you can discuss the request's importance with sales to make appropriate business decisions.

When presenting information, coordinate with sales about who will present what information. Review each other's material before the meeting to check for inconsistencies and redundancies. Advance planning can make for a smoother presentation with fewer unpleasant surprises. You might find it helpful to practice delivering your presentation in front of the development team before you present it to a client.

Closing the Deal

Sales people focus on closing deals with clients in ways that satisfy the client and are useful to the company's bottom line. Sales people need to listen to the client's requirements, then talk to others in the company about what

DOING ALL THE TALKING

One of my worst customer sales presentations was a joint presentation with my company's sales rep. We were both expected to present our product offering to the customer, but we did not meet and clearly divide the presentation topics. I assumed that I would talk about the product technology and he would discuss sales and marketing topics. At his request, I sent my presentation to him the day before the meeting for his review. He did not send me his material, although I asked for it.

At the meeting, the sales rep went first; he delivered my presentation, and did it poorly. I was stuck rehashing the same slides quickly. He admitted that he had not prepared his own presentation, so he used mine. I never trusted him again.

—Hardware engineer

can reasonably be accomplished and in what time frame, and finally work to close any gaps to please the client. This process is usually iterative for larger sales of software products and services.

In a well-run company, management has created a process for sales request validation. A sales request process usually requires rapid engineering response because the company needs to close deals and clients need the information to make decisions.

If your company doesn't have a sales request process, set one up. First, talk to sales about its needs and time frames. Then work out what information you generally need from sales to make estimates. Splitting estimates into *firm quotes* and *rough quotes* can be useful in a cooperative environment. You can generate rough quotes faster than firm quotes and use ranges of delivery dates that require less information to create. Rough quotes can be useful for establishing the feasibility of concepts, but they should not be used to close a deal.

A sales request process with buy-in from the sales department is essential for the success of a small company. Not having a process in a company with poor controls will lead to problems.

When the Sales Team Overpromises

If a sales person wants to close a deal and earn his commission, he listens to the client's needs and then makes promises on what can be delivered to match those needs. Unfortunately, on occasion, sales people will promise clients engineering deliverables without first consulting you. In a poorly managed company, the CEO gives the sales team incentives to sell but enforces few controls over what they can sell. If the client's needs are greater than the product can deliver, a naïve, less-than-ethical, or uninformed sales person can promise the additional functionality without first confirming that those promises can be kept.

Of course, such promises frustrate because they can and often do impact other, more reasonable, development team deliverables. Almost every engineering manager has run into the problem of unexpected customer promises by overeager sales people, leading to a complete redefinition of the product release schedule. Sometimes even a relatively small client can "hijack" the development calendar, ultimately stunting future growth that depends on some planned functionality.

A mishandled new sale can shift the product direction away from the sweet spot of the market and toward one particular customer's needs. Instead of each sale demonstrating the market potential for the product, this sale diverts the company from creating the product that many customers really want. Small and growing companies need to keep to their product roadmap and continue to build on their whole product offering instead of bolting new features on to the current offering for one customer.

In some cases, your company will need to adjust the development calendar to close a particularly important deal. The CEO or executive team should be consciously making these types of decisions, as they will best understand the impact of the choice on the business.

To stop a cycle of unchecked sales promises, talk with your boss and the management team to create guidelines for a sales request process. You can make a strong business case for creating this process: Letting individual sales deals drive a small company's development strategy can lead to company stagnation or worse—failure. If requests for customer features as part of a large sale appear to drive the product off track, review the requests with senior management and, as a team, make an appropriate choice as a logical business decision. You may need to coach other team members if frustrations continue about business decisions that lead to inefficient delivery schedules or less-than-ideal technical solutions.

Requests for Quotes

Long sales cycles (6 to 12 months) are common for expensive and complex software. Long sales cycles are also common for *software as a service (SAS)* offerings in which the long-term customer costs of the relationship are high. For these types of software purchases, customers investigate the product and service thoroughly before making a purchase because of the potential impact to their businesses. This investigation often starts with a *request for quote (RFQ)*, sometimes called a *request for procurement* (or a *proposal*). An RFQ usually requires that engineering contribute information.

Customers will issue RFQs for expensive software and expect a quote from the company that indicates price and often specific services and new program features. Typically, the sales team will be responsible for supplying RFQ responses. Sales will send customer requests to development and other teams to provide the information required to complete the quote. Most RFQs include questions appropriate for engineering that help the customer assess how the software works as well as its risks and reliability. Typically, the RFQ requires a quick turnaround from engineering. Responses must be factually accurate, compact, and understandable, and they must highlight the positive aspects of the product.

Because supporting sales to respond to RFQs means development must quickly deliver information, preparation is critical. First, engineering must work with sales to devise a request process that defines how the sales team communicates requests to you, what information is included in the RFQs, and how engineering will respond. Failing to create a process will lead to mistakes, such as the following:

- Sales failing to inform engineers of the need for a quote until the day it is due

- Sales failing to provide crucial information

- "Guesstimates" provided by individual engineers being treated as true estimates

- Development time being wasted in collecting information or preparing the wrong information

- Schedule dates being misunderstood in the quote

Second, devise a quick method of providing estimates to the sales team. The quicker the estimate, the more extra time you can insert to make sure that deliverables are released on time. When you create time estimates, make sure you clearly describe the quoted functionality and the accuracy of the estimate. In some cases, providing estimates based on rough time ranges can be useful to sales and the customer as long as sales doesn't use them to price and sign the deal. (Chapter 12 has more information on estimates.)

Third, build up a list of common RFQ questions. Most requests include common questions that you can anticipate in advance. If you build this list in advance, you will need to supplement it only with those few questions you did not expect. If you receive your first RFQ without having prepared for it, use the opportunity to start a list of questions and answers. As new questions come along, add them to your RFQ list.

Here are some examples of questions that might appear in an RFQ.

Describe the system.

Create a customer-facing system diagram. The diagram can be simple and fit on a single page, but it should provide a clear overview of the system. Supplement it with a written explanation of how the system works. The explanation can also be short and need not rely on internal technical terminology. Work with marketing and the technical communications group to make this material customer ready.

Describe the software technology.

This is an open-ended question. Be prepared with an overview of how your product works and specific technical innovations: Prepare a list of what libraries are used in the product, what languages were used in building it, and what standards your product follows. The customer may be looking for technical issues and support risks, so be prepared to explain known issues.

List third-party code or applications used by the product.

Ask the senior architect to create this list in advance. The customer may be looking for system and security risks.

Describe the product's risks and reliability figures.

Collect the statistics that best reflect your system in advance. This data can take considerable time to collect, as it usually requires testing and analysis of the system to understand its reliability under different conditions. Performing product and system risk analyses requires knowing the types of risks that are of most concern to customers, such as data integrity, mean time to failure, security risks, or throughput reduction risks.

Describe the new development risks if the product requires extra development.

Development risks become important when part of your work involves developing new code to support a customer's particular needs. They might be concerned that product changes won't be delivered on time or that the changes impose some technical challenges that can't be easily solved. Identify standard development risks and provide some discussion of development's risk-mitigation process. Be prepared to add specific risks when responding to the RFQ.

Describe the development process.

Prepare an overview of your development process, including drawings. A customer may need to understand how you build quality and security into your system.

Describe the quality of the product. (Alternatively, list measures you take to ensure high quality.)

Provide quality statistics from the product's latest release. You can provide customer-facing statistics based on problems found in production and describe the quality process and metrics.

Define the product's limitations.

Customer concerns may include speed, database size, and scalability. Be prepared for follow-up questions about how you collected the data you provide.

Describe how you ensure that the system is secure.

> Provide assurances that security processes are installed and that the security technology used is sufficient and up to date.

With a request process in place and a document providing the answers to the most common technical questions, you can usually provide a quick turnaround on a customer RFQ. Even if the RFQ includes a few surprising questions, you will be able to complete the request quickly if you are properly prepared.

It's easy to forget how long it takes to respond to RFQs when you're creating the overall product schedule. Be sure to factor in time to the schedule to allow for RFQs, as they can be time consuming and can require customer visits and multiple conversations. Depending on the nature of your company's sales, you may also need to allow for some unplanned customization time for new orders.

Support and Customer Requests

Every project seems to encounter customer requests and changes that crop up after the deal has been signed. Customers often discover issues and more specific requirements for a newly ordered software system. This information can help you improve your product.

Since you can be pretty sure that new customer requests will appear after development begins, add time up front to accommodate them in the production schedule. Account for a percentage of development time to support current customers. Scheduling without allowing for late requests often leads to delays. Even more importantly, make sure that your company has implemented a *change control process*. If no such process exists, work with other teams to create one. More information on a change control process can be found in Chapter 14.

Your company's customer service team is also a great conduit for information gathered from customers. Maintain a good relationship with the team to get the best information. Even the best relationship between engineering and customer service can become adversarial, however. The customer support team empathizes with the customer's problems and may insist that you handle development requests and issues immediately.

From a practical point of view, the development manager must balance customer requests with ongoing development. Allowing the customer service team some control over how development handles client requests can improve the relationship between support and development. Set aside a fixed percentage of time and resources for dealing with customer service requests. Then, ask customer service management to set priorities for requests while considering other company stakeholders, including QA and the product manager. Ask customer support to order requests and grant them the budgeted engineering hours and quick estimates on their requests. In some cases, you may need to create a "bug repair release" to support client services if a history of deferring defect repairs exists.

EMPOWERING CUSTOMER SUPPORT

At my company, customer support had many ongoing requests from customers. Meeting with customer support became an intense weekly discussion. Customer support management wanted all customer requests fixed in the code quickly.

From my perspective, 25 percent of development time went to dealing with customers' defect and minor enhancement requests. The remaining new development consumed the rest of our time, and those schedules were under pressure. Not enough time was available to devote to customer requests.

I decided to shift the perspective of the customer support manager by pulling him into the solution. I gave him a budget equal to the maintenance time available and calculated in advance how many hours of time were available per release. We would provide quick estimates for him so he could decide how to spend his time per week. He would make the requests, spending his hourly allotment; we would schedule the work and tell him when it would go out in a release.

He was happy with this approach and began to appreciate the difficulty of servicing all customer requests when the budget was limited.

—Engineering director

PART IV

MAKING WORK FLOW:
PROJECTS, PROCESS, AND QUALITY

In addition to working with people and technology, the development manager must strive to enable efficient workflow. Project management, development processes, and quality are significant topics—and many books have been written about each. This section cannot provide a complete discussion of each topic, but it does offer an introduction to each, with an emphasis on applications for small software companies. If you want to read more, you'll find a list of references provided at the end of each chapter.

12

PROJECT ESTIMATING

As soon as someone asks "How long will the project take, and how many staff hours are required?", your reputation as development manager is on the line. You could offer up a quick estimate that gets the task off of your to-do list, or you could take the time to create a thoughtful project estimate and be confident that you can actually make it happen.

Winging it by providing a quick estimate might be the fastest way to provide an answer, but it's also an easy way to "get fried." And after being cooked a few times over poor estimates, most development managers start looking for a better estimating recipe.

For new managers, the best estimating method isn't always obvious. At the extreme end of the spectrum, you can't make an estimate until a complete definition of the effort has been proposed and analyzed. Unfortunately, this is not always practical for small companies whose approaches must be systematic, simple, and relatively straightforward.

This chapter covers the process of estimating a single project and creating a model to help you improve future estimates. Estimating models can take some effort to set up, but they can be very effective in helping you improve both the speed and quality of your estimates.

Building an Estimate

Building a good estimate is a skill and an art that requires following a reasoned process and using your experience—even intuition—to make adjustments. You will rarely have the exact information you need to create a highly accurate estimate for a project. Part of improving your estimating skills is realizing that you will be making many assumptions and guesses, some of which will be wrong. You will succeed when your assumptions and guesses are mostly right and when you can successfully split the larger processes into smaller pieces to estimate.

When crafting an estimate, do it in a systematic way. Start by defining what data you need to collect and how you need to assemble it into the estimate. Then collect the data for your estimate: This will require that you dig through past estimates and data and discuss the project and its requirements with others. Finally, you'll construct the estimate by assembling the pieces of data into a coherent picture that lets you determine the amount of time and effort required to finish the work.

When you have completed your estimate, you'll need to deliver it. Your method of delivery can have a large impact on the project's success. Let's consider estimating and delivery in more detail first.

Creating a Task List

How you build the estimate depends on the project complexity. A simple project estimate might comprise a short series of steps with an estimated *cost in effort* and *cost in calendar days*. *Cost in effort* refers to the time required to complete a task, assuming the worker is devoting all of his time to the task. This is often captured in hours or days of work. *Cost in calendar time* refers to the time required to complete a task, assuming the employee won't be able to devote all of his time to the task because of overhead tasks, company meetings, vacations, and sometimes other projects. This is often recorded in calendar days. For example, a cost of effort of 20 hours for a person who works 8-hour days and can work on the task 60 percent of the time yields 1.5 calendar days (20 hours × 0.6 ÷ 8 hours = 1.5 calendar days).

Ideally, the project has been sufficiently divided into tasks that each make up no more than 5 to 10 percent of the project duration and last less than two weeks. To estimate a project with dozens of tasks to track, you need to split apart the project into smaller tasks, understand the assumptions, identify the risks, and then assemble the results. Dividing the project into a series of smaller tasks improves the accuracy of your estimate, because estimates of time required for smaller tasks are more likely to be accurate, as the pieces are easier to understand and often relate to previous work for which effort is known. If smaller estimates are created properly and without *estimation biases* (discussed later in this chapter), they will, on average, be more accurate. Per-task estimates that miss the mark on the high or low end tend to average out statistically for the entire project if no single estimated component is considerably larger than the others. If a single estimated component is considerably larger than the others, break it down into smaller tasks and estimate these tasks.

When building your estimate, first gather information from development team members about the issues that will affect the project creation and delivery. Consider each developer's unique productivity level: The same task might take considerably more time if undertaken by one engineer versus another with different skills, attitude, and experience. Estimates also need to account for time necessary to work on other projects assigned to team members.

Next, create a list of tasks (the *approach*) required to complete the project. You can review the list of tasks required for other recent projects for comparison. A common estimation mistake is omitting important steps, including those that are not in the "critical path" or those that seem uninteresting. As you might not remember every task, consider the following list of easy-to-overlook tasks as you compile your estimate:

Testing	Customer requested changes
Systems integration	Staff vacations
Build and packaging time	Buffer times
Documentation	Alpha/beta release customer support

Marketing support	Project risk allowance
Training	Technical risks and discoveries
Peer reviews	Technical integration
Customer reviews	

Your approach to estimation will differ based on the type of business and the product it creates. If the business provides many small and similar type jobs, an estimating model with a list of choices and a quick summary can work well. If the business builds large projects over a period of several months, creating a custom spreadsheet for each estimate might be necessary. Another alternative for projects with many dependencies is to use a *Gantt chart program*, such as Microsoft Project, to prepare your estimate. Gantt chart programs allow you to test sample schedules and calculate costs based on those schedules.

After you have created your task list and approach, you can start creating task estimates.

Creating Task Estimates

To collect task length estimates, you can take several approaches. You can look back at past projects and use the time required to finish each project step as a rough guide for what you'll need for the current project. This approach requires that you keep information on past estimates and the amount of time each task actually took to implement. Adjust these values only as needed to scale the task to your current estimate needs. In addition, consider that historic project data is valuable for identifying tasks that didn't get considered in the original estimate.

A second approach to get task estimates is to talk individually to developers and ask for their opinions. This approach requires that you engage in multiple conversations in which you explain the task and ask for help in creating the estimate. Make sure you ask what assumptions the engineer is making (for example, are the estimates in calendar time, or is the engineer counting on any specific tools or approach?) to ensure that these assumptions match your understanding of the efforts required.

A third approach is to select two to five senior engineers to be your "elite" estimation team. This group would meet to create estimates for new projects and evaluate change requests to projects. In the course of the work, each engineer can become a specialist in a particular area and offer insight into the expected costs of tasks in that area.

A fourth approach is to schedule an estimation meeting to estimate the tasks as a group. With this approach, you can describe each task to everyone and request that each participant create an estimate independently. Moving around the table and asking for suggestions can provide estimates, but people can show a first speaker bias, in which everyone adjusts their numbers to be closer to those of the first speaker. Consequently, you can ask that everyone write down his or her number and show the estimates at the same time. An alternative is to use a specially made estimation deck of cards that team members can use to hold up their estimates simultaneously.

After everyone in the group estimation meeting offers input, ask the high and low estimators about their figures. Often they might have realized a key point about the task that other estimators have forgotten. Some discussion of the point can be useful as you settle on the most reliable estimate.

If limited information is available when creating task estimates, you and other developers might be more comfortable suggesting *rough estimates*. A reasonable scale is roughly based on factors of 2: 1 hour, 2 hours, 4 hours; 1 day, 2 days; 1 week, 2 weeks, greater than 2 weeks. Break down tasks that take longer than 2 weeks into subtasks and provide estimates for those. If you draw a size line on the whiteboard, you can mark estimates up as they are made and view them in total, as shown in Figure 12-1.

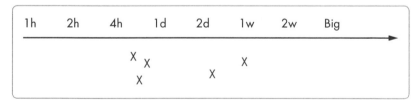

Figure 12-1: Sample estimating size line

Considering Estimation Bias

Before you can create an estimate, you need to adjust numbers to account for *estimation bias*. Estimation biases have multiple causes. For example, engineers are generally optimistic, especially about tasks they *want* to do. On the other hand, they might forget about a few mundane details. Since estimates turn into schedules by which the engineers are judged, some engineers will pad time estimates—as a matter of human nature. Another common bias is estimating more time required for tasks that an engineer doesn't want to do, especially if he or she believes the solution is technically inferior. Finally, some engineers might not be interested in estimation and will spend too little time thinking through what is involved.

Once the team estimates are in, you can revise estimates from team members based on their history, especially if you are getting information from only one or two engineers. Knowing a bit about each person's past predictions will help you know how to adjust their current estimates. You might multiply their estimates by a factor to account for past biases. For some engineers' estimates, the multiplier is as high as 2 to 3 times, implying that a job with a 20-hour estimate will actually take 40 or 60 hours to complete.

An engineer's desire to perform a task can also affect his estimate. If he looks forward to doing the work, his estimate may be low. If he has no interest in the task, the estimate may be higher than it should be. You'll need to use your management sense to detect how much bias is present in the estimate.

After you have collected the estimate data, you need a simple approach to pulling together the final estimate.

Building the Estimate

With all the estimates in hand, you'll begin assembling the pieces into a cohesive picture. This picture should show estimates for all the elements involved as well as totals so that you can review your assumptions and make changes to the estimate.

As soon as you have finished an estimate draft, "What if?" questions will arise:

- What if we implement some features and not others?
- What if we add or remove staff?
- What if we start earlier or later?

Build your estimates to make it easy to answer such questions. A spreadsheet estimating approach is an excellent way to explore different options, because it can be set up to try out different options. If built correctly, it should make it easier for you to see the impact of different feature sets, more or less staff on the project, and different start dates. A well-made spreadsheet will be designed so that single-cell entries allow for shifting feature sets, staff size, and start dates.

Figure 12-2 illustrates an estimating spreadsheet with key construction features highlighted. The tasks are entered in column B (Item). The *xs* in column A (Use) control whether the task is to be included in the total. Column C contains the engineering estimates in desired units (hours in this example) that are multiplied by the factor in column D (Est. Mult.) to obtain adjusted totals in days in column E. Column D allows you to add in extra time based on your experience with individual engineer's estimates. Similarly, QA estimates for the tasks are entered into column F, QA multipliers are in column G, and column H contains the total cost for that task in days.

In Figure 12-2, some estimates are multiplied by 1 (no change) and others are multiplied by other factors up to 2. These factors allow you to see the original data and scale the information to account for estimation biases.

	A	B	C	D	E	F	G	H	Formulas
	Use	Item	Eng Est. (hrs)	Est. Mult.	Eng Cost (days)	QA Cost (hrs)	Mult.	Total Cost (days)	=D3*C3/$C$26/8
1									Copy to E4:E12
2									
3	x	Feature 1	32	1	5.3	12	1	2.0	=G3*F3/$C$26/8
4		Feature 2	16	1	2.7	4	1	0.7	Copy to H4:H12
5	x	Feature 3	8	2	2.7	4	1	0.7	
6	x	Feature 4	24	1.5	6.0	20	1	3.3	
7	x	Feature 5	16	0.8	2.1	2	2	0.7	
8	x	Feature 6	8	1.2	1.6	1	1	0.2	
9		Feature 7	40	1	6.7	4	1	0.7	
10		Feature 8	32	1.5	8.0	8	1	1.3	
11	x	Feature 9	24	1	4.0	4	1	0.7	
12		Feature 10	16	1	2.7	4	1	0.7	
13		TOTALS	216.0		41.7	63.0		10.8	=SUM(H3:H12) and
14									sum columns F, E, C
15		Start Project	8-Jun						
16		Eng Calendar Days	41.7						=E13
17		Effective Eng team size	3						
18		Calendar Days	13.9						=C16/C17
19		Eng. Done Date	25-Jun						=WORKDAY(C15,C18)
20									
21		QA Calendar Days	10.8						=H13
22		Effective QA Team Size	1.5						
23		Calendar Days	7.2						=C21/C22
24		QA done date	4-Jul						=WORKDAY(C19,C23)
25									NOTE: WORKDAY function
26		Percent Availability	75%						is an Excel free "add-in." See Excel Help.

Figure 12-2: Cost and schedule estimate spreadsheet

The number in cell C26, set here at 75 percent, is the *percent availability* to assign to the overall engineering and QA team estimates. All calendar day estimates in columns E and H are adjusted by $1 \div$ (*availability constant*) to represent the increased time required to complete a project because engineers can't work 100 percent of the time on the effort. (However, if they can, then you can set the percent availability to 100 percent.)

Also near the bottom of the spreadsheet, calendar days are added and a done date (completion date) is estimated by dividing total calendar days for engineering and QA by the size of the teams. Recognize that dividing by full team size is a crude approach that works only for smaller teams with tasks that have few dependencies. (For more information on these estimates, read *The Mythical Man-Month* by Frederick P. Brooks, Jr.)

This example is *not* intended as a "working spreadsheet" for general purpose estimating, but instead serves as a teaching tool. If you want to work through it as an example, construct the spreadsheet by copying the data elements into your spreadsheet and then type in the formulas. Reread the introduction that covers the spreadsheet construction approach used in this book. Also, pay attention to the lowercase *x* character used in this example. In addition, keep in mind the difference between the separators used in OpenOffice.org Calc (semicolon) and Microsoft Excel (comma).

You can start with this example spreadsheet and modify it for your specific estimate in a number of ways, such as adding rows to correspond to features or tasks. You can also expand this spreadsheet to cover other teams, including technical documentation and product marketing teams.

This example illustrates how to build an estimation worksheet to solve a common estimation problem: projecting the end date for a project and the total number of staff hours required, while providing quick "What if?" estimates based on different features. You can use similar formulas and approaches to create templates that fit your projects and estimating style.

Writing and Delivering the Estimate

After you've completed the hard work of collecting data and creating the estimate, you can write up the estimate and deliver the information to the person who requested the quote.

An estimate should consist of a high-level description, assumptions, the type of estimate you've created (rough or exact), resources required, a delivery date, and a total cost including labor, expenses, and materials. Keep the information short, succinct, and in list form when possible, ideally limiting the estimate to a single page. Describe the exact parameters on which your estimates are based, and clearly state each assumption, especially any make-or-break assumptions. Be clear about the total cost and weeks to delivery, and accompany the proposed completion date with a required start date. If necessary, attach an appendix to describe specific technology in more detail. Estimates can provide ranges of possible costs and timelines (rough estimates) instead of exact hours (exact estimates). Add the delivery date and cost at the end of the estimate, because often the person receiving the estimate will not read anything other than those key pieces of information if the cost delivery dates are at the beginning.

Even when your estimate considers every detail of the project and is written clearly and succinctly, things can go wrong. For example, when the job finally arrives in engineering, you might discover that the sales person sold something quite different than what you expected, the customer wants a different technical solution than the one proposed, and you have to start work immediately, even though two of your team members just left for three-week vacations. As you go into hyperdrive trying to clean up this mess, you realize that something went wrong between the point at which you completed the estimate and the point at which the job arrived in engineering. In the interest of avoiding future pain, you resolve to change your practices when it comes to delivering estimates.

Here is some general advice for anyone who has been burned by a new job that differs from that described in the estimate: *Provide a written estimate and deliver it in person.* Anything else will adversely affect your health. A written estimate gives you the opportunity to identify mismatches between the customer's requirements and the estimate provided. These mismatches can be highlighted if you deliver all your estimates in person and talk through the details with the receiver. The combination of a written estimate for references and the interactive discussion adds considerable clarity about the estimate and about the assumptions made by the requestor and estimator.

Delivering the estimate in person is the best case, but it could be delivered by email as you talk on the phone with the person who's receiving the estimate. If you deliver the written estimate prior to talking to the person who receives it, it is possible that the estimate may be delivered to the customer and even approved by the customer before you can fully explain your assumptions and the estimate's intentions. Often the development team will be asked to bear the costs of fixing any problems created by misunderstandings or other miscommunications.

Verbal estimates with no written documentation usually lead to confusion and misunderstandings after a project is underway. Common misunderstandings occur because of miscommunications concerning the project start date, because engineering assumptions are not taken into account, customer assumptions are not passed on to engineering, rough estimates are taken as exact estimates and used for contracts, and customer requirements are not fully understood.

That said, don't count on estimate assumptions being taken seriously unless you emphasize them verbally along with the written descriptions. The person accepting the estimate might focus only on cost and delivery time, ignoring other factors.

For assumptions that critically affect the company, make sure your CEO buys into them—consider, for example, a new project that requires that development delay working on another business-critical project to focus on the new one. In general, make sure that all stakeholders are aware of all the impacts resulting from performing work on the projects you estimate. If your company has a marketing group or product managers, include them in your estimate delivery process as well.

Collecting Raw Project Data

Planning and creating estimates requires that you understand how people spend their time. Efficiency and process improvements benefit from time breakdowns as well. Any company that might be considering purchasing your firm will also want to see information on project and team efforts. You won't usually need to collect this data during the company startup or foothold stages, but it becomes important during the growth stage.

One common approach to collecting time-effort information is to buy a software package that tracks time per project per individual. Such packages generate reports to show the staff breakdown in different ways. Software consulting firms, agencies, and large companies often use these packages.

However, a "time card–tracking" package has some disadvantages for small firms: Some developers resent individual time recording systems and might leave the firm because of them, and these packages are expensive to set up and maintain.

Collecting coarse-grained time data in a spreadsheet can be an efficient solution for tracking project time at a growing firm. To set up such a system, you need to define project efforts and how you want to report data, and then collect the information in a particular format. The spreadsheet can have simple reporting built into it. You can ask engineers to summarize their hours in an email once a week. If you use a less formal approach for collecting data, you can simplify the process.

An informal spreadsheet approach provides information that is not *strictly* correct, so don't use it for accounting or billing purposes. However, this data is *mostly* correct, so you can use it for estimating purposes. Creating a high-level view will reveal information about where and how developer time is spent relative to where and how it should be spent to get maximum return.

One caution with this approach: Do not use this data collection process as an opportunity to micromanage your team. If you start nitpicking about why one week shows 10 percent more overhead hours than the next, your team members will become resentful and might start providing incorrect information.

To avoid this, make sure that the team knows how you are using the data. You can present the collected information to the team to show how you will be using the data in an estimating model. Explain to your team how this information benefits them, and they will be more enthusiastic about the process. Potential benefits of this information include improved planning, schedules that are not overloaded (forcing everyone to work weekends), justifications for more staff to handle more work, and clarity to executive management about the true costs of each request. When presenting the information to your team, also describe your efforts to make the overall data collection simple and lightweight. It is difficult for engineers to feel enthusiastic about an unnecessarily complex data collection effort that consumes their time.

Summarizing Data Using a Spreadsheet

Figure 12-3 illustrates a spreadsheet of projects versus weeks for a development team. This example shows seven weeks of data collected by the development team. Using this approach, you can assign a worksheet to each team. Each week, add an additional column to the chart and insert that week's data.

	A	B	C	D	E	F	G	H	Formulas
1		Week	Week	Week	Week	Week	Week	Week	
2	Project	3-Jun	10-Jun	17-Jun	24-Jun	1-Jul	8-Jul	15-Jul	← Date format
3	Project A	0	55	200	300	280	50	0	
4	Project B	100	0	0	0	0	0	0	
5	Project C	200	200	50	0	0	0	0	
6	Project D	0	0	0	0	0	165	220	
7	Overhead	20	25	30	20	40	25	20	
8	Vacation	0	40	40	0	0	80	80	
9	Totals	320	320	320	320	320	320	320	← =SUM(H3:H8) Copy to B9-G9

Figure 12-3: Worksheet tracking engineering time

You can use the hours-tracking spreadsheet approach to collect information for multiple teams and summarize them on a single worksheet. To store other teams' information, copy the engineering worksheet and rename and modify the underlying data. To create the summary worksheet, first copy the engineering worksheet and rename it *Summary*. See Figure 12-4.

	A	B	C	D	E	F	G	H	Formulas
1		Week	Week	Week	Week	Week	Week	Week	
2	Project	3-Jun	10-Jun	17-Jun	24-Jun	1-Jul	8-Jul	15-Jul	← Date format
3	Project A	0	110	340	503	483	152	120	← =Eng!H3+QA!H3 Copy to B3 to H8
4	Project B	294	97	0	0	0	0	0	
5	Project C	298	299	151	102	82	0	0	
6	Project D	0	0	0	0	0	285	320	
7	Overhead	40	50	59	40	80	50	40	
8	Vacation	0	80	80	0	0	160	160	
9	Totals	632	636	630	645	645	647	640	← =SUM(H3:H8) Copy to B9-G9

Figure 12-4: Example of summary worksheet in an hours-tracking spreadsheet

Figure 12-4 illustrates a very simple example of a summary worksheet as part of a larger spreadsheet containing two worksheets—one for engineering (called *Eng*) and one for quality assurance (called *QA*). Each worksheet has collected data for each team. In this example, the summary worksheet adds the contents of the two groups together to show a combined sum of hours.

Engineering Maintenance and Overhead

Project estimating also requires that you have an idea of how much time engineering is spending on maintenance and overhead, separate from the actual project work. You must know this information to plan future project work and create estimates, because it helps in translating project days to calendar days.

You can use the raw time data you collect to create *average available percentages*. Consider this example: Suppose your development team spends, on average, 67 percent of its hours over 8 weeks on project work (33 percent overhead) with no significant overtime. You can convert project hours into calendar hours like so: $100 \div 67 = 1.49$. Using this information, you can determine that a task that takes 12 engineering hours to complete will require $12 \times 1.49 = 17.91$ calendar hours, or about 2.4 days ($17.91 \div 8 = 2.24$), to complete.

An automated approach to calculating overhead percentage can be incorporated into the data collection process. Figure 12-5 illustrates this approach, using the total time and total project time to calculate overhead.

SIMPLE TIME SUMMARY

I worked for a small company that grew fast. We did not have a method of estimating how much time teams spent per project. At the time, tracking packages were too expensive to purchase, as the business was not doing well. Individuals resisted time reporting.

The manager summary approach worked reasonably well for giving a bird's eye view of where time was going. As it turns out, this estimate was reasonable enough that the management supplied it to a company that ultimately purchased our company. The data met the buying company's needs.

—Planning director

	A	B	C	D	E	F	G	H	I	Formulas
1			Week	Week	Week	Week	Week	Week	Week	
2	Project		3-Jun	10-Jun	17-Jun	24-Jun	1-Jul	8-Jul	15-Jul	
3	Project A		0	55	200	255	240	50	0	
4	Project B		40	0	0	0	0	0	0	
5	Project C		200	160	50	0	0	0	0	
6	Project D		0	0	0	0	0	165	160	Enter and then copy to columns C and H for that row:
7	All Overhead		80	50	30	70	120	60	70	
8	Vacation		0	40	80	0	0	80	120	
9										
10	Totals		320	305	360	325	360	355	350	← =SUM(I3:I8)
11	Project Totals		240	215	250	255	240	215	160	← =SUM(I3:I6)
12	Overhead %	33%	25%	30%	31%	22%	33%	39%	54%	← =1-(I11/I10)

=AVERAGE(C12:I12)

Figure 12-5: Calculating overhead

Be cautious of data that includes significant overtime hours, especially if it's calculated based on 40-hour work weeks and not total hours. Significant overtime hours can skew calculations even if total hours are used—unless, that is, your team's standard practice is to work excessive amounts of overtime. (And if that's the case, your calculations will be correct, but you should reread the first section of this book, because you and your team probably don't have a healthy work-life balance.)

Another caution is to consider how vacation time is averaged into your data. Vacations tend to be taken in May through August and in December, rather than being distributed throughout the year. Consequently, you should separate out your vacation time when collecting data. In addition, look for vacation patterns such as many vacations during summer and the second half of December, and plan your projects accordingly.

Don't be surprised to discover that your team's non-project hours are in the range of 25 to 50 percent of the normal work hours per year. A typical technology company has 3 weeks of vacation, 7 days of holidays, plus sick leave. These factors alone make up 10.4 percent of the workdays per year. Meetings, maintenance tasks, and other regular duties can take up a large slice of your team's time—from 10 to 40 percent, depending on the company and culture. With project hours being a percentage of total calendar hours, the inverse ($1 \div$ percent availability) is used to convert estimate hours into calendar days. So, for example, 60 percent availability is figured like so: $1 \div 0.6 = 1.67$ (1.67 is the multiplier); therefore, 3 work days is $3 \times 1.67 = 5$ calendar days for this situation.

Additional Reading

Here is some additional reading on topics presented in this chapter:

Controlling Software Projects: Management, Measurement, and Estimates, by Tom DeMarco (Prentice Hall PTR, 1986)

Developing Products in Half the Time: New Rules, New Tools, by Preston G. Smith and Donald G. Reinertsen (Wiley, 1997)

Estimating Software Costs, by T. Capers Jones (McGraw-Hill Osborne, 2007)

Manage It! Your Guide to Modern, Pragmatic Project Management, by Johanna Rothman (Pragmatic Bookshelf, 2007)

The Mythical Man-Month: Essays on Software Engineering, Anniversary Edition, by Frederick P. Brooks, Jr. (Addison-Wesley Professional, 1995)

13

STARTING A PROJECT

Starting a new project can be similar to planning a trip. You need to choose a destination, decide who is going with you, figure out the costs, determine how you'll get there, plan for the unexpected, and finally take the first step out the door. With a project, you define the goal, assemble a team, set the priorities, create a plan, prepare for risks, define the framework for carrying out the project, and take the first step with a kickoff meeting. In both scenarios, planning your start before you take off will make the rest of the journey more pleasant.

In many small software firms, engineers jump directly to the middle of a project by immediately starting to write code and seeing if it works. However, forgoing a properly planned start will guarantee that the end product will face difficulties with delivery, customer satisfaction, quality, and cost.

Imagine getting up one day, driving to the airport, and hopping on a plane you choose at random. It might be exciting at first, but it probably won't be much fun once you get there.

With any project, or trip, you should first focus on understanding the goal.

Understanding the Goal

At the start of the project, the goal might seem obvious: Build the software. The customer wants a particular problem solved and wants to purchase software to solve it.

Creating a general-use software program is not just about one customer's goal, however. A customer might ask for a very specific software solution but will not be sure that this solution will truly provide the answer to a core problem until after the software has been delivered and used in a production system.

As you begin to fully understand the customer's problems and solution requirements, you will begin to understand your *company's* project goal. If you're building a product for a single customer, you can directly ask the customer to specify what is needed. If, however, you are selling a product to many customers with which you don't have direct contact, your product marketing team is responsible for understanding the market and acting as the development team's customer. Keep this information in mind as you consider how you need to understand the customer or user of your software and how your company and development team fits into the picture.

Once you understand your customers' problems and needs and see your company's role in providing the solution, your next step is to agree on your *common* goals. For example, consider the following questions: Is the customer looking for the software to reduce operating costs? Does the customer need the improved functionality to offer better customer service? Is your product part of a larger sale the customer is making with a fixed time frame? Is the customer trying to offer a totally new product or service to its customers? Is the customer hoping to produce a highly scalable system of which your product is one component?

The larger and more important the project, the more important it is for *you* to talk to the customer *directly*. Without directly conversing with customers to understand what they are trying to achieve with a solution, you will likely miss the mark with the software you deliver. When you talk to individual customers, echo what you hear in your own words to be sure you understand. Ask about their current needs and understand their plans for using the product after rollout.

After the customer meeting, create a memo recapping the information and requirements as you understand them, and send this to the customer for review. This approach will help avoid potential misunderstandings in the future.

Once the project's goals and requirements are clear, you can start the planning process by selecting a project development team.

Assembling the Project Team

If your company is working on one large project, assembling your team is not a project issue, but a general staffing issue. Follow good hiring practices and build the best team you can (as described in Chapter 4). Many small companies work on multiple projects that draw from a common team of engineers. In this environment, choosing the right team for each project is critical to each project's success.

Many managers choose team members by focusing on each developer's availability at the time the project needs to start. However, availability shouldn't be your sole criteria: Consider the candidate's interest and enthusiasm for the effort; the project's priority within the company's workload; the candidate's familiarity with the technology, ability to work with customers and stakeholders, and diversification of assignments; and whether the project will help or hurt the developer's career.

Interest and enthusiasm for the effort are important criteria for a team member who will contribute to the project's success. An engineer who is excited to work on the project will be more likely to contribute in positive ways, especially if he or she has asked you for a chance to work on it.

The higher the priority of the project for your company, the more important it is to assign your strongest engineers to work on it, as long as they are enthusiastic about the effort. In addition, consider whether an engineer has experience working with the technology required for the project, or whether he or she will need to spend time learning it. If a candidate needs to learn, can you build this into the project costs and timeline and still deliver a successful project on time? Training as you go increases the overall project risk, which must be considered for high priority projects.

Furthermore, if working on the project requires considerable interaction with the customer, does the engineer have a positive attitude toward building customer relationships and working with customers? If not, you would do better to assign an engineer who enjoys working with and listening to customers.

Next, consider whether you are assigning the same tasks to the same engineers again and again. This poor management practice doesn't help engineers build up their skill sets, which is important in helping team members gain flexibility in handling a wide array of tasks. You will need such flexibility if team members become sick, leave for vacation, or leave the company. Also note that engineers get bored performing repetitive tasks, so assigning them new challenges can help them stick with your company.

Finally, consider whether working on the project will help or hurt a developer's career. Offering a senior engineer routine or low-level assignments can reduce his attractiveness to future employers. Many engineers realize this, and they'll start looking for new jobs if they see their assignments causing their careers to stagnate.

Spending time considering the best fit for the job is a valuable use of your time. Properly matching people to efforts not only boosts productivity, but also reduces risks and improves employee morale.

Substitutions

Projects do not always unfold neatly—problems crop up in the process as team members' availability changes: Perhaps the project requires different numbers of engineers during different parts of the development process, or team members become unavailable during part of the project cycle. In such cases, you have more than general staffing issues to consider.

Substituting one development engineer for another short term does not work well, especially if the substitute engineer's time involved is less than three weeks and his or her work does not result in a *clear deliverable* (a clearly defined section of the code that can be evaluated on its own when the work is accomplished). First, the replacement engineer doesn't have the same level of project identification as the full-time team member, which can lead to low-quality work. Second, the substitute engineer doesn't have the full-product perspective. He or she might make assumptions that can cause problems that are discovered only later. Finally, many engineers find it easier to rewrite others' work than to spend time understanding it, leading to wasted effort—which sometimes occurs twice, if the original engineer returns to the project and reinstates the original code.

Substitutions work best when a clear deliverable is defined as the engineer's goal, when the engineer has enough time and expertise to understand the code, and especially when the engineer has a positive attitude toward working with another engineer's code. If these requirements are met, spend time describing the requirements of the project to the new engineer in detail and walk through the specific deliverable with the engineer. Having another kickoff meeting with the entire team can be very effective—it allows the team to describe project status, open issues, and changes made from the original requirements. Finally, make sure that the new engineer agrees that the deliverable makes sense before sending him off to do the work.

Political pressure from outside engineering can try to force you to swap in a new engineer to show that "everything possible is being done" to finish a critical project. As development manager, you must explain the costs of this approach to others. If a substitution is warranted, consider keeping the substitute engineer longer term on the project instead of releasing him or her after the original team member returns.

Game Delays

Some projects are delayed at the start due to the unavailability of the team. You will be tempted on such projects to pile on engineers to help make up for the lost time, especially if you have a fixed completion date. If you feel so tempted, take a day off and read *The Mythical Man-Month* by Frederick P. Brooks, Jr. (see "Additional Reading" on page 243). The next day, change your game plan. You can make up considerable time on a delayed project by starting with a single senior engineer instead of a team. Together, focus on clarity of requirements, functional definitions, and system architecture. This will save you considerable time lost by delayed staffing. Come to think of it, you could start your projects that way even if the project did start on time and with a full team coding.

Some projects are delayed because a key team member isn't available at the start. If a project has a hard completion deadline, consider whether starting the effort without the key team member makes sense. If the project can be reorganized to allow the starting team to do useful work, it may make sense to do that.

One other case of interest is a project that requires technical expertise your team currently doesn't have. It may be in your company's best interest to ask for a delay of release so you can get the expertise—either through a consultant or a team member doing research or getting additional training. Charging ahead without key expertise can be very wasteful of your company's time and resources.

Setting Priorities

Before creating a project plan, you also need to examine priorities. Every project has different criteria for success that directs its priorities. For some projects, the schedule is the top priority because a firm delivery deadline is required. For other projects, the security of the product cannot be compromised, even at the expense of the schedule. Additional aspects of a project that need prioritization include features, costs, resource usage, quality, operational policies (how the project is run), reporting, and technology choices. Despite what a customer might say and want, not every aspect of a project can be top priority.

Make a clear choice about your project's top priority. Identify the top priority along with the second and third most important priorities. The choices you make determine how you make trade-offs in your planning as well as how you make decisions during project execution.

A common top priority for software product is schedule—often, you're told, because "The Release Date Cannot Move." This is often the case when your company requires the project for display at a trade show that occurs on a fixed date. Knowing this up front will allow you to make ongoing adjustments to your project tactics to increase your chance of success. For example, if schedule is top priority, followed by quality, and your project is running late, you might consider reducing features to ensure that you will release a high-quality project on schedule.

Regardless of where functionality falls in your priority list, you will also need to prioritize the parts of the functionality you plan to build. A good way to evaluate what is most important is to ask yourself this question: If the project had to ship early with only one or two features complete, what would those features be? Working on the most important features first, instead of the easiest features to build, is beneficial if you are forced to ship early because schedules and priorities change. This happens far too often on software projects, so you should consider the feature priority order in advance.

With a plan in place, consider the framework for how you will organize the effort.

Selecting the Framework

A common framework defines *how* a team will work on the project. Consider four areas: interaction, process, standards, and tools. Without formalizing the process, you'll experience a status quo approach: *We will do this the same way, using the same tools and processes we used in the last project.* This might be fine for completing the project, but failing to consider your framework carefully will lead to unpleasant surprises.

Interaction defines how you want to work with the team and how team members want to work together, including collaboration, meetings, and reports. Some projects include specific instructions regarding interaction. For example, the *Scrum process* (an iterative incremental process of software development) requires a daily standup meeting. Other projects might or might not include definitions of all the interactions of the team. A new project is the logical place to change the interaction style if you see the need.

Process is the predefined, repeatable set of steps that the project will move through as it's being developed. In addition to repeatable steps, software development processes have different characteristics, some defining required meetings, reports, or specific types of communications as the project progresses. You should define the process that will be used for the project instead of defaulting this decision to the team. Chapter 15 describes different types of processes in more detail.

Standards define the technical practices and languages used on the project, including coding languages, minimal coding conventions, and file interchange formats. Your choice of standards can greatly impact the quality and maintainability of the code your team provides. Typically, general technical standards are not clearly set at a small company, so you can use new projects as opportunities to define solid standards.

Tools describe the choice of software tools, software libraries, and hardware systems to be used on the project. Some projects are set up as a "free-for-all," in which any tool or system is okay to use as long as it pleases the engineers working on the code. While granting some flexibility to engineers on their choice of tools can be a good idea, not considering the business impacts of some tool choices is negligent. Either define the tools to be used or review the team's choices to understand the potential impacts of the choices before the project begins. See Chapters 7 and 8 for more information on tools, methods, and technology.

Mapping out the Timeline

A project timeline improves the product and process by mapping out initial task order. Start by creating a list of tasks and dependencies, and then put them in a reasonable order considering constraints such as staff availability. Next, estimate the cost of each step, both in hours of effort and projected time required. When calculating schedules in calendar time, consider that your staff isn't available to work on your project full time every week because of disruptions such as meetings, vacation, holidays, and illness. You can use a spreadsheet to build up your estimates and track time to complete the project as it progresses. All these techniques are covered in more detail in Chapters 12 and 14.

Now let's pull these pieces together into a project plan.

Creating a Project Plan

Creating a clear, written agreement with the project stakeholders that details the project's direction and goals greatly increases your chances of providing a solid product that meets those goals. This agreement should describe the project's deliverables, when they are expected, the project's costs, and what documents describe the effort in detail. Equally important is an agreement regarding the project's risks, constraints, and open items (undecided issues).

A simple approach is to define all of this information in a one-page *project plan*. Figure 13-1 illustrates a sample project plan template that can result in a one- to two-page plan.

Project Title

Author: *Author(s) name*
Date: *Revision date*
Version: *Revision number*

1. Purpose
   Describe the purpose of the project in one to two paragraphs. This is not a functional specification.

2. Deliverables
   Provide a short list of the project's deliverables with limited detail.

3. Applicable Documents
   Describe reference documents including the functional specification.

4. Schedule
   Provide the schedule range of outcomes based on the expected and potential risks.

5. Resources and Costs
   List the staff and external costs required to build the project.

6. Constraint Priorities
   Provide agreed-upon prioritization of the project constraints: schedule, costs, resources, features, and quality.

7. Risks
   List risks identified at the start of the project, including technical risks, schedule risks, external vendor risks, and risks to sanity. Include mitigation for top risks.

8. Open Items and Assumptions
   List any items included with the project that require time or effort to clarify.

Figure 13-1: Sample project plan template

A short project plan might seem like an unnecessary formality in a small company. However, the plan can serve as a useful communication device, because it frames the project for all the stakeholders, helping them understand your vision of the project and the problems it will face. The exercise of creating the project plan will also help you in understanding the scope of the project.

Building the plan will require that you collect information on the project risks and priorities. Getting agreement on the project plan will require some negotiation about different project variables. Take care of this at the start of a project to eliminate some of the dissatisfaction that can result later from differing expectations for the project.

A one-page graphic, such as a Gantt chart or other device, representing the development effort can also be helpful at this phase of the project. A clear, single-page illustration can help project stakeholders easily grasp the efforts about to begin.

With the plan defined, you are ready to kick off the project.

Kickoff Meeting

What is the best way to start the project? Even a short and informal *kickoff meeting* improves project success and decreases time wasted, but make sure you schedule it so that all team members can attend.

At the kickoff meeting, review the following areas:

- Project team members and roles
- Goals and requirements of the project
- Customer, team, and corporate perspectives for this project
- Timelines and other resources
- Potential risks
- Successful outcomes

The kickoff meeting is also your opportunity to build team enthusiasm for the project and its success. Set a positive tone, allow time for questions, and keep the discussion at a high level. You can fill in the lower-level details later in separate discussions.

The kickoff meeting also serves as a ritual that defines a start of a new journey. Without a kickoff meeting, team members can feel like they are wandering toward the project rather than heading along a welcoming path toward a positive final goal.

With a successful kickoff, you have positioned your project for success. Now you're ready to start tracking and managing the project.

Additional Reading

Here is some additional reading on topics presented in this chapter:

Controlling Software Projects: Management, Measurement, and Estimates, by Tom DeMarco (Prentice Hall PTR, 1986)

Developing Products in Half the Time: New Rules, New Tools, Second Edition, by Preston G. Smith and Donald G. Reinertsen (Wiley, 1997)

Manage It!: Your Guide to Modern, Pragmatic Project Management, by Johanna Rothman (Pragmatic Bookshelf, 2007)

The Mythical Man-Month: Essays on Software Engineering, Anniversary Edition, by Frederick P. Brooks, Jr. (Addison-Wesley Professional, 1995)

Waltzing with Bears: Managing Risk on Software Projects, by Tom DeMarco and Timothy Lister (Dorset House, 2003)

14

PROJECT EXECUTION AND TRACKING

Results matter. As a development manager in a small, growing company, you will be judged by the work and results of your development team. Your team must deliver quality software projects on time, and that software must please your customers.

As you drive your development team toward success, you should expect to encounter some detours and hazards along the way. Few plans are executed as originally envisioned, so you will need to track and direct a project throughout its development cycle.

The good news is that you don't need to use complex project management skills to manage most projects in small companies. The general practices discussed in this chapter will help you locate and use the proper tools to drive project execution forward.

NOTE *Before you can manage a project in execution, you should have started the project in an appropriate way. If you haven't read Chapter 13, do so now and establish your project goals, plans, and priorities up front. Then put together a winning development team.*

Managing a Project's Execution

Successful project management starts with an accurate picture of the current project status and realistic estimates of tasks and goals to be accomplished. Your primary goal is clear: You must drive the project toward a successful conclusion. Study the final goals and objectives relative to the current development status of the project. Revise your plans at least weekly based on tasks that still need to be accomplished and new challenges that arise.

It's not enough simply to measure your team's progress as a percentage of tasks completed based on estimates from your original schedule. Sticking to your original schedule when the project or its components have changed can lead you to rationalize why development might be behind schedule with thoughts like "So what if we're behind schedule? We have plenty of time to catch up." Instead, you need to be realistic and adjust your plans as the project progresses; don't wait for your team to fail. Respond quickly to project delays with project reassessments, and implement appropriate changes to improve the schedule and outcome. You can make adjustments early by rearranging tasks, applying more development resources, changing functional deliverables, and sometimes optimizing a step in the process.

The Five Rules of Project Management

To understand and communicate your project's actual status, you'll need more than the right strategy and the right tools. You'll need the right attitude. Use the following five rules as a guide to managing your projects realistically and successfully.

Don't lie to yourself.

This common error for development managers can lead to some less-than-constructive behaviors. For example, if you can't deal with the truth about development delays or problems, you might be tempted to ignore a forecast of late delivery because a particular due date has not yet arrived. You might convince yourself into thinking you can still make the deadline. Or perhaps you decided that a task will take only half the time it normally takes, just to make the plan look good on paper (and to make yourself feel better). If you haven't come up with a realistic plan for reducing the time for the effort, don't fool yourself. Take the opportunity to recognize such serious problems before you're forced to do so.

Don't lie to others.

Keep your project schedule honest. Don't let the project predictions echo the original plan because upper management doesn't want to hear bad news. Some development managers mirror their initial delivery schedules when describing the development team's status—in the worst cases, this deception continues up until the software is due to be delivered. This results in a huge impact due to delays, with little chance to resolve serious problems. Instead, as the project progresses, you must provide factual information to those who have a stake in your project's outcome, including management and the development team.

Deal with bad news early, and let everyone know the details.

In many workplaces, people tend to reveal bad news just before delivery is due. In low-trust environments, this behavior is actually encouraged. Some senior managers don't want to know about potential problems: Don't tell me about it; just fix it! This attitude leads to delays in investigating or acknowledging problems until events force the discussion and a crisis ensues. Instead, inform the appropriate people of problems as soon as possible, and include your plans for resolving these problems. Dealing with and revealing issues early on will lead to better solutions overall.

If your forecast shows your project will be late no matter what you do, you are late.

Finding problems early on in the process is ideal, because you obviously have more time and options for solving the problems. Problems discovered late in the game are more difficult to resolve, as time and options are few. Not acknowledging future delivery delays is similar to asking "Am I going to be late?" when your appointment is in 10 minutes but it takes 50 minutes to get there. *You are late. Period.* Make the call immediately and let people know.

Large, last-minute schedule surprises are not acceptable.
People can be reluctant to admit that a project for which they are responsible has encountered serious problems and will not be delivered on time. When a project is going to miss a key date, such as a delivery date, it's human nature to put off telling management and customers the bad news until you absolutely must. Remember, however, that customers make strategic business plans based on what you tell them; their success can depend on your meeting your roll-out promises. Waiting until the last minute to inform a customer that a project will not be available on time will ruin your credibility and quite possibly your business. And it can ruin your customer's business as well.

Now with some basic rules to help guide your steps, let's look at an approach to tracking your project during execution.

LAST-MINUTE SURPRISE

My company had multiple engineering managers reporting to the same general manager (GM). One manager worked on a project with a six-month schedule. The GM of the group held weekly staff meetings to review the progress of everyone's projects. Every week this manager would report that the project was on track. Six weeks before delivery, he said it would be on time. Five weeks before delivery, he indicated it was on time. Four weeks before delivery, he said it was on time. Marketing told customers that the software would ship in four weeks. At three weeks before delivery, the manager indicated it was on time. At two weeks before delivery, he said the project needs an extra three months.

This was a jaw-dropping moment. Either this manager had so little insight into the project that he did not know until two weeks before delivery that it would be late, or he had misled everyone until he was forced to admit there was a problem.

—Peer engineering manager

Project-Tracking Approaches

Two project-tracking approaches work well for small software companies. One approach uses a *Gantt chart* that lets you graphically track a project's progress against your original plan and predict a schedule outcome. As illustrated in Figure 14-1, a Gantt chart uses horizontal bars that each represent the length of time required for a task shown at the left. Arrows connecting bars are called *dependencies*. A dependent task requires the completion of an earlier task before it can start. In this example, the pizza must be delivered and the table set before dinner can be eaten. Diamonds are used to mark milestones—in this case, the diamond marks that dinner is over.

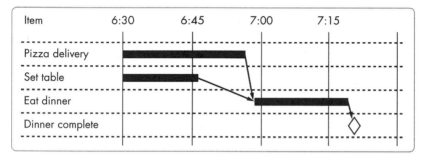

Figure 14-1: Simple Gantt chart

The second approach is a *tracking spreadsheet* that measures progress against original estimates and predicts likely outcomes using predetermined formulas. You can expand a tracking spreadsheet to show a range of final delivery dates using minimum, expected, and maximum values for each step.

A Gantt chart works best when the project has many *task dependencies* and when a moderate number of parallel tasks are required to complete the project. As Gantt charts typically allow for only simple calculations, they are not appropriate if you need more complex numeric analyses, such as the ability to track multiple ranges of outcomes or base times for events on formulas.

In contrast, tracking spreadsheets work best for projects with fewer task interdependences, more steps in parallel, larger task counts, and complex calculations. Table 14-1 provides comparisons of the two approaches based on project characteristics. For large projects, complex tools may provide the best results, but they are rarely needed in small software companies.

Table 14-1: Comparison of Gantt vs. Tracking Spreadsheet

Characteristic	Gantt	Tracking spreadsheet
Number of interdependencies among tasks	Many	Few
Number of parallel tasks	Few	Many
Performing best-case, typical, and worst-case delivery estimates	Difficult	Relatively easy
Calculations	Some	Many
Visualization—quick assessments	Easy	Can be more difficult

You can use both approaches to track multiple-step efforts contributing to a single release. In addition, you can adapt either approach to correspond to different process workflow and milestones. Consider the following simple example cases of projects and choices of approach.

Case 1: You are asked to implement a new data interface feature to your online application. The data interface requires negotiating a data format with the customer and defining a user interface. You need to include a certification review step, and several intermediate code development steps need to follow a sequence. The project requires a data scheme change after your team has completed the initial interface definition. For this case, a Gantt should work reasonably well: The project involves multiple interdependencies, a relatively small number of team members, and parallel tasks.

Case 2: Marketing requires that development create 44 new customer reports for delivery in two months. You decide to split the tasks among your team of five engineers dedicated to completing the reports. After estimating the time required for the reports, the estimates vary considerably among them. You need to schedule each report separately for engineering, QA, and the documentation team. In this case, a tracking spreadsheet is appropriate, because the tasks are relatively independent and a large number of tasks are being assigned. A spreadsheet will allow you to shift tasks easily among individuals.

Now that you have the big picture, let's get to the particulars of using Gantt charts and spreadsheets as project management tools.

Gantt Chart

Most project management software tools can be used to create Gantt-style charts. Commercial project management tools, such as Microsoft Project, offer considerable flexibility in the ways they can be used to configure and label a chart. The advantages of the chart include easy visibility of dependencies and project progress, and the ability to print out the chart for others to review. However, you won't enjoy these advantages if your chart is designed poorly or used improperly.

One common mistake is to provide only the underlying data in a row-and-column format instead of using a Gantt, as illustrated in Table 14-2. The Pred column here shows the prerequisite tasks that must be completed.

Table 14-2: Data in Table Format

Task name	Duration	Start	Finish	Pred	Resource names
Task 1	2 days	9/15	9/16		James
Task 2	1 day	9/16	9/16		John
Task 3	4 days	9/17	9/22	1,2	Megan
Task 4	3 days	9/23	9/25	2,3	Adam
Task 5	2 days	9/23	9/24	3	John
Task 6	1 day	9/25	9/25	5	James

This information is much easier to visualize in the Gantt chart shown in Figure 14-2.

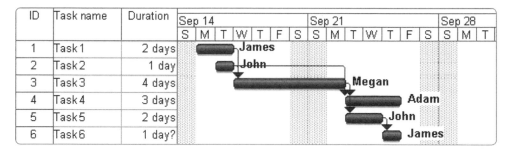

Figure 14-2: Information in a Gantt chart is easier to understand.

Once the Gantt chart is set up properly, your team should be able to see the following at a glance:

- Task status

- Prediction of the most likely project delivery date

- Milestones based on process

- Staff assigned to each step

- Each step's task interdependencies

Figure 14-3 shows a *Gantt chart layout* approach. Each task has its own row. Having two columns on the left make the chart easy to read. Using two columns works well, but you can add a third or fourth column without distracting from the main information. For example, you could add a third column to this example for task start date.

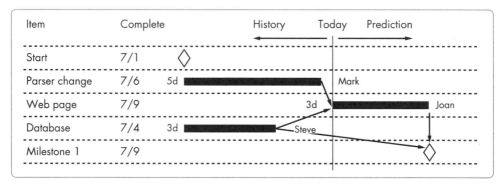

Figure 14-3: Gantt chart layout example

In this layout, rows show either a diamond milestone marker or a solid bar representing a task timeline. The text to the right of the bar shows the person assigned to each task. The text to the left of each bar shows the total task time in consistent units (in this case, days); the task time information should be in consistent units—that is, you shouldn't switch among weeks, days, and hours in the timescale, because this complicates quick calculations and leads to errors. The arrows represent dependencies between tasks. In this simple example, Web page task starts after Parser change task and Database task are completed.

The value of the Gantt chart increases as the number of tasks increases. A project with 30 to 50 different tasks with dependencies can be demonstrated and visualized directly in a Gantt chart.

As you construct a Gantt chart, consider these guidelines:

- Set the timescale so you can see the Gantt chart on a single screen or page whenever possible. Viewing a chart that covers many pages limits the ability of the reader to fully understand all the particulars of the tasks and interdependencies among them and makes it difficult to plan for required changes.

- When making timeline assignments, enter all the numbers using the same units, ideally in days or weeks.

- Make sure the line representing today is bold enough to see easily.

Like any management tracking tool, a Gantt chart is a *living plan*. Update the Gantt at least weekly to reflect the actual project timeline and tasks. Performing regular updates makes the chart an accurate and complete record of the project's history. As you update, save copies of the older versions. Use version control software to save copies of the file, or save files under different filenames based on dates or other pertinent information. Do not overwrite these files or you will lose historical data.

A useful feature of Gantt chart software is the vertical line that indicates today. As the project progresses, regular review cycles will occur daily, every other day, or weekly. At each review, you can adjust lengths and starting points of the bars to the left of the today line to reflect project history. If a task started late, move the task start to reflect the reality of what happened. If a step took more or less time, change the bar length to reflect that. If a staffing assignment changes, reflect this in the chart.

Times to the right of the today line reflect your best estimates of the future—the tasks that need to be completed and the time to complete them. Avoid the temptation to shorten future task lengths to maintain the end goal if past tasks took too long. Future task lengths should remain unchanged unless something has changed to justify shortening your estimate of the time required for an upcoming task.

In addition, maintain dependencies of future milestones based on past tasks unless a dependency no longer exists. For example, if step B follows step A, and step A was three days late, then step B will end three days later than originally expected. Stay honest.

Following this approach, you'll appreciate the Gantt chart's features. First, you can use the chart to communicate status. In addition, the Gantt continually predicts the future end dates of the project during development, based on dates and deadlines already passed along with your current best estimates. Good predictions help you plan for the future (or change a potential outcome before it happens) by adding staff, removing features, or sometimes rearranging tasks. Finally, the Gantt stores project history, which is especially useful after the project is complete, during improvement reviews. In addition, you can use this information to create estimates for new projects in the future and to compare how engineers performed on their estimates versus actual delivery times.

A useful variation of this basic chart is the *dual-bar tracking Gantt*, which you can use to compare an original plan against the current status. The Gantt chart illustrated in Figure 14-3 works well in a dual-bar display as well, as shown in Figure 14-4. In this figure, the black bars show the original plan and the gray bars show the updated numbers. Microsoft Project lets you create dual-bar tracking Gantts; in this product, the original plan is called the *baseline*.

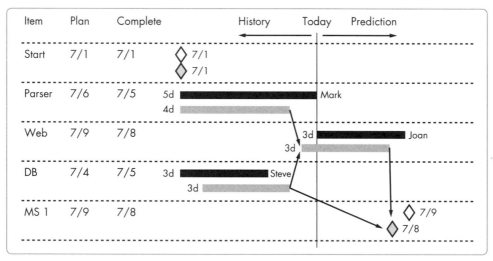

Figure 14-4: Dual-bar tracking Gantt chart

Project management tools, such as Microsoft Project, offer considerable capabilities that are well worth investigating as you progress in your Gantt charting experience, including the following:

- Establishing complex dependencies among tasks, such as adding different delays or start/end relationships among tasks

- Calculating resource usage and cost views once the Gantt chart is set up

- Grouping series of tasks together
- Viewing workload per person

Now with the basics of Gantt chart setup under your belt, let's review the spreadsheet-based approach.

Project-Tracking Spreadsheet

Use a tracking spreadsheet when the interdependences of tasks are few, when the number of tasks is large, and when the number of parallel tasks is large. You can use common spreadsheet tools such as Microsoft Excel or OpenOffice.org Calc to create a tracking spreadsheet. Like a Gantt chart, a tracking spreadsheet allows you to compare results against the original plan as well as predict the likely outcome date. However, a spreadsheet also allows you to use complex calculations when making projections.

Figure 14-5 shows a simple tracking spreadsheet. You can add tasks and subtasks fairly easily. Task times should be broken down into small increments of up to a few days.

	A	B	C	D	E	F	
1	Task	Plan	Spent	Left	Done?	Notes	
2	Task A	4	5	0	X		
3	Task B	3	0	3			
4	Task C						
5	Task C1	2	2	0	X		
6	Task C2	3	2	0	X		Formulas
7	Task D	4	3	4			
8	Totals	16	12	7 ←			=SUM(D2:D7)
9	Team Size	2					Copy to B8:C8
10	Cal days for team	8	6	3.5 ←			=D8/$B$9
11							Copy to B10:C10
12		Dates					
13	Start Project Date	7-Jun					
14	Plan Estimate	19-Jun ←					=WORKDAY(B13,B10)
15							
16	Today	14-Jun ←					Today's date or =TODAY( )
17	Projected Date 1	19-Jun ←					=WORKDAY(B16,D10)
18	Projected Date 2	20-Jun ←					=WORKDAY(B13,C10+D10)

Figure 14-5: Tracking spreadsheet

This example uses calendar-day estimates for all data, instead of work hours or continuous time estimates. As discussed in Chapter 12, a *calendar-day estimate* incorporates any non-project time expected for the person doing the work. In making an estimate, the engineer accounts for other tasks and overhead tasks required during the week in addition to the task at hand. So if the estimate is for five days, the engineer is accounting for not only time directly working on the task, but time for overhead tasks and work on other projects.

The alternative to using calendar days is to track work hours expected for each task. Work hours are the actual hours required to complete the task if the engineer were working on the task full time. To create this estimate, use a multiplier to convert work hours into calendar days. The multiplier accounts for overhead and other tasks that prevent a worker from spending 100 percent of his time on only assigned tasks. Software company overhead percentages can vary, but a common number is 30 percent, which leads to a multiplier of $1 \div (1 - 0.30) = 1.42$. See Chapter 12 for a more detailed discussion of this topic.

The spreadsheet calculates calendar date outcomes directly. Figure 14-5, for example, illustrates two different approaches to calculating end dates. The calculations can be based on today's date with time estimates added as required to complete the project (from the Left column), as shown for Projected Date 1. Alternatively, you can calculate the end date based on the project start date, plus the spent time, plus the estimate for time remaining (from the Left column, or column D) until the project is complete, as shown in Projected Date 2. The Projected Date 1 approach will shift the end date as you check the worksheet daily unless you continually update the Left column values or type in today's date as a number instead of using the today() function. The Projected Date 2 approach will not shift daily but can accumulate small errors in the Spent column that can lead to day errors near the end of the project. Both approaches require vigilance to ensure accuracy.

You can use the tracking spreadsheet as a project management tool. If necessary, you can modify work assignments as the schedule progresses. If you need to add a step, you can add an entire row, but set the Plan column value to *zero (0)* and add a note, as you've added an unplanned item. To drop a step, leave the row in place, but set the Left column value to *zero* and add a note. As with the dual-tracking Gantt, the spreadsheet will allow you to compare your original plan against the work history when the project is complete.

As mentioned, proper project management requires that you accurately track project status throughout the project effort. If you construct a model, it can be combined with project status information to predict future outcomes. If you don't like the outcomes, you can make changes to your project by asking *what if* questions through your model. Change happens in most projects—staff changes, requirements change, and new opportunities and problems arise. A good model lets you deal with change rather than being buffeted by it.

Because this planning tool predicts the likely outcome each day, it allows you to make changes to improve the outcome. You can identify improvements through *what if* calculations—What if I remove a task? What if I add a feature? What if I increase staff? Try the approach, view the revised outcome, and judge whether the change makes sense and gets the plan closer to the desired goal.

With the basics of the tracking spreadsheet covered, let's consider a common problem that projects with many parallel tasks can face: balancing the workload among developers as the work progresses. The following sections show you how to make these changes using a spreadsheet.

Staff Assignments and Workload Balancing

As the project progresses, the plan will change as estimates change due to actual times and as new tasks are entered into the plan. Simply adjusting lengths of tasks will often leave you with an unbalanced set of assignments—that is, some engineers will be done with their assignments while others are still toiling away. Some rebalancing of workload can help, and you can use a simple approach to see what shifts make the most sense. Of course, you do have to account for engineers' skills and background knowledge while assigning tasks.

You can change team assignments to balance workloads during the project and to reduce the overall time required to complete tasks. This approach works best for projects in which flexible engineering assignments are made. Figure 14-6 shows a modified version of the sample spreadsheet shown in Figure 14-5.

	A	B	C	D	E	F	G	H
1	Task	Plan	Spent	Left	Done?	Who	RC	JB
2	Item A	4	1	4	X	JB		4
3	Item B	3	0	3		RC	3	
4	Item C							
5	Item C1	2	0	2	X	RC	2	
6	Item C2	3	2	0	X	RC	0	
7	Item D	4	2	2		JB		2
8	Totals	16	5	11			5	6

Formulas and Notes

Create one column for each person, putting the name or initials at the top. Use the same names in the Who column.

=IF($F7=H$1,$D7,"")
Copy to rectangle G2:H7

=SUM(H2:H7)
Copy to B8:D8,G8

Figure 14-6: Balancing team workload

This spreadsheet allows quick *what if* calculations based on time remaining on the project. In this simple example, adding initials in the Who column (column F) affects the days of work remaining for each engineer (columns G and H). This allows you to make a quick assignment and balance the workload based on time remaining for the project by adjusting assignments until RC and JB have approximately the same amount of work to do. With dozens of tasks involved, performing load balancing manually can be a complex task. Of course, this spreadsheet can be easily expanded to cover a larger team.

Let's look at another variation of the tracking spreadsheet, the minimum-typical-maximum spreadsheet.

Minimum-Typical-Maximum Tracking

A tracking spreadsheet can be set up to predict a range of outcomes. With the addition of *minimum-typical-maximum* value columns of data for each task, the best case, the likely case, and the worst case scenarios can be examined at the same time. The "min-typ-max" tracking approach can be useful for dealing with risk management issues when the risks are known. It can help you visualize and address potential schedule risks early on.

Figure 14-7 illustrates an example min-typ-max spreadsheet. You can enter the range of task times from the original engineering estimates. As work progresses, enter spent time into the Actual column (column G). The Spent plus Remaining columns should provide a range of estimates for the total project effort in End Estimates. This spreadsheet uses the same formulas used in Figures 14-5 and 14-6; the key difference here is the addition of min, typ, and max columns for the plan and the remaining time. An additional row (row 9) sums the spent time and remaining time estimates.

In this example, the original plan had a range of min-typ-max outcomes of 15-19-31 days. With tasks A and C done, the expected time outcome is now 21-23-28. The outcome is still in the predicted range, but it's closer to the worst case predicted in the original plan.

	A	B	C	D	E	F	G	H	I	J	K	L	M
			PLAN				Spent			Remaining			
1													
2	Task	min	typ	max		Done?	Actual		min	typ	max	Who	Notes
3	Task A	4	5	8		X	5					JB	
4	Task B	2	2	2			2		1	1	1	RC	
5	Task C												
6	Task C1	2	3	4		X	1					JB	
7	Task C2	3	3	6		X	6					JB	
8	Task D	4	6	11			2		4	6	11	LT	
9	Totals	15	19	31			16		5	7	12		
10	End Estimates								21	23	28		

Formulas: =SUM(B3:B8) Copy to C9, D9, G9, I9:K9

=$G$9+K9 Copy to I10:J10

Figure 14-7: Min-typ-max tracking spreadsheet

Change Control Process

Every software project experiences changes from the original plan, and a *change control process* is necessary to keep changes from turning into chaos. A change control process is an agreement of how a change request will be handled in these areas: decision, communication, payment, and documentation. For small product companies, a simple method of designating who makes the decision, how it will be communicated, and agreement on a recording mechanism should be sufficient. For a company selling billable services along with the product, a more formalized process may be necessary that should result in a written change order to be approved by the customer requesting the change.

Without a change control process in place, several undesirable results can occur:

- Projects increase in cost.
- Projects are delayed.
- Small, less important requests can overtake the overall project goal.

- Clients are not charged for work they requested. This is a missed revenue opportunity and encourages clients to make more last-minute requests because they are free.

The change control process should distinguish between customer-requested changes and internally requested changes. For internal changes, agreement between marketing and engineering about the project features, costs, and delivery changes should be required. In addition, you should inform your team promptly of any changes.

A change control process should account for approval and implementation:

Approval

- How the requests are made
- Who is responsible for estimating the cost of the change and the method used for the estimate
- Who needs to approve the change
- Who should be consulted
- How the decision will be communicated to the customer if it is a customer request
- How and if the customer will be billed for specific requests
- What is the priority of the change relative to other tasks

Implementation

- How the change is communicated to the team
- Whether the process communicates changes to the documentation team with ample time to ensure that changes are in place before the release
- How QA tracks the change to ensure its completion; as the change was not part of the original plan, it's easy to miss during development

For customer-requested changes, the process must involve your company's sales team as well as engineering and marketing. Larger changes might require discussions with your company's executive team.

The right time to put a change control process in place is *before* your company's growth phase. The amount of review and delay in responding should be smaller initially and larger as the company grows as every change affects more customers. In the early startup phases, making ad hoc and quick changes to meet customer needs can be desirable. In the growth phase, dealing with customer requests without a change control process will impose a high cost on your overall ability to deliver satisfaction to all your customers.

Risk Management

In addition to tracking projects and dealing with changes, a development manager needs to manage project risks. Every software project faces risks, such as external dependencies causing delays, unexpected development problems, team member unavailability, and late changes to requirements. Finding risks early and working to minimize those risks leads to successful project deliverables. Waiting until risks become reality leads to unnecessary delays. A simple risk management approach can improve your delivery success considerably.

Small company risk management need not be complex. The effort involved in tracking and mitigating risks should match the size of the problems. Typically, medium-sized projects lasting several months are good candidates for risk management. Risk tracking for projects lasting under a month often has less utility, unless the project is on the critical path or it will directly affect a release date or a larger project.

A simple risk management approach is to create a risk list and review this regularly with the team during the project effort. The risk manager should consider tracking the following for each identifiable risk:

- Risk ID: identification assigned to track that risk

- Project title: optional if multiple projects in a release are tracked

- Risk title

- Category of risk: schedule, quality, or other

- Probability of risk occurring: different scales can be used, but three, four, or five values work best (for example, low, medium, and high, or a percentage)

- Impact if risk is realized: if it causes a delay, it could be represented as weeks added to the schedule

- Person assigned to monitor the risk

- Notes: can include triggers, mitigations, and contingencies

A spreadsheet or a table can be a practical way to track risks. Table 14-3 shows a sample table.

Table 14-3: Risk-Tracking Example

#	Risk title	Category	Probability	Impact	Assigned	Notes
1	Third-party software doesn't work as advertised	Schedule	Med.	Med.	Smith	Make it work, buy alternative package, or write internally
2	Possible vendor delivery delays	Schedule	Low	High	Jones	Explore other vendors

A reasonable risk management process requires that you regularly review the tracking table in a team meeting. A reasonable time frame is weekly for complex projects but less often for smaller projects. At the team meeting, anyone in attendance can identify a new risk. The project team determines risk value and who to assign to mitigate the risk impact. For existing items, the assignee reports on the status weekly. The assignee can work to reduce the risk's probability and impact. In some cases, the project manager will monitor low and medium risks and treat them as acceptable risks for the project. The team meeting can also be a time to brainstorm mitigations for any of the risks identified.

For most small company projects, your proactive efforts should focus on mitigating the high- and medium-impact risks. A risk is *mitigated* when it goes away or is reduced to a low-impact or low-probability risk. For low-impact or low-probability risks, monitoring them for changes throughout the project is usually sufficient.

Team members should be encouraged to point out risks in team meetings. Tell your team that finding risks early makes them much easier to fix or prevent and helps ensure project success. Note that it is always better to point out a potential risk before it has occurred, instead of dealing with the aftermath of it. In some companies, the corporate culture discourages risk identification, because anyone who points out risks is considered to be too negative. The development manager can set a positive example by listing his or her own observed risks.

The earlier risks are identified, the more time-risk leverage is available to make adjustments at the lowest cost. *Time-risk leverage* describes how the effort today is more effective (has more leverage) when the time before risk realization is long instead of short. The more weeks ahead of risk becoming reality, the less work effort you need to mitigate the risk and obtain a desirable outcome. Waiting until a few days before a problem becomes a critical reality means that it can take a large effort to change the outcome, if you can change it at all.

Consider a hypothetical scenario: A contractor cannot guarantee a security review of a key module when you need it, 10 weeks from now. A team member discovers this risk and reports it to the assigned risk mitigator, who starts calling other contractors to find an alternative. If, instead, the team member had discovered this risk a week before the critical help was required, finding an alternative contractor would be far more difficult, as few, if any, would be available on such short notice. You can calculate the expected risk impact on your schedule. If you enter percent probability along with risk impact in days for each risk, the effective impact can be determined by multiplying the two numbers. For example, 20 percent probability and a 10-day impact gives $0.2 \times 10 = 2$-day risk impact for that risk. Summing up all of the schedule risks will show the probable unmitigated impacts of all the risks. Knowing this number tells you the current total schedule risk to your project.

This example focuses on schedule impact while maintaining the other aspects of the project such as functionality. If the risk is realized, you would use the 10 days if they were required for the success of the project. For many projects, priority of different features varies considerably. If the work involves a lower priority feature and the schedule is of the highest importance, the customer might decide to forgo a feature to meet the schedule. When you're considering how to determine the impact of different risks, focus on the core deliverables for the project and discount less essential tasks.

Figure 14-8 illustrates the cumulative schedule impact of the outstanding weighted risk on the project. Given what you know when you updated the chart, the risk-adjusted schedule will likely result in a 12.5-day slip. If the risks in this case were identified at the start of the project, you could examine your abilities to mitigate those risks quickly. Otherwise, adding 12.5 days to your project schedule would be prudent.

	A	B	C	D	E	F	G	H
1	#	Project	Risk Title	Category	Probability	Impact (days)	Effective Impact	Assigned to
2	1	Module A	3rd party API missing key function	Schedule	50%	5	2.5	Smith
3	2	Module B	Vendor delivery delays	Schedule	20%	30	6	Jones
4	3	Module C	New features	Schedule	80%	5	4	Mark
5		TOTALS					12.5	

Formulas =E2*F2 Copy to G3:G4 =SUM(G2:G4)

Figure 14-8: Outstanding weighted risk

In summary, risk management allows you to see the impact of potential problems early on and take action while it is easier. If successful risk management processes are used, fewer crises will affect your projects—they will run more smoothly and will have a better chance of succeeding.

Additional Reading

Here is some additional reading on topics presented in this chapter:

Code Complete: A Practical Handbook of Software Construction, by Steve McConnell (Microsoft Press, 2004)

Controlling Software Projects: Management, Measurement, and Estimates, by Tom DeMarco (Prentice Hall, 1986)

The Deadline: A Novel About Project Management, by Tom DeMarco (Dorset House Publishing Co., 1997)

Developing Products in Half the Time: New Rules, New Tools, by Preston G. Smith and Donald G. Reinertsen (Wiley, 1997)

Manage It! Your Guide to Modern, Pragmatic Project Management, by Johanna Rothman (Pragmatic Bookshelf, 2007)

The Mythical Man-Month: Essays on Software Engineering, Anniversary Edition, by Frederick P. Brooks, Jr. (Addison-Wesley, 1995)

Waltzing with Bears: Managing Risk on Software Projects, by Tom DeMarco and Timothy Listner (Dorset House Publishing Co., 2003)

15

DESIGNING A SOFTWARE DEVELOPMENT PROCESS

Process can be the friend to everyone involved in a growing software company. A useful development *process* represents everything a company has learned about creating and developing successful software products. It provides a foundation for efficient and successful future projects and gives a company a competitive edge. A development manager who picks the proper process, trains his team based on it, and then maintains practices for that process will likely have an effective team with high morale.

Unfortunately, problematic processes have earned poor reputations in some companies, where processes can be bloated, out of date, difficult to change, awkward to use, senselessly enforced, and generally responsible for slowing everyone down. These companies treat their processes not as tools for improving outcomes, but as ends in and of themselves. Workers bearing the weight of a misapplied process grow resentful, particularly of the concept of development processes in general.

Many startup companies begin without having created a development process. As problems appear following the first few releases, it becomes apparent that some sort of order needs to be made out of the chaos. These companies need a development process, but they might not know how to choose, create, or implement one.

This chapter introduces you to software development processes, including types of processes and process selection.

What's in a Software Development Process?

A *software development process* defines a systematic, repeatable approach to building software and usually involves a series of steps or a diagram showing activities and decision points. A development process formalizes the steps involved in defining, developing, testing, and releasing software.

Although many formal software development processes exist, they all set out to do the same thing: make software development predictable while supporting corporate goals. Processes do this through a repeatable recipe, with measureable steps along the way. The process inputs are product definition, desired schedule, workers, resources, and money budgeted. The measurable process outputs are delivery schedule, quality, functionality delivered, and money spent.

Different development processes use different strategies in their definitions. For example, some processes work to fix the functional definition early on and allow the schedule to vary, while other processes fix the development time per release and reduce functionality as needed. Processes also vary regarding number of iterations of the main tasks, the amount of feedback between steps, the nature of milestones, and the length of the development cycle. Because of these variations, different processes can emphasize different results, such as the following:

- Minimal time to completion
- Accuracy of schedule prediction

- Quality of end product
- Cost of activity
- Risk reduction
- Most accurately meeting customer needs

Stepping through some of the more common processes used in software development can introduce you to different variations and what they optimize. The next section covers the most common processes in use.

Types of Development Processes

Each process has its place, and no single process is the best solution for every situation. In some cases, sensibly customizing a process will provide the best results.

The following sections offer brief overviews of various processes. You can consult with experienced process users or read a book about a particular process to learn more details. (See "Additional Reading" on page 284.) Each process has its advantages and disadvantages. Consider the environment of your company as you decide which process to use. Keep in mind that, in some cases, company political issues can render a great process unusable.

WARNING   *For process advocates who believe there is one ~~ring~~ process of power that rules over all other processes . . . well . . . lighten up. After all, engineers have to learn about the others to understand the rest of the story, don't they?*

For process learners, these sections provide an overview of development processes, but not enough information is provided here to allow you to understand every detail of any single process. You can read a book or undergo training to learn more about a particular process. (And you can just ignore those "there is only one process" advocates for now!)

In general, small companies can use a *lightweight process* due to their need for limited overhead and maximum speed. A lightweight process has a few basic steps, few key milestones, clear requirements, limited reporting, few sign-offs, and a few alternative paths. A lightweight process must be simple—so simple that a diagram of the process fits easily on one page, along with a short description.

The following sections discuss several process alternatives, starting with the ad hoc approach, which is the most common starting place for small development projects.

Ad Hoc

Startup companies often design their first code without a formal process—that is, in an *ad hoc* manner. Such an effort usually goes like this: The developer gets an idea, writes the code, and keeps adjusting it until he likes the result. This approach can be effective (and fun) on small projects.

On projects that require more than one or two developers, however, ad hoc approaches produce unpredictable results in quality, delivery, and functionality. The results are generally poorer than those achieved by using a repeatable process. Ad hoc work is difficult to schedule accurately, and the overall cost of development increases exponentially as the size of a project increases.

Ad hoc works best for efforts involving the following:

- One or two developers
- Tiny to small efforts
- Prototyping an idea
- Technology experimentation

Waterfall Process

In its simplest form, a *waterfall process* includes four major steps: define, design, implement, and test. Each step must be completed before the next one is started. Most companies implementing a waterfall process provide feedback paths, but they require special reviews, which can be slow or difficult, especially in some larger companies. The process diagram shown in Figure 15-1 indicates how the process earned its name.

Process advocates often point out the deficiencies of the waterfall process. One problem is that many projects lack a clear definition at the beginning,

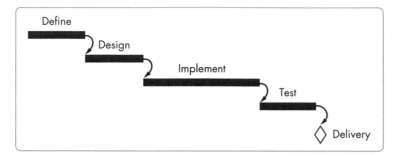

Figure 15-1: Waterfall Gantt chart

so completing the definition step first can be very difficult on a major project. Without a clear definition, many long feedback loops are incurred as the team discovers development problems later in the development cycle. In addition, if the team finds problems in an earlier step after that step has been completed and the project has moved forward, the process of changing the earlier step can be cumbersome. Because each step must be completed and approved before the next one can start, development can be slower than other approaches.

The waterfall process also has its advocates, however. This process can work well when the following criteria are met:

- Customer requirements for the project are reasonably well known—for example, they require a variant of an existing program.

- A dispersed team is working on a joint effort.

- The project is medium to large in size.

- The project does not decompose into smaller deliverable pieces.

- The project requires large amounts of interaction between different functional teams.

Modified Waterfall Process

Many companies use a *modified waterfall* variation. Modified waterfalls allow some later steps to begin before the team has completed earlier steps. Most modified waterfalls provide monitored feedback loops so that when people find a problem while tackling one step, they can rework an earlier step to help fix it. For example, if the team detects a definition problem in the

WATERFALL WORKED BETTER

I was working for a company making a complex, semi-custom software product, which my company sold to a few dozen customers. Most engineers consistently took about a year to complete each product. On my first effort, my manager told me to add features iteratively after creating the skeleton of the program. As I got to later features, the work slowed down—to get clarity from customers, to redesign the system, and to add support throughout the system.

I switched to a waterfall approach for my next program. I spent considerable time getting a clear definition from the customer. I then carefully designed and reviewed the system before coding. Coding was rapid and successful. Including testing, the project was done in half the time. My later projects matched or exceeded this result.

—Software engineer

design step, the team reopens the definition step to work on it. Modified waterfalls usually define what to do in the feedback loops to keep the effort from turning into chaos. Figure 15-2 illustrates a version of the modified waterfall.

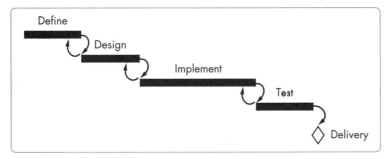

Figure 15-2: Simple modified waterfall process

Companies use many variations of a modified waterfall, such as adding tests between steps, using different steps, and using different checkpoints depending on the need and company policy. A lightweight waterfall process can be created by limiting the overhead of hand-off steps while meeting the needs of the company and the project.

The modified waterfall process can work well if the following criteria apply:

- The project definition is partially known or can be discovered early and can be clearly stated.

- Marketing or customers will make some changes to the product definition during development.

- Your company requires some very specific structures and controls.

- A project does not decompose into smaller deliverable pieces.

- The project is of medium complexity.

Iterative Process

The *iterative process* splits the project into sections, with "mini-waterfalls" in each. Development teams can use an iterative process to develop usable code in functional sections. Marketing can develop requirements either as part of each development section or in advance of the iterations. The team performs code integration and system tests at the end of all the iterations. Figure 15-3 illustrates an iterative process workflow.

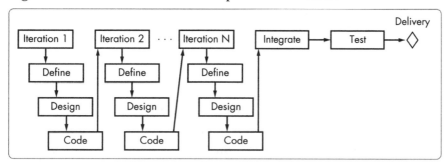

Figure 15-3: Iterative process workflow

Iterative processes work well for the following situations:

- Projects with high risk-reduction requirements

- Projects that can be decomposed into smaller, usable segments

- Projects with components much simpler than the whole project

- Projects without clear definitions up front

- Projects that benefit from multiple small releases of functionality

- Projects that require medium to large efforts

Spiral Process

The *spiral process* combines prototyping with a series of waterfall models, each sequence forming one loop of the spiral when drawn. A standard spiral has three iterations, as compared to an iterative process for which the number of iterations is undefined. The first spiral of the standard process consists of prototype creation. In each subsequent spiral, developers add increments of functionality to the project. At the end of each spiral, management evaluates the risk and makes the decision of whether or not to go forward. This formalized risk evaluation is a unique feature in the spiral process.

The spiral process steps are as follows:

1. Define the requirements or objectives (usually by interviewing users and customers).

2. Create a preliminary design.

3. Create a prototype (first loop) or iteration of the system (second and later loops).

4. Evaluate the risks and decide whether to continue.

5. Plan for the next iteration.

The spiral model offers advantages for larger projects. First, as the work moves through different spirals, planning and estimating become more realistic. Second, it provides a useful way of mitigating risk by constructing the project in stages and evaluating each stage. Third, it provides a way to evaluate the feasibility of the system as the work progresses. Finally, the model can cope with user requirement changes.

One disadvantage of the spiral model is the emphasis on risk reduction, which can increase overall costs compared to other processes.

Spiral process can work well for the following:

- Projects that lack a clear definition up front, so that the project effort might change during discovery

- Projects for which minimizing project risk is very important

- Projects of medium to large size

- Complicated projects
- Projects with experimental- or research-type subprojects

Agile Processes

Agile processes are not a single process, but a family of processes with similar characteristics. *Agile processes* are considered lightweight processes that solve core problems with software development, including unclear definitions at project start, limited progress indicators, slow development, and an unacceptable product being created.

Agile processes have a number of common characteristics:

- Customer focus and participation throughout development, not just during definition
- Limited formal documentation early in the project
- Emphasis on customer involvement in the definition throughout development phases
- Working software as the key success measure
- Daily communication between team members
- Self-organizing teams
- Very short delivery cycles measured in weeks, with two- to six-week ranges being common

NOTE *Some agile teams use short integration cycles instead of short delivery cycles.*

Agile processes have many proponents who appreciate the short development cycles, the value of continuous customer feedback, the ability to be ready to deliver at any time, and the feeling of continual progress. Many people contend that agile processes save time overall, because the product definition does not have to be complete to make progress and because the end result is likely to be acceptable to the customer as built.

WARNING *It is possible to encumber an agile process so that it is no longer lightweight.*

Agile processes have detractors as well. Some people believe that daily status meetings, short timelines, and pair programming of *extreme programming (XP)* are inefficient. In addition, some agile processes do not clearly define QA's role in the effort. Getting good software test coverage with short development cycles is a huge problem, especially for larger projects. Not having clear documentation greatly reduces the effectiveness of the QA team's work. In addition, short development cycles make it difficult to create complex code or systems that developers can split into short, complete sections.

WARNING   *Some companies claim their development process is agile, which does not make sense because agile is not a process but a group of processes. Such a company tends to focus on short delivery cycles and changing requirements. It dresses up its ad hoc behavior with the* agile *terminology.*

Several popular agile processes are XP, Scrum, Feature-Driven Development, Dynamic Systems Development Method, Adaptive Software Development, Crystal Clear, and Evolutionary Development (Evo). The next two sections discuss the XP and Scrum processes.

Extreme Programming

An early popular agile process is commonly known as *XP*. Kent Beck and Cynthia Andres' book, *Extreme Programming Explained* (see "Additional Reading" on page 284) helped popularized XP, which consists of a number of interrelated practices, including the following:

- Pair programming
- Story cards
- Short timelines
- Continual building and integration of the code
- Evolving designs
- Getting solutions into production early
- Unit testing

Two of these practices may need some explanation: *Pair programming* describes two engineers working together at a single computer—one writes code while the other provides feedback. The joint development can lead to better designs and higher-quality code, which minimizes debugging and test repairs. As part of planning, the team creates *story cards* using index cards to describe small tasks associated with the software.

XP also emphasizes short time frame releases with minimal features in each release. This makes sense for certain classes of software problems, especially smaller projects being developed from scratch in which the customer does not fully understand the nature of the problem or solution.

Extreme programming works best for projects that meet the following criteria:

- Projects with teams of 3 to 12 members
- Projects that can be built in usable pieces
- Projects for which delivery date is more important than ensuring specific functionality
- Projects with unclear definitions for the larger project
- Projects of small to medium complexity
- Organizations with cooperative customers willing to participate actively
- Projects whose testing lends itself to being accurately and rapidly completed

Scrum Process

Another popular agile process called *Scrum* is named after a rugby term. Scrum uses fixed-length release cycles called *sprints* that are usually 30 days long. At the start of the cycle, the team negotiates the definition for the sprint. A *Scrum master* holds daily standup meetings and creates specific reports showing progress of the work toward completion. The team builds functioning code daily. When projected delivery exceeds the sprint length, the scrum master decreases the functionality until the team can meet the original delivery date. If marketing determines that the functionality must change, then the sprint resets and the team starts a new sprint. Scrum also uses specific project management methods during the cycle, which include daily reviews and specific reports.

Scrum has the benefit of fixing the maximum functionality along with fixing the timeline at the beginning of the cycle. The functionality planned does not increase or change during a sprint, but the Scrum master can reduce it to fit the time available. The staff size remains constant for a cycle. Having potential variables fixed up front makes a Scrum process predictable.

WARNING   *Scrum does not allow functional changes during a cycle without resetting to a new 30-day cycle. However, some Scrum users do not follow the reset requirement because their management will not allow them to do so—this seriously compromises the effectiveness of the process.*

A modified version of Scrum delivers working functionality at the end of a sprint that will later be integrated into the end product.

Overall, Scrum is an effective agile process to consider. Figure 15-4 illustrates the Scrum process that produces a shippable product.

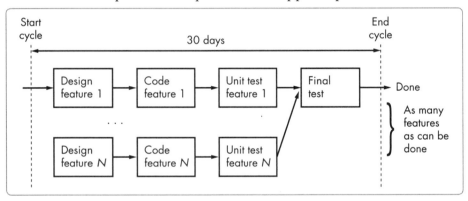

Figure 15-4: Scrum process workflow

Scrum works best when the following critera are met:

- Team sizes of 3 to 12 members
- Projects that can be built in usable sections
- Projects for which delivery date is more important than ensuring specific functionality
- Projects for which the definition of the full product is unclear
- A corporate culture based on cooperation

- Projects for which marketing wants to leave options open and allow for later changes

- Projects for which testing can be accurately and rapidly completed

Other Processes and Approaches

Two other approaches that are not complete processes but are often included in process discussion are test-driven development and model-driven development.

Test-driven development describes the practice of first creating tests for each module, and then writing the code for the module. This is more a development practice than a full process. Creating tests up front aids in the creation of the code as it clarifies the definition of the functionality.

Model-driven development describes the practice of creating a software model to define the software, and then writing the code to match the model. This is effective when a model can be programmed at a high level to form a useful definition but not provide a usable software product.

Customizing a Process

The development manager can create a custom process by modifying one of the processes discussed in this chapter. Customization of a process can better align development with the company's needs and the served industry's requirements. Being familiar with multiple processes gives the development manager a number of different options and features to consider in the design.

Here are some guidelines to consider when customizing a standard process:

- Notify the right people at milestones, but keep sign-offs to a minimum.

- Accommodate changes to requirements.

- Keep definitions short and to the point.

- Allow for feedback loops and iteration.

- Plan to create prototypes early or create an early working version.

- Consider a small number of intermediate milestones and deliverables for each milestone.

- Use the minimum cycle time for releases that is practical given all the constraints.

- Ensure that milestones support efficiency, not control.

- Consider how quality assurance fits into the picture.

- Determine how to handle system integration in the process.

A customized process can provide advantages for your company because it can support specific company goals, allow for efficiency in development, meet the needs of other teams, and deal with regulatory requirements. However, a custom process should never be created purely for political reasons: It will lead to team resentment and will not solve core problems.

WAITING TO GET THINGS DONE

I worked for a company where I was the only engineer on my project and was, effectively, the project manager. This company used an extensive process that required many approvals at milestones. Most of the milestones required multiple signatures to get approval to move on. Some required eight different signature approvals.

One way to handle this was to route the forms with documents to eight different people. This process could take a week or two if a person was slow or out of the office. Making appointments was another slow and time-consuming approach. My solution was to walk the documents and sign-off forms around to each person and wait outside their office until they were available. I could typically finish this in one or two days.

I learned that many people signing really did not care to review the documents provided, but just wanted to ensure that they had a copy they could review. Others had only limited questions. My early conclusion was to minimize the signature approvals required in a process because they typically did not add value and did cost time.

—Engineer

Selecting a Process

A small company needs to properly choose and introduce a process so that team members understand how it works and what its benefits are. Scale your process introduction effort for the size of the development organization. A tiny team in a small company usually requires a minimal amount of training, review, and documentation as compared to a larger team with multiple differing roles and perspectives.

Choosing or improving the best process is not easy. Different processes meet different company needs and produce different results.

To plan process improvements, first examine the intrinsic needs and the constraints of your company. Then review common processes and techniques in use. Next, map out the process and create the training materials. Finally, train all staff who will be using the process.

Selecting a new process requires collecting information about the current processes and practices. A good approach is to compare the collected information against standard practices and make adjustments as needed. Consider the following when selecting or designing a new process:

- Length of release cycle
- Nature of development task
- Test and approval constraints
- Business requirements
- Company culture
- Team size and distribution

One more thought: Do not make the process choice alone. Get advice and feedback from your peers, your boss, your team, and people with process experience. This will help you set up a strong process as well as gain buy-in from your company.

Introducing a Process

Introducing a new process to your company is never as simple as telling the team to use a process you have chosen. Process introduction usually requires a fair amount of preparation and training. The steps in introducing a process usually go like this:

1. Select and analyze a process.

2. Document the process.

3. Train the team on the process.

4. Kick off the process.

Once the process is in place, maintaining the process requires the following:

- Promoting the process

- Monitoring and enforcing the process

- Training new team members

Let's review some of the areas not covered earlier.

To document a process, start with a one-page flow chart and a one- to three-page summary. When you have a more complex workflow, people using the process will have a more difficult time understanding the process during training and will not have a simple or useful reference. However, you can provide supplementary information or reference books that describe the process in more detail.

You can promote a documented process by talking about it, demonstrating the benefits, and highlighting the potential successes. The benefits of a new process are not always clear to the team. In some cases, people grumble about having to change the way they do their work. If you continue to promote the process, gaining your team's acceptance will be easier. Promoting a process may be your most important action toward assuring its acceptance.

Training people on the software development process is crucial to its success. The best approach is to train people with an in-service workshop instead of sending them material to read. At the workshop, you can step through the process in detail and answer questions. Failing to train the team on the process indicates that you are not serious about putting it in place.

After your team has been trained, let everyone know the start date for switching over to the new process. For many small companies, the switchover can start immediately. In other cases, however, waiting until the next release effort starts will minimize disruptions to the current product development cycle.

FOUND IT ON THE INTERNET

The manager of our group was concerned that one of the engineering managers was not following a development process and it was affecting quality. The engineering manager did not want to put a process in place, so he continued to sidestep the issue. The group manager was not familiar with software processes, so he found one on the Internet and told the engineering manager to use it. However, the group manager never followed up, so the engineering manager and the team ignored the new process.

The result was continued development without a process by the engineering team. It also lowered the team's respect for the group manager because of his inappropriate choice and lack of enforcement. After this, his job became more difficult.

—Software engineer

A process succeeds only if you monitor it and enforce it. You must set up a definition, measurable schedule, and quality goals. When you detect problems, spend time understanding the core issues. Processes usually require enforcement, which can mean talking to people when the process isn't followed to understand what happened. (You may need to modify the process if problems are uncovered.) Without enforcement, some people will skip steps to wait to see if any repercussions follow. Ensuring that the team follows the process is key to its success.

A great topic for an end-of-project "post-mortem" discussion is a review of the process, especially if its first use was on this project. Ask team members to examine the process to see whether it meets the company's and team's needs. Actively review the process steps one at a time to ask for suggestions for improvement.

Establishing a new software development process can take six months to a year, depending on the situation. It usually takes that long for people to understand it, realize its benefits, and become familiar with using it during the development process. Stick with it through the difficult times and enjoy the rewards later when you are more productive as a team.

Additional Reading

Here is some additional reading on topics presented in this chapter:

> *Controlling Software Projects: Management, Measurement, and Estimates*, by Tom DeMarco (Yourdon Press, 1986)
>
> *Developing Products in Half the Time: New Rules, New Tools*, by Preston G. Smith and Donald G. Reinertsen (Wiley, 1997)
>
> *Introduction to the Team Software Process*, by Watts S. Humphrey (Addison-Wesley Professional, 2008)
>
> *Manage It!: Your Guide to Modern, Pragmatic Project Management*, by Johanna Rothman (Pragmatic Bookshelf, 2007)
>
> *The Mythical Man-Month: Essays on Software Engineering, Anniversary Edition*, by Frederick P. Brooks, Jr. (Addison-Wesley Professional, 1995)
>
> *Managing the Software Process*, by Watts S. Humphrey (Addison-Wesley Professional, 1989)
>
> "Software Development Process," from Wikipedia, *http://en.wikipedia.org/wiki/Software_development_process*

Here is some additional reading on agile processes:

> Agile Alliance organization home page, *http://www.agilealliance.org/*
>
> *Agile & Iterative Development: A Manager's Guide (Agile Software Development Series)*, by Craig Larman (Addison-Wesley Professional, 2003)
>
> *Agile Project Management with Scrum*, by Ken Schwaber (Microsoft Press, 2004)
>
> *Extreme Programming Explained: Embrace Change, 2nd Edition*, by Kent Beck and Cynthia Andres (Addison-Wesley Professional, 2004)

"Agile Software Development," from Wikipedia, *http://en.wikipedia.org/wiki/Agile_software_development*

"Manifesto for Agile Software Development," *http://agilemanifesto.org/*

ScrumAlliance home page, *http://www.scrumalliance.org/*

"Scrum Development," from Wikipedia, *http://en.wikipedia.org/wiki/Scrum_development*

16

PROCESS IMPROVEMENT

A process is not a static item that you design once and leave in place. You need to maintain it, and you need to review it periodically in search of opportunities for improvement. Any process, whether a development process or any other type, can benefit from analysis and improvement.

Improving a process can be exciting and fun for a development manager; it can have a significant impact on team and company productivity and morale. An improved development process can help make the development team more productive. Of course, when working with short development cycles and firm delivery dates, a significant process change can be risky. However, if the process is seriously broken or would benefit from a simple improvement, fixing it immediately can help you make a looming delivery date that once seemed impossible.

Larger companies often use heavy tools such as Six Sigma Analysis[1] to conduct thorough analyses and revisions of their processes. Some managers have been put off while working for larger companies, however, where encumbering process improvement programs took too much time and offered too few results. Some larger firms use fossilized processes with unnecessary steps. At these companies, a manager's attempt to improve the process can result in political maneuvering, unnecessary studies, and long delays. Worse yet, the Six-Sigma improvement approach is too often applied to problems better suited to a simple analysis. The result can be worker cynicism in general at the mention of "process improvement."

Process improvement need not be intimidating, but heavy Six Sigma–type analyses are usually too time-consuming for a small company. Instead, a small company can benefit from the simple modeling described in this chapter.

Creating a Process Model

Development managers in small companies rarely model processes. Many development managers do not focus on process modeling, because their primary focus is to deliver the required software on time. They also might not have the tools or experience required for simple process modeling.

By skipping this step, however, you'll miss an opportunity to make important time-saving adjustments before your company begins rapidly growing.

The steps involved in creating a process model are straightforward:

1. Define the process boundaries.
2. List the process steps.
3. Create a flow chart.
4. Estimate a range of times.
5. Create a spreadsheet model.
6. Verify the model.

---

[1] *Six Sigma Analysis* involves a set of methods that were invented at Motorola for analyzing and improving complex processes. For readers who are statistically savvy, a Six Sigma book is included in "Additional Reading" on page 299.

Define the Process Boundaries

In defining the process boundaries, you identify the beginning and end points of the process: Which step initiates the process, and which step occurs at the end? This might seem like a trivial issue, but it is important and should be considered carefully. Improvement solutions can become difficult if the wrong boundary is chosen. For the inputs to the process, define a single item which initiates the process, when possible. This might be a detailed description of what is desired, or it could be a set of requirements. For the outputs of the process, multiple deliverables are acceptable, but define clearly what they should be. For example, an estimating process might start with a form describing the requirements of the estimate, while the output might be a high-level definition and a separate cost or delivery estimate.

List the Process Steps

Write down a list of steps and number them. Keep it brief: A single sentence for each step works well. If a step requires a decision that will affect two or more steps that follow, label the step as a *decision* step. If a step leads to *parallel* steps, label the next steps as parallel. Processes often include *recursion* (one step that repeats multiple times usually with changing input conditions) or *iteration* (one step that leads back to an earlier step); you should describe the decisions that lead to recursion or iteration when listing the steps.

Create a Flow Chart

For a simple analysis, a flow chart that uses boxes for steps and diamonds for decision points will do. Each box should correspond to a process step and use the same number scheme used for the process steps. Add a two- to three-word title in the box to represent the step, and add the name of the group, team, or person responsible for completing the step in brackets at the bottom. For decision steps, use a diamond-shaped box and add the decision keywords. Decision step boxes should show two or more arrows leaving them, showing the step choices resulting from the decision.

Estimate a Range of Times

Write down minimum, typical, and maximum (min-typ-max) times for each of the steps on the flow chart. At branch points, indicate the likelihood for each option as a percentage, along with its min-typ-max values. Be sure to indicate parallel workflow paths.

Create a Spreadsheet Model

Create the spreadsheet model with each step in the spreadsheet corresponding to the steps in the flow chart. Although a variety of commercial modeling programs can be used, a simple spreadsheet model works remarkably well to track the process at a small firm.

A simple approach is to use one row for each step in the process. Each row will use the appropriate step number, step name, and min-typ-max times expected. The total time for each step can be summed up at the bottom.

A *decision branch point* occurs in a process when a decision is made that results in more than one next step option as the outcome of the decision. In the spreadsheet, decision branch points can be handled by shifting their calculations out of the main path. You can put multiple calculations based on branch choices off to the side and list them all along with percent of time occurrence for each and min-typ-max times. With two or more branch decisions, the minimum for the different branches should be the shortest of the minimum choices. Similarly, the maximum times will be the largest of the maximum choices. Typical times will be the percentage weighting of the typical times of the different choices.

Processes often require *parallel tasks*, in which a task spurs multiple sub-steps that occur in parallel before the step is complete. For example, an estimation step might require that you ask two developers for estimates, and though each estimate can be created independently, both estimates must be completed before the step is complete. Parallel tasks can also be calculated to the side of the main column of a spreadsheet. To simplify calculations, consider all parallel items as a single process step. For the entire process step, the minimum total time will be the largest value of the minimums of the parallel tasks. The typical total time will be the largest value of the typical parallel tasks. The maximum time will be the largest value of the maximum parallel tasks.

Iteration or feedback paths are difficult to incorporate into a simple model. However, this situation can be modeled by turning the iteration path into its own workflow path. For example, if the steps in the process are A and then B, and B is a decision either to go back to A or go on to C, then you can convert the "go back to A" path to step D.

An example spreadsheet is illustrated in the next section, which should help clarify the spreadsheet layout potential.

Verify the Model

Pass the model through the "smell test." Does it "smell" right? Do reasonable inputs provide reasonable outputs? If you make changes to an element, does it produce reasonable results? Have you reviewed the model with stakeholders (anyone who works on a process step)? If so, then the model is ready for detailed analysis.

Analyzing the Process Model

Once the model is built, you should analyze it and look for opportunities to improve the result. Using the process model, investigate "what if" scenarios. Others may request specific improvement goals, and you will be asked to find ways to meet them. Here are some common examples:

- Reduce the maximum time throughout the process.

- Reduce the typical time.

- Reduce the minimum time throughout for special cases.

- Allow for an increase in time for one step and maintain the same time throughout the process.

- On a decision point, decrease the percentage of time for the more expensive decision.

- For parallel tasks, focus on the most expensive task for time reductions.

Let's look at a simple process example that moves through the analysis steps.

Process Analysis in Action

The process modeled in this example will be used for engineering estimates in response to sales team requests for quotes. The example illustrates a simple approach to modeling a process and making improvements.

Let's start by defining the boundaries of the process. In this case, the entry point is the sales manager submitting the request to the engineer you have designated as the *quote engineer* responsible for the quoting process. The exit point occurs when the development manager delivers the quote to the sales manager who asked for it.

With the process boundaries defined, you can step through the steps and assign who completes the step. These are the high-level steps in the process:

1. [Entry point] The sales manager sends a request for an estimate.

2. The quote engineer reviews sales information.

3. [Decision] The quote engineer determines whether enough information is available to complete the quote.

    *   If information is sufficient, move on to the next step.

    *   If it is not, the engineer requests additional information from the sales manager and the quote stalls until a complete response is received.

4. After a response is received, the quote engineer writes up a description of the request so that it is clear to the development team. This description will be used for the estimate and returned with the quote delivery. The description will include any assumptions that are made.

5. The quote engineer requests estimates from a Java programmer and a database programmer.

    *   [Parallel] (A) The Java engineer makes his estimate and returns it to the quote engineer.

    *   [Parallel] (B) The database engineer makes her estimate and returns it to the quote engineer.

6. When both estimates are returned, the quote engineer writes up the quote and sends it to the development manager for review.

7. The development manager reviews and edits the quote.

8. [Output] The development manager delivers the estimate to the sales manager.

If you write the process steps as a sequential list, they might look like those in Table 16-1. This example shows every step, including delivery steps. This simple process also illustrates parallel tasks in steps 6a and 6b. Note the decision point in step 3.

Table 16-1: Steps in Quote Process Example

What	Who
1. Quote request to engineering	Sales
2. Quote request is reviewed	Quote-Eng.
3. [Decision] Quote needs more information	Quote-Eng. -> Sales
4. Quote write-up	Quote-Eng.
5. Estimate requests to DB and Java eng.	Quote-Eng.
6a. [PARALLEL STEP] DB eng. estimate	DB Eng.
6b. [PARALLEL STEP] Java eng. estimate	Java Eng.
7. Quote write-up prepared	Quote-Eng.
8. Quote eng. reviewed	Dev. Management
9. Quote delivered	Dev. Management

Turning this table into a workflow is useful for visual analysis and discussion. Figure 16-1 illustrates the workflow.

Your next step is to write down the time required for each step in the workflow drawing. If you write min-typ-max time estimates, you can use an abbreviated format, such as 10-13-20. For decision points, show approximate percentage weighting of the typical time requirements of the different choices that go with each decision path.

After completing the drawing, you'll find it easier to visualize the process workflow and convert it into a spreadsheet. Figure 16-2 shows the workflow diagram directly translated to a spreadsheet. It also shows total min-typ-max times for the simple quote process at the bottom. The surprising thing is that while the typical time is a long 3.8 days, the worst-case time for the process is more than 10 days! Stepping through the construction of this estimate shows how modeling works.

The decision point in step 3 has two different options: Half the time, more information will be required. For this decision point, the minimum is the smaller of the two options for more info needed—yes or no. The typical

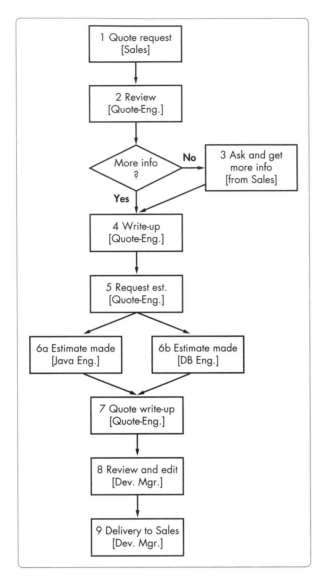

Figure 16-1: Workflow for quote process

value is weighted for the typical of each option—50 percent each is typical. The maximum is the maximum for the two cases. A sales worst case takes 2 days to respond to requests, and this could cause a significant process delay.

The parallel tasks in 6a and 6b are estimates provided by the Java engineer and the database engineer. Given typical tasks and their schedules, these numbers suggest that the database estimate is shorter than the Java

	A	B	C	D	E	F	G	H	I	J	K	
1			**Main Flow**					**Branching Workflows**				
2		Item	Min	Typ	Max		Item	Min	Typ	Max	%	
3	1	Request	0	0	0							
4	2	Review	1	2	8							
5		Decision: more info?				=>	SPLIT WORKFLOW					
6							no	0	0	0	50%	**Formulas**
7							yes	1	8	16	50%	
8	3	More Info Result	0	4	16	<=	3. Weighted	0	4	16		=MAX(J6:J7)
9	4	Description Write-up	1	2	4							=I6*K6+I7*K7
10												=MIN(H6:H7)
11	5	Request Est.	0.2	0.2	0.2							=J8
12												Copy to D8:C8
13		Estimate Parallel Tasks				=>	PARALLEL					
14							6a Java Est.	2	4	8		
15							6b DB Est.	1	2	4		
16	6	Estimates	2	4	8	<=	6a,6b max	2	4	8		=MAX(J14:J15)
17												Copy to H16:I16
18	7	Quote Write-up	1	1	4							=J16
19	8	Mgr Review	1	8	16							Copy to C16:D16
20	9	Delivery	0.2	0.2	0.2							
21		**Totals (hrs)**	**6.4**	**21.4**	**56.4**							=SUM(E3:E20)
22		**Total (days)**	**1.143**	**3.821**	**10.07**							Copy to C21:D21
23												=E21/$C$24
24		Hrs to Cal Days	5.6									Copy to C22:D22
25		assumes 8 hr days, 70% availability										

Figure 16-2: Quote process workflow spreadsheet

estimate. As the process shows the task steps in parallel, the calculation uses the larger of the two. Note that improving the min-typ-max values for the database engineer will have no impact on the process outcome, as they are all smaller than the Java engineer's values. The Java engineer's time values are in the critical path of the process for most quotes.

After you create the model, you should carefully examine it: Does the result seem reasonable? To verify, keep track of the quotes you receive and measure the delays through each step. Do the individual numbers look right and is the typical time close? If so, you know the model is reasonable. If not, you need to make revisions.

Using the Model to Improve the Process

You can use your spreadsheet model as a tool to help you improve the process schedule. By adjusting times, you can determine the impact on the process total schedule. In general, fine-grained tweaking of numbers won't yield significant reductions, but the model will help you identify bottlenecks and experiment with the impact of the reductions.

A few reduction cases follow, targeting reduction in maximum process time and the typical time.

Case 1: Reducing the Maximum Time

Sales is complaining about some quotes from engineering that take a week or more to produce. Your first goal is to reduce the maximum time from 7 days to 5 days for a quote. Start by examining the largest numbers in the maximum columns: the sales delay and the manager review. If you could reduce each of these to 8 hours maximum, then the maximum time is reduced to 5.1 days. The next potential reductions are either the Java engineer's maximum time or the quote engineer's write-up time, each at 8 hours max. Changing the Java engineer's time to 7 hours maximum adjusts the total maximum to less than 5 days.

If possible, further reduce maximums to allow time buffers for unexpected events. One common unplanned event is the absence of key people, which requires a backup person to complete each step. Providing a second or even a third person as backup for the person primarily doing the work can help considerably when the worst case time is critical. Figure 16-3 illustrates these reductions in steps 3, 8, and 6.

	A	B	C	D	E	F	G	H	I	J	K	
1			Main Flow					Branching Workflows				
2		Item	Min	Typ	Max		Item	Min	Typ	Max	%	
3	1	Request	0	0	0							
4	2	Review	1	2	8							
5		Decision: more info?				=>	SPLIT WORKFLOW					
6							no	0	0	0	50%	Formulas
7							yes	1	8	8	50%	
8	3	More Info Result	0	4	8	<=	3. Weighted	0	4	8		=MAX(J6:J7)
9	4	Description Write-up	1	2	4							=I6*K6+I7*K7
10												=MIN(H6:H7)
11	5	Request Est.	0.2	0.2	0.2							=J8
12												Copy to D8:C8
13		Estimate Parallel Tasks				=>	PARALLEL					
14							6a Java Est.	2	4	7		
15							6b DB Est.	1	2	4		
16	6	Estimates	2	4	7	<=	6a,6b max	2	4	7		=MAX(J14:J15)
17												Copy to H16:I16
18	7	Quote Write-up	1	1	4							=J16
19	8	Mgr Review	1	8	8							Copy to C16:D16
20	9	Delivery	0.2	0.2	0.2							
21		Totals (hrs)	6.4	21.4	39.4							=SUM(E3:E20)
22		Total (days)	1.143	3.821	7.036							Copy to C21:D21
23												=E21/$C$24
24		Hrs to Cal Days	5.6									Copy to C22:D22
25		assumes 8 hr days, 70% availability										

Figure 16-3: Case 1: Reduction in maximum time

Case 2: Reducing the Typical Time

The sales team is pleased that the worst case will be less than a week for new quotes. However, the sales manager now says that they need most of their quotes in 2.5 days. Your goal is to look at the typical cases and determine what reductions you can make. For typical cases, look at decision points and determine whether you can reduce the percentage for the slower decisions. In this case, can you reduce the percentage of time that the quote engineer needs to ask sales for more information from 50 percent to 10 percent?

One approach to doing this might be to create a standard form that the sales requestor must fill out so all the required information is present. Entering 10 percent for the time sales uses cuts the typical time down to 3.25 days. If you ask sales to give their responses in 4 hours on average, the time drops to 3.2 days. The other expensive typical time is the manager review at 8 hours. You could require that the manager complete review in 4 hours or drop the step all together. Dropping the manager review time to 4 hours makes the total time typically 2.5 days, which meets the goal. Figure 16-4 illustrates this example.

	A	B	C (Main Flow)	D	E	F	G (Branching Workflows)	H	I	J	K
			Min	Typ	Max		Item	Min	Typ	Max	%
3	1	Request	0	0	0						
4	2	Review	1	2	8						
5		Decision: more info?				=>	SPLIT WORKFLOW				
6							no	0	0	0	90%
7							yes	1	4	8	10%
8	3	More Info Result	0	0.4	8	<=	3. Weighted	0	0.4	8	
9	4	Description Write-up	1	2	4						
10											
11	5	Request Est.	0.2	0.2	0.2						
12											
13		Estimate Parallel Tasks				=>	PARALLEL				
14							6a Java Est.	2	4	7	
15							6b DB Est.	1	2	4	
16	6	Estimates	2	4	7	<=	6a,6b max	2	4	7	
17											
18	7	Quote Write-up	1	1	4						
19	8	Mgr Review	1	4	8						
20	9	Delivery	0.2	0.2	0.2						
21		Totals (hrs)	6.4	13.8	39.4						
22		Total (days)	1.1429	2.4643	7.0357						
23											
24		Hrs to Cal Days	5.6								
25		assumes 8 hr days, 70% availability									

Formulas

=MAX(J6:J7)
=I6*K6+I7*K7
=MIN(H6:H7)
=J8
Copy to D8:C8

=MAX(J14:J15)
Copy to H16:I16

=J16
Copy to C16:D16

=SUM(E3:E20)
Copy to C21:D21
=E21/$C$24
Copy to C22:D22

Figure 16-4: Quote process with typical improvement

You can also consider whether any steps can be dropped altogether or replaced with something else. Dropping the manager's review provides an interesting result. If the step is dropped, the total days dropped to a minimum of 0.96, typical of 1.75, and maximum of 5.61 days. Dropping the review might be a possibility if most of the delay is caused by the availability of the manager and not the total time it takes to perform the review. If the 4 hours is due to availability and the review is short, you can work with the manager to allow others to respond to a review request if the manager is unavailable. Understanding the reason for the review can provide some insight as well. If the step is due to the quote engineer not having enough experience to be trusted, perhaps the situation can be improved over time. If the delay is due to manager review, and the manager is the only expert at the firm who knows a lot about some particularly complicated issue, dropping the review may not be a good approach.

You can also look for ways of reducing the typical time required for a step. Approaches include adding more resources to the task, splitting up the work in a different way, providing improved tools for the person completing the step, redefining the step to reduce its effort, and providing training to the person who is completing the step.

Although these examples are simple, they illustrate effective approaches to analyzing process workflows. Using a spreadsheet allows for experimenting with "what-if" questions in pursuit of particular time goals. For a small company, direct effective approaches work the best.

Working with Other Teams

When the process workflow involves several teams, the challenge of making process improvements can be greater. If improving the overall process requires work shifting or reduction from someone other than an engineer, a development manager can lose perspective on the other team member's needs in the workflow. Instead of simply making requests, involve people outside your team in discussing process improvements and the impacts on their work. Negotiate for changes you would like others to make and be flexible in requests made of you. You might discover that changes in your team's steps can greatly ease the efforts for other groups.

Getting It Going

After you have made your process improvement design changes, spend some time planning how you will roll it out to the teams. You'll find more advice in Chapter 15, which deals with rolling-out processes.

Additional Reading

Here is some additional reading on topics presented in this chapter:

Developing Products in Half the Time: New Rules, New Tools, 2nd Edition, by Preston G. Smith and Donald G. Reinertsen (Wiley, 1998)

The Mythical Man-Month: Essays on Software Engineering, Anniversary Edition, by Frederick P. Brooks, Jr. (Addison-Wesley, 1995)

The Six Sigma Way: How GE, Motorola, and Other Top Companies are Honing Their Performance, by Peter S. Pande, Robert P. Neuman, and Ronald R. Cavanaugh (McGraw-Hill, 2000)

Winning at New Products: Accelerating the Process from Idea to Launch, 3rd Edition, by Robert G. Cooper (Basic Books, 2001)

17

UNDERSTANDING QUALITY ASSURANCE

As a company matures and changes, quality requirements grow and change as well. From the early startup stage, to the foothold stage, to the growth stage, basic quality practices are required to keep the company from stagnating or failing to grow to the next level.

A quality assurance (QA) team is devoted to evaluating and improving the quality of the company's software product. Effective QA requires much more than simply testing new products, however. As discussed in earlier chapters, QA teams should also be involved in the product's definition, development process, and customer feedback.

In a small company, one manager is often in charge of both QA and development teams. In this role, the manager needs to coordinate both teams to locate and resolve core quality problems. A good foundation in QA practices provides insight in how to improve the productivity of the QA and development teams and the quality of the product. This chapter covers the basics of quality assurance for a small company development manager who has limited QA experience.

Importance of Quality

Small growing companies must focus on rapidly meeting their customers' needs. As customers continue to pour more requirements into the development mix, and as the company grows, the development manager faces challenges other than simply insuring that the team implements the new features. In fact, an exclusive focus on implementing new features is a trap that can make a manager lose focus on important, core issues. Continually adding new features and ignoring core issues is comparable to adding new floors to a building that has a weak foundation.

If a manager focuses solely on the short-term development goals and loses sight of the bigger picture, the result will be a poor-quality product. Engineers might produce more features rapidly, but the features aren't as quality built as they should be, and the product and customer will suffer. Lack of quality critically affects small companies and development departments, as old issues take up time that should be spent for ongoing development. Quality problems can consume huge amounts of the development and QA teams' time.

Engineering can "sweep poor quality under the rug" when the company has a single customer and is working on a groundbreaking new product, but as the customer list grows, past quality issues will come back to haunt you. They can also lead the company into a *crisis mentality*, where each new customer crisis results in the team scrambling to patch together a solution. Poor-quality products lead to lost sales and drive existing customers to other companies' products. Once customers label your company and its product's quality as poor, you will find it difficult to change their impressions.

QUALITY MATTERS

My company never left the startup phase of quality practices, although we had a number of large- and medium-sized customers. Poor quality cost us some of our earlier customers. Quality problems continue to affect our ability to work on new features; we are discovering major defects in our released software that require intense effort by engineering and QA to resolve. For a while, the development team spent half of its time fixing defects in the released software.

We are now setting up reasonable quality practices to dig ourselves out of this hole and are making some progress. The team noticed the improvements after about four months of effort.

—New QA manager

Quality Defined

What defines quality? Ask a dozen people and you'll often get a dozen different answers. Some will answer that quality means including the latest features in the product. Others will talk about mean time to failure or lack of defects. Others will describe a product that gives the customer a positive impression.

Defining quality ultimately comes down to the customer's perception. For most customers, a quality product meets the following criteria:

- Meets or exceeds the expectations of the customer (includes all aspects, such as capabilities, performance, and security)

- Functions as intended

- Handles unexpected conditions in graceful ways

- Is easy to use and intuitive

- Is easy to upgrade

- Is consistent across its feature set so customers are not surprised or confused by operations in different parts of the product

When measuring software quality, many developers focus on known *defects*, or problems in the software that prevent it from being used as intended or expected. Such an approach, however, has several problems: First, who defines the *intended use* of the product? And who determines whether an issue is a *defect* or merely a *feature change*? From a development perspective, an issue can look like a feature change, while the customer sees the same issue as an obvious defect.

By focusing only on defects, developers can miss other aspects of quality. Although keeping track of prerelease and post-release defects is very important, other aspects of quality should also be examined, such as accurate requirements, elegant design, utility, and long-term customer satisfaction. Finally, defects are only detected by way of focused efforts to locate them. Without a focused QA effort to reveal problems under the hood, a shiny new product's quality might appear better than it really is.

In addition, quality does not equate to the number of defects repaired in a release. Engineering and QA can identify and repair a large number of defects in a product, yet the product can still be of poor quality due to many undiscovered defects or because the product does not meet the customer's expectations. In fact, products with a large number of defects found and repaired are often still plagued with more defects yet to be found. Extensive testing of high-quality products often results in fewer defects, because they were built with quality in mind by a development team that used good design, best development practices, careful code construction, and attention to quality. A great QA team can assist by encouraging positive practices, providing valuable feedback, helping instill an attitude of quality, and measuring the results with thorough testing.

A high-quality product exceeds the customer's expectations and meets the customer's core needs. With the bar set so high for software quality, how do you create a truly quality product? It boils down to starting with a culture that values quality.

Valuing Quality

A company with a culture that values quality produces a high-quality product. A company that lacks this culture will not produce a high-quality product, because quality isn't the focus. If your company has a culture that values quality, your quality improvement effort will be easy. If not, talk to your CEO about the business impact of poor quality, and seek his support to improve quality overall.

To begin fostering a culture that values quality, train developers and QA staff to think about quality as an *attitude* rather than simply a product goal or state. Building a "quality attitude" among members of the development team improves quality more than even the best QA practices. Why? Because having an attitude that values quality from the start will encourage the development team to build a quality product by getting clear requirements and by spending time understanding those requirements—through thoughtful design and with careful coding and review. In contrast, quickly coded solutions that are only polished through limited testing and repair will result in a product with poor quality baked in.

In addition, a good QA team can be an effective partner to the development team; although both teams focus on quality, QA personnel consider the product requirements differently from how developers think about the product. Engineers often focus on getting the product to work properly, while QA focuses on finding ways to break the product.

You can promote a quality attitude in a number of ways. Encourage developers to focus on checking their code before sending it to QA. Pairing a QA engineer with a development engineer during unit testing can prove effective in producing higher-quality code. Show your concern for defects generated during coding; this will encourage the team to create fewer problems. Set up development processes and methodologies that encourage quality to emphasize its importance.

You can improve your team's attitude toward quality by encouraging people to view the entire product as the outcome, rather than the blocks of code each team member is writing. To encourage teamwork and help developers appreciate the product from a quality perspective, assign individuals as architects or leads for each product (or project when appropriate). The architect will coordinate the product coding and encourage the team members to act like a team rather than independent agents.

Improving quality can be a long and painful process if the issue backlog is high. Projects that suffered in the past from poor quality can serve as obstacles to success in many small firms. A development team cannot maintain a focus on quality if its products continue to be defective. Focus on fixing existing problems built into the product. Depending on the extent of the problems, you might be able to set aside time during a longer release cycle to undergo extensive bug repairs. If the problems are too extensive for a single release, schedule major defect repairs (sometimes called "bug scrubs") for the next few releases.

A key development control over product quality is the team's ability to repair defects. Improving the success rate of defect repairs by the development team will have a big impact on productivity and quality. Engineering attitude drives the repair success rate. This is addressed in detail later in "The Impact of Defects on Quality and Productivity" on page 330.

As the team's focus on quality improves, product and work quality will improve as well. Your team can make improvements with each release; realize, however, that major improvements can take months or longer. Keep up the focus on quality for the long haul.

Quality Assessment

After you have successfully encouraged a culture that values quality among members of the development and QA teams, you can assess the efforts toward that. A quality assurance assessment requires that you examine your teams and the tools, processes, practices, and measures they use to perform their work. Take note of the following specifics:

QA Team

> Assess the background, skill, and organization of members of the QA team.

QA Tools and Environment

> Assess tools used to measure and track software quality, especially a defect and enhancement tracking program. Additional tools can assist with testing automation.

QA Activities and Processes

> Assess the activities and processes that describe the efforts the teams make to ensure quality.

QA Metrics

> Assess the success of the quality effort. Quality metrics allow you to judge the product's quality and the processes used to create the product.

With these definitions in mind, let's examine each area in more detail, starting with the QA team.

The Quality Assurance Team

Your QA team can drive a major movement toward a culture of quality in your company. Build a team of experienced QA engineers who share that culture. The best QA people are passionate about quality as the most important aspect of their jobs. The best QA engineers take it personally when a problem eludes them. Because they are continually looking for ways to improve quality, good QA engineers want to work for companies that care about it. These engineers make the effort to learn more about and apply the best QA techniques and approaches.

In contrast, some QA engineers see their work as all about testing. They care about it, but not enough to go the extra mile. These engineers do not look for clever ways to break the product or improve it. A strong QA team will support you in your efforts to improve quality. A weak team will want to focus only on testing.

Team Skill Levels

Build a QA team of engineers who offer the skill levels and attitudes that best match the needs of the company and its products. QA engineers come in all skill levels—from "push-the-button" website testers to gurus who write code to test other code. Do not expect people with low QA skills to shine at testing complex systems.

Compare your QA team's abilities with the complexity of the work that needs to be accomplished to see if a mismatch exists. Review the artifacts they have created and observe the types of problems that get past them; this can help you assess their overall QA skills. QA artifacts include any item created to aid in testing, including documentation, test plans, test suites, test process, testing infrastructure, and test software. When talking with QA team members, assess their communication skills, as these are crucial to the job.

To assess your QA team's abilities, ask them the following questions:

- How many years of QA experience do you have?
- Do you consider yourself a senior QA engineer?
- How do you see the role of QA in the company?
- Could you review a test plan you created with me?
- What quality measurements do you recommend?
- How does the current process promote quality?
- How do you prefer to work with development engineers when resolving QA problems?

To understand your QA team's effectiveness, observe the team's work habits. Some engineers work hard at continually improving the product and are well integrated into all stages of the development process. Others work in binges: When the product reaches QA, these team members work long hours to test the product, but when the product is out the door, they invest little effort until the next binge. This behavior, however, is not good quality assurance, but is purely a testing function that occurs at the end of the line.

Staffing Levels

At each company growth stage, different QA staffing levels are required and should be anticipated. In the startup phase, the QA staff can comprise a single person; this QA engineer should be a senior engineer who is well versed in quality practices. Hiring junior QA engineers with the goal of keeping costs low is a mistake, as they will not position the department for high quality as the company grows.

When your company starts getting established in the marketplace—the "foothold" stage—hire an experienced QA manager to direct the team. A company in a growth stage should hire a small QA team with a manager and should employ well-established quality practices. A successful team needs a strong set of tools and the appropriate QA computing environment. Poor-quality products will consume too much of your development time and eventually drive fledgling customers away.

QA Tools and Environment

The QA software tools and computing environment provide the foundation for the quality effort. Don't skimp on providing your team with the appropriate equipment and enough use licenses to get their jobs done. Doing so is unwise—and plain foolish.

A number of quality-focused software tools are available. For a small company, the tools and environment should focus primarily on three aspects: a defect-tracking tool, QA test environment, and test automation software.

Defect-Tracking Tool and Process

The defect-tracking process defines the workflow for handling defects. The defect-tracking tool is the primary method of tracking the status of defects and issues discovered by QA and development teams. These factors must be aligned to work together to provide the quality required by your company and its products. Because the defect-tracking tool enforces and enables the process, this section discusses them together.

The defect process should follow a simple workflow, such as the following:

1. Defect is reported.
2. Defect is reviewed and ranked. It may be put on hold (for the future) or until more information is provided. If not held, the next step ensues.
3. Defect assigned for investigation.
4. Defect fixed.
5. Defect fix verified.
6. Defect closed.

Figure 17-1 shows this workflow as a flow chart, with the decision point at step 2.

Your defect-tracking tool must serve the needs of the organization and should not be a general-purpose task entry tool. Task tracking is fundamentally different from defect tracking. Combining the two into one system leads to a system with too much information requested that is too difficult to use properly.

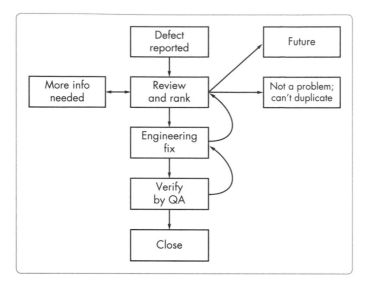

Figure 17-1: Simple defect workflow diagram

Your defect-tracking tool should be set up and used only for tracking defects or entering enhancements, not for other purposes. A dedicated defect-tracking tool improves the quality of the data collected and ensures that important information is easy to view, because the tool administrator can create data entry screens best suited for defect tracking. A dedicated defect-tracking system makes it easy to review and report on the data. In addition, a dedicated tracking system allows the defect workflow to match the stages defined in the defect-tracking tool.

NOTE   *A variety of defect-tracking tools are available. Chapter 7 discusses different tools and considerations. A list of resources appears in "Additional Reading" on page 333.*

To align the defect-tracking tool with the defect process, think systematically. Use your process workflow as your blueprint and make the defect tool conform to it. Then, follow this advice:

- Map each process step (block in the diagram) to tool states. This way, the tool will retain defect state information and step transition information as it goes through the process. With a clear map of process steps to tool states, the process workflow is encouraged and enforced by the tool workflow. If this isn't done, the tool workflow will be followed to the detriment of the process workflow.

- Choose states and process steps that clearly identify the activity.

- Define the current subsequent states in the workflow and set up the tool to enforce transitions. This eliminates people skipping states or putting items in the wrong states.

- Look at decision and branch points and check to see that proper decision paths are covered.

- Consider carefully what information is required at each process step and keep the information to a minimum. Limit the number of fields required for each entry screen. The more data requested and required, the less likely a submitter will fill them out completely and the more likely the defect won't be submitted at all.

- Consider who has access to the defect-tracking tool. The "submitter" might be a customer or anyone in the organization if a clear gatekeeper is assigned to clean up entry. Alternatively, entry can be restricted to development and QA team members to ensure that higher-quality data is entered, leaving people outside of development and QA to submit their problems to a designated development or QA team member.

- Before building the system, decide what reporting and quality metrics interest you and those that are required for the product. If you are not sure, review metrics first (see "QA Metrics" on page 324). Retrofitting a system to capture metrics can be difficult and awkward.

WARNING   *Metrics may be required outside your company if your product has safety, medical, or public risk. In those cases, standards for reporting metrics are defined by external companies or agencies.*

Your defect-tracking process should include a step for evaluating the defect. In this step, provide a simple rating mechanism that can be useful for comparing one defect's priority against those of other defects.

Some defect systems are set up to require that the submitter be responsible for closing the defect. This adds overhead to the process, however, because the submitter takes on a secondary role of reverifying the defect fix. This approach usually results in a backlog of defects waiting for the submitter to close them; submitters often do not want to verify many defect closures because of the time required, and the task typically is not their primary task. Avoid this approach, because it will result in many defects left unresolved.

Another system approach to avoid is using a separate state for verifying the defect after production release, because this adds complexity to the process. Instead, require that the QA engineer add a test for the defect into the test plan so that QA will automatically test for each defect repair in future releases.

Once you have set up the system, ask a member of the QA team to monitor the defects in each state. The monitor can review defects that "stall out" in any part of the system. The system can also be monitored to avoid a backlog of defects that surprise you at the end of the release cycle.

Keep the system simple and use it to track state information. Using a clearly mapped definition makes it easy to get statistics and to identify quality process problems.

Building a Test Environment

Small growing companies have limited money to invest in QA testing. Most initial technology investments go toward the workstations and servers that are required to create and deploy the software. With budgets tight, management often neglects to set up the environment needed to duplicate the customer's system, making the QA job of testing and evaluating problems very challenging.

A lack of a properly configured test environment may not lead to disaster in the short term if a company has only a few customers. With few customers, the team might hear about a few problems post-release directly, and the cost of fixing the errors might not be devastating. As the company grows, however, the costs of post-release problems left undetected because of an inadequate QA testing environment will increase significantly and affect the company's bottom line.

When a customer experiences a problem with a product post-release, that problem must become an immediate focus for your QA and development teams. Investigating and resolving production problems incurs a large immediate cost, especially if the customer's problem cannot be duplicated internally. Quickly setting up a test environment with the same equipment, memory, operating systems, application programs and settings, and program versions might not always be possible. Without the appropriate equipment, properly configured and available for immediate QA use, however, a post-release problem can prove devastating to productivity and customer perception of your product and your company.

Small companies benefit more from having the proper test environment set up from the start. Waiting until your company has grown to establish this environment will drag down productivity and customer satisfaction. As development manager, push to ensure that a proper QA test system is set up from the beginning.

SYNCHRONIZE YOUR SYSTEMS

My company had a major problem and had lived with it for years before I joined. The infrastructure did not match production in engineering, QA, or the preproduction staging. Too often, we were surprised in production by code behavior we could not see in test environments.

I pulled together a plan to build out a proper test environment in stages. The first stage was a properly configured QA environment. The second stage was a speed test environment. We started the QA environment work immediately. As the cost of the speed testing was expensive, we provided several scalable options to allow for partial system testing initially, and we then built up to full system testing.

—Development manager

Test Automation Tools

The requirements for test automation tools vary considerably for small companies. Test automation makes sense when the product is stable enough that repeatable testing is cost effective. For startups with rapidly changing products, test automation may not be effective because of the cost of maintaining a rapidly changing product. As the company enters the foothold and growth phases, test automation can be more practical and its value increases considerably. Automation can increase test accuracy while significantly reducing testing time.

QA uses automation tools to input a set of conditions into the software quickly and compare the resulting outputs against past results. Differences in results do not necessarily indicate an error in the code; differences can be caused by intended changes in the code since the last regression results were stored, for example. When QA has reviewed all the results for accuracy, the outputs are saved as the correct values for later comparisons.

Test automation tools are effective for graphical user interfaces (GUIs) that are relatively stable and for products available for use on multiple platforms. Commercial tools that focus on GUI testing are available, such as Borland SilkTest (*http://www.borland.com/*).

Test automation can be effective for testing files and data. Either commercial tools or manually created scripts can quickly cycle through standard tests and identify the differences between releases. To see how effective automation will be for your product, evaluate the rate of change in the automation output per release versus the cost of maintaining the scripts. If more than 20 percent of the automation output changes per release, the product may not be a good candidate for script automation.

Another test automation approach is *white box testing*, in which a *test harness* (a software framework to simplify the creation, running, and evaluation of unit tests) is used to test internal sections of the code. Often, the engineering team creates the unit tests and continues to maintain them. Test harnesses are worthwhile even if the GUI and features in code are changing, because maintaining them is not as expensive as maintaining external testing efforts. Test harnesses isolate code sections, many of which will not change per release. JUnit (*http://www.junit.org/*) and NUnit (*http://www.nunit.org/*) are example frameworks for unit test automation.

Test automation has huge advantages when the product is relatively stable but time consuming to test. Otherwise, think twice before investing in test automation.

QA Activities

The QA team performs key activities that are independent of the QA processes used. During the definition phase, QA should review requirements, specifications, and use cases created by product marketing. QA management should also review any outstanding defects and identify those that require repair in the next release. During the design and coding phases,

QA should prepare test plans and work on test automation as required. During the testing phase, QA should execute test plans, identify defects, and back-check repairs made. In addition, QA should take measurements that identify the quality of the code during all phases.

Figure 17-2 illustrates these activities against major steps of a software life cycle. The following sections discuss each of these activities in detail.

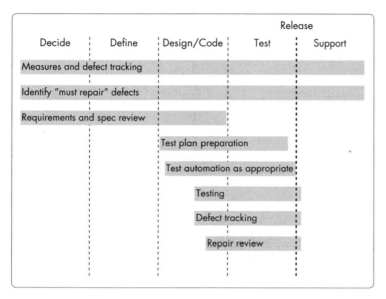

Figure 17-2: QA activities versus software life cycle

Requirements and Functionality Review

Organizations that emphasize quality will promote the QA team's efforts throughout the software development life cycle. QA team members can offer insight into product utility and ease of use, so allowing them to comment before engineering starts building the code will help ensure a higher-quality product. QA team members also need to understand exactly what engineering is building to determine how best to test the product. Before testing, QA will produce test plans to optimize the testing process and create a repeatable set of tests.

QA should be involved in reviewing the requirements and functional specifications of every product and should have an opportunity to review prototype designs. The development and QA teams should meet, listen to feedback, and make appropriate adjustments to the product definition.

The only thing worse than not allowing QA a voice in requirements and functionality is not listening to and heeding what QA has to say.

Test Plans

A test plan helps create a repeatable method for testing a product. Without a repeatable method, testing will be ad hoc—gaps will appear in the testing process that can result in post-release problems. Consequently, the QA team should create test plans for all products.

Each test plan should be based on a standard template (see the next section) to assure consistency across the team and from product to product. This will allow each team member to use a reliable test plan to ensure consistency in construction.

Determining the scope of the testing to do is not always easy; for example, in small companies, some parts of a system may be overlooked and not tested. QA often neglects to test the internal tools used to maintain the product. Internal tools can require less strict testing than customer-facing products—especially regarding error messaging. However, testing still is required if the maintenance tool affects customer outcomes. Consider the following questions regarding internal projects:

- Does the code function properly for the administrators?
- Will any usage side effects impact the customer?
- Is the entry error checking acceptable for an internal project?

Produce a list of all the products and modules you use and review it with both the engineering and QA teams. Maintain this list as the product line changes. Each item on this list should have its own test plan.

Test Plan Template

Standardizing the test plan format by using a template makes it easy for any member of the QA team to run the appropriate tests. A test plan template provides a common layout and format for all test plans. Using a template makes it easy to review and execute test plans consistently.

A spreadsheet-based template allows for easy data entry, status summaries, and progress tracking through summary worksheets. The layout should include multiple worksheets that correspond to different components to be tested. A Summary Worksheet can offer an overview of the entire test plan.

Summary Worksheet

Summarize the test plan data on this worksheet by collecting information from the component worksheets:

- Percent complete of all worksheets in the spreadsheet
- Name of the program or module being tested
- Build number of code being tested
- Date of the test
- Pass/fail summary showing tests and number that failed

Component Worksheets

Create a worksheet for each area of the product to test. Each worksheet ideally shows one test per row, so that the sheet is easy to work through and scan. Each test worksheet should cover these areas:

- Functional testing for the intended use cases
- Functional testing for edge cases (tests that push right to the edge of what is allowed)
- Functional testing for error cases

Each test in a component worksheet will use a unique number. The combination of the worksheet name and the number creates a unique identifier, which is useful for reporting and discussing problems. For example, Security worksheet, test 44, could be written like this: *security-44*.

Each worksheet will feature one test per row with multiple field columns. The choice of fields varies based on need, but here's a typical list of fields for the plan:

- Test number
- Description (with enough detail to describe the test clearly)
- Expected behavior (details the product behavior)
- Expected outcome (short description—for example, "the first line should be 53")

A row can include additional fields that are set each time the test plan is used:

- Actual outcome for this test run (for example, pass, or fail; sometimes it is useful to use a spreadsheet "pick list" to only allow a specific set of choices from a list)

- Defect-tracking number (from the defect-tracking system, where you find a problem and log it)

- Traceability matrix information (information on how this test corresponds to the requirements or functional definition; the nature of this varies considerably per project but can simplify evaluation of test completeness)

- Notes (notes about the test case not covered earlier)

Creating Automated Tests

Automated testing often requires a test plan strategy that differs from that of manual testing. QA can perform test planning with a higher level description, defining what types of tests fit the automated testing approach. The individual test instructions are encoded into the automated system, while the results of the testing are usually listed in an output file. It is still possible to create a summary worksheet that covers both automated and manual testing.

Increasing the percentage of automation can improve speed and accuracy of testing, because automated testing is faster to run and the tools identify correct results quickly. Automation improves the quality when multiple delivery platforms exist or when time to perform complete manual testing is limited.

The workflow for test automation should cover these steps:

1. Collect information about the tests.
2. Write test scripts.
3. Edit and build test data.
4. Run the automated tests.

5. Correct problems in one of three ways: Fix the script, fix the correct results data, or have the engineer fix the problem the scripts identified.

Keep in mind that you can invest too heavily in automation at the expense of under-testing some parts of the product line. Review the cost of creating automation against the time saved during the test phase. Evaluate the benefit and cost of automation if more than 20 percent of an application is changing per release.

QA Processes

Basic *QA processes* are essential for any company, especially for small start-ups. Without a clear process defined, work will not be repeatable and cannot be improved over time. Good QA processes allow you to control, measure, and improve product quality.

Establish core QA processes as soon as you acquire the responsibility for the QA team. Set up a development process, a defect-handling process, a defect-ranking process, and a defect-selection process. The first two processes have been covered in earlier chapters and earlier in this chapter. The following sections cover defect-ranking and defect-selection processes.

Defect-Ranking Process

Defect ranking requires a method of determining in what order defects should be dealt with. Many different methods can be used to rank defects, including ranking each defect using several different categories, such as severity, priority, and business impact. Ranking scales vary considerably from company to company, with some choosing alphabetic ranking, some choosing text (such as Very Severe), and some using numeric ranking. The problem with a technique that uses multiple scales is that it engenders arguments about which defect to tackle first: How do you compare a 7 severity, B priority, 6 business, against a 2 severity, A priority, 8 business?

One solution is to use a single number to encapsulate all the information. This number is the *overall priority* of the defect (or feature). As many companies already use the term *priority* for a specific purpose, this discussion uses a new term called *ranking number* or *rank* to distinguish this process. The ranking number is the overall ranking of one defect relative to the other defects.

The ranking number makes use of a simple range of numbers. Five categories works well, with 1 being the lowest and 5 the highest. Assigning a larger number to the most severe problem simplifies calculating *defect impact*, as described later. You can use more numeric categories, but you may end up wasting time trying to fit defects into the range (for example, with a scale of 10, it can be difficult to select whether the defect is a 3 or a 4, and so on).

You can use a table to encapsulate all the information into a ranking number. The table columns will list the categories of items to rank, and the rows will represent each ranking number. You can expand the number of categories as necessary by adding columns. Here are some potential categories:

- Security

- Business need

- Functionality broken

    How important is the broken feature relative to how often the feature is used?

- Customer-facing GUI

    A spelling error on a main page may not break the product, but it looks bad. Ranking GUI errors independently emphasizes their importance.

- Data integrity

    Risks to internal or customer data may require a separate category.

- Safety

- Legal liability

Functionality and Usefulness as Specified and Built

Table 17-1 shows an example table with sample categories. The example table does not show values in the boxes that need to be filled in with descriptions of the conditions to qualify for each rank. These values are *decision drivers*—they help you make the choice of appropriate rank value for each defect being considered. When you create your table, define appropriate drivers for each box.

Table 17-1: Corporate Quality Values Ranking Table

Rank	Security	Business need	How badly broken?	Customer-facing GUI
5				
4				
3				
2				
1				

To create decision drivers, place a description of criteria that would represent that ranking for that category in each empty field. For example, a Business need rank of 4 could represent an important revenue opportunity of $100K or more; a Security rank of 5 could be a severe security risk that affects many customers with data exposure.

You can leave fields empty to indicate that the choice of category and value cannot be ranked. For example, a Security rank of 1 may be omitted if no low-priority security issues exist.

After you have filled out the table corresponding to the company's values, you can use it to evaluate defects. You can consider defects in more than one category. For example, a defect can be a Business need as well as a Customer-facing GUI. To rank a defect, read down each relevant category column until a description matches what actually exists. The highest ranking becomes the defect's ranking number. So, for example, if a defect is a 4 in Security and 3 in Business need, its ranking number is 4.

Once a defect has been ranked, this information will be stored in your defect-tracking system. Most systems can show tables of outstanding problems, making it easy for you to sort outstanding defects by their rank, which allows you to focus on the highest-ranking defects first.

Ranking numbers provide for consistency over time. This method allows you to compare the ranks of defects found a year ago against those of new defects, so you can avoid long sessions of reviewing hundreds of historical defects with every release. A ranking number should be changed only if the information associated with it changes. In general, QA is the best arbiter of a ranking. Do not change a ranking because someone insists that the defect be repaired faster.

You can extend this approach to cover enhancements as well as defects by creating a ranking table for enhancements. Because of the larger cost associated with enhancements and the quality impact of defects, it is better to treat enhancements and defects as separate categories of decisions.

Defect Selection Process

If you have a long list of defects, you might find it difficult to select which to tackle first. You can use a systematic approach to ordering defect repair. The following system triages defects when it is clear that not enough time is available to remove them all in the release cycle. This system works well for defect lists of moderate length, with perhaps 200 or fewer items.

The *return-on-investment (ROI)* project concept is the model for this approach. The *return-per-cost (RPC)* of effort allows you to rank different defects. RPC is a calculation of benefits that requires you to assign benefit values to ranking numbers. In this example, a rank 5 defect is twice as important as a rank 4. A rank 4 defect is twice as important as a rank 3. A rank 3 is twice as important as a rank 2. And a rank 2 defect is 1.5 times as important as a rank 1. This example assigns a rank 1 defect a value of 10 so that you can set up a relationship between defects and the repair benefit. (Using 10 as the smallest value has calculation advantages, which will be made apparent shortly.) Table 17-2 shows an example mapping of ranking numbers against a weighting factor.

Table 17-2: Importance Weight of Each Ranking Number

Rank	Weight
1	10
2	15
3	30
4	60
5	120

To implement the ranking tool, create a spreadsheet table with columns, as shown in Table 17-3. Ensure that all the defects have a ranking number. Next, make a quick estimate of the cost of the item. Many experienced developers can provide a rough estimate of costs by reading the description of the issue. The estimate does not need to be exact, because errors should average out over the entire list of defects.

Table 17-3: Table Column Setup Example

Defect #	Description	Rank	Weighted value	Cost	RPC
432	Button "continue" on error A page broken	4	60	4	15

You can calculate Weighted value directly from the Rank using a *lookup table*. The table manager can override and increase or decrease the Weighted value based on reading the description. For Cost, use estimated effort in hours. Calculate RPC as Weighted value divided by Cost. Figure 17-3 shows a simple spreadsheet example with ranked defects and RPC with the rows sorted by RPC. Note that defect 124 is the best one to tackle first, because it shows the best return for time spent. Occasionally, simple 1- and 2-ranked defects are good choices to implement first if their costs are low enough. However, the heavy weighted values of rank 4 and 5 defects will often be near the top of the list unless the cost of tackling them is huge.

	A	B	C	D	E	F	Formula
1	Defect #	Description	Rank	Weight Value	Cost (hrs)	RPC	
2	124	File format I...	3	30	4	7.50	=D2/E2
3	235	GUI problem...	4	60	12	5.00	Copy to F3:F6
4	488	Startup Sequ...	1	10	2	5.00	
5	425	Export mode...	4	60	18	3.33	
6	444	Customer A...	2	15	8	1.88	

Figure 17-3: Defect RPC calculation

You can extend the table to perform date calculations if you know how many engineers are available to perform the work. A simple approach is to total the hours and divide by the number of engineers available to work on the defects. From there, calculate how many hours per day the team will work on defects to translate days to repair. As described in Chapter 12, conversion of hours of effort on tasks into calendar days requires accounting for percentages of the time engineers can work on the project and what the normal work week looks like. The sorted list can then show estimated completion dates. You can estimate the number of defects likely to be repaired in the time available.

Figure 17-4 shows an example calculation: Starting the effort on the morning of May 4 with one engineer working on the defects, let's figure out a timeline for defect repair. Assume that the engineer is able to work only 6 hours per day on defect repair. Delay in days becomes Cost in hours divided by 6 hours/day. Calculate Date done using the Excel function =WORKDAY(*start date, day increment*) with start date being the last day and day increment being your calculated days' effort for the defect. If the deadline is May 16 for finishing the defect work, then you can estimate how far down a long list of defects will likely be completed.

	A	B	C	D	E	F	G	H	Formulas
	Defect #	Description	Rank	Weight Value	Cost (hrs)	RPC	Delay (days)	Date Done	=E3/$C$9
1									Copy to F4:F7
2		START						7-May	
3	124	File format I...	3	30	4	7.50	0.67	7-May	=WORKDAY(H2,G3)
4	235	GUI problem...	4	60	12	5.00	2.00	9-May	Copy to H4:H7
5	488	Startup Sequ...	1	10	2	5.00	0.33	9-May	
6	425	Export mode...	4	60	18	3.33	3.00	14-May	*deadline*
7	444	Customer A...	2	15	8	1.88	1.33	15-May	
8									=D7/E7
9		Work Hours/Day	6						Copy to F3:F6

Figure 17-4: RPC ordering with data calculation and deadline

If your quality policy requires completing all higher-ranked defects ahead of lower-ranked defects, you can still use the table approach. However, you will not need to calculate RPC. Effectively, this policy says that a rank 5 defect is infinitely more important than a 4, a rank 4 defect is infinitely more important than a 3, and so on. In this case, sort by two fields: Sort by rank first, and then sort by cost, and work on the lower cost defects first.

QA Metrics

QA metrics are tools used by the QA team to "keep score" of the quality of the product or the development process. Proper metrics allow for better prediction of timelines for testing, development, and release. Metrics can also help the management team decide whether the product is ready for release. Metrics provide insight into problems the team is facing and how to improve performance and process. A well-run QA team will have collected metrics on many aspects of quality from past releases. In a strong, quality-oriented team, these metrics will be created and *used*.

Companies collect metrics based on need, processes used, and team preferences. In general, a small company needs only a small set of metrics targeted at its specific needs. This set should be designed to be easy to collect and review in a reasonable amount of time.

The following sections cover some common metrics that can be collected along with simple approaches for collecting the data. Use these approaches as starting points for your quality metrics. Not all are necessary and not all will work best in every situation. Don't stop with this list, either; look for other opportunities to create metrics consistently and act on the results. Your team's quality awareness will improve in no time.

Defects Found per Week Post-Release

Defects found per week post-release is a simple count of defects found after the release of the product until the next non-patch release. To calculate, start counting defects at the product release and stop counting at the next non-patch release. Group the defects into weekly totals and report the totals each week. You can organize this information in a table format and plot it, as shown in Figure 17-5. This data will help you anticipate what to expect for future releases.

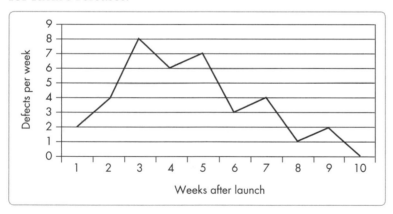

Figure 17-5: Defects found post-release

If the defects per week continue to increase after a few weeks, the product may be in trouble. Sometimes, during the first three or four weeks, no defects will be reported. This can indicate an excellent release, or it could mean that customers have not yet fully used the product. Once you have collected data on one release, you can use it for planning for defect repair time with the next release.

Weighted Defect Count per Week

Weighted defect count per week is an ongoing count summing up the weighted value of each defect between releases. The *weighted value* represents the impact of each defect relative to that of other defects. The highest rated defect (5) can be many times more important than a middle-rank defect (3). Setting up a table in advance that shows relative impact to your company of ranked defects will allow you to weight the impact of problems found post-release.

Table 17-4 shows a sample weighting table. In this example, the highest ranked defect (5) has an impact 25 times more than the lowest level defect (1) and 2.5 times more than the next lower defect (4). Your weighting tables will vary, but most impacts will be different from the rank number.

Table 17-4: Rank vs. Impact Weighting Table

Rank	Impact
1	1
2	3
3	5
4	10
5	25

To calculate the weighted value, sum up the weighted values of all post-release defects. For example, if the post-release defects had ranks of 3, 2, 4, 4, 2, 1, and 5 in week one, then the total would be: 5 + 3 + 10 + 10 + 3 + 1 + 25 = 57. Track this information weekly and examine the totals. You can compare the data to past releases to get some insight into what to expect after the first few weeks post-release.

You can also use a spreadsheet to calculate weighted defects per week. Figure 17-6 illustrates an example spreadsheet showing the proper formulas to use.

Weighted defect tracking post-release is also valuable for tracking *post-release trends*—tracking the length of time between the release and the peak of reported problems per week. This can vary based on product and customer. For products with simple setup and customers who are very anxious to use them, the peak will probably occur early.

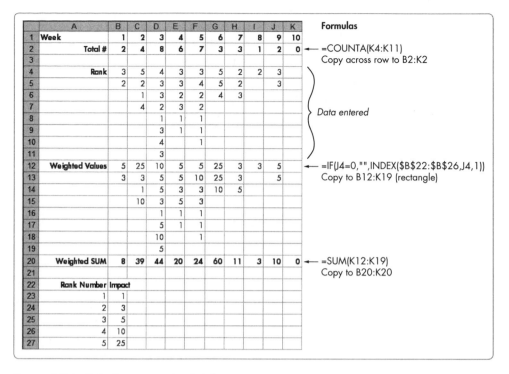

	A	B	C	D	E	F	G	H	I	J	K	Formulas
1	Week	1	2	3	4	5	6	7	8	9	10	
2	Total #	2	4	8	6	7	3	3	1	2	0	← =COUNTA(K4:K11)
3												Copy across row to B2:K2
4	Rank	3	5	4	3	3	5	2	2	3		
5		2	2	3	3	4	5	2		3		
6			1	3	2	2	4	3				
7			4	2	3	2						Data entered
8				1	1	1						
9				3	1	1						
10				4		1						
11				3								
12	Weighted Values	5	25	10	5	5	25	3	3	5		← =IF(J4=0,"",INDEX($B$22:$B$26,J4,1))
13		3	3	5	5	10	25	3		5		Copy to B12:K19 (rectangle)
14			1	5	3	3	10	5				
15			10	3	5	3						
16				1	1	1						
17				5	1	1						
18				10		1						
19				5								
20	Weighted SUM	8	39	44	20	24	60	11	3	10	0	← =SUM(K12:K19)
21												Copy to B20:K20
22	Rank Number	Impact										
23	1	1										
24	2	3										
25	3	5										
26	4	10										
27	5	25										

Figure 17-6: Calculating weighted defects

Knowing when to expect the peak number of problems is useful for planning purposes. You can use the information to ensure that the proper staff is available to support customer issues and anticipate when the issues will require additional staff. You can also plot the data in a graph to compare the current release's quality and defect counts against those of past releases. These comparisons document the progress your teams are making to improve product quality.

Figure 17-7 shows a sample graph of data. In this example, notice that the weighted customer-reported defects are higher six weeks post-release than they are at the earlier peak at three weeks. This could be a sign of serious quality problems that might not be easily noticed in a nonweighted chart.

Weighted defects per week can also be used as a prerelease measure during testing. It can tell you about the quality of the code before it is released and help you predict total testing time to lower the defect count to an acceptable range. The quality measure is useful for releases with substantial new functionality as well as older products. However, initial defect counts

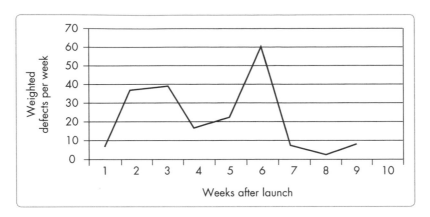

Figure 17-7: Weighted defects per week post-release

will likely be proportional to the amount of code changes. This can have a smaller effect for product lines with consistently long release cycles and a consistent amount of changes. But it can be significant for highly variable releases in terms of amount of changes, and you can apply a normalization factor to compare releases or set a standard. With a consistent testing approach and a normalization factor to account for scope of the change, you can use the data as a guide to help determine when a product is ready for release.

Setting a normalization factor can be tricky, as accounting for relative amounts of change in a release can't be based merely on lines of code written. Sometimes changes take considerable effort, and the effort involves refactoring existing code. A practical normalization approach is to use an approximate calculation of number of hours of development effort planned for the release. If a release has twice as many engineering hours planned as the last release, for example, use 2 as the normalization factor—divide defect counts by 2 to compare these against data from the last release.

Weighted Customer-Found Defects

A variation on the previous approach is to count only *defects found by customers*. This will reflect the customer's perception of the product. Sometimes the internally detected defects will skew the picture for better or worse relative to what customers have identified. Remember that customers do not report most defects; they tend to focus only on problems that annoy them or affect their work. Even so, customer-reported defects can give you a handle on how customers perceive your quality.

Percent of Tests Run During Test Pass

The QA team can execute *test passes*—which consist of a barrage of tests to evaluate the product, a log of found defects, repair of defects, and verification of the repairs. Releases often consist of multiple test passes; you will find it useful to know the percentage of total tests QA has completed, because the percentage is a progress indicator. Predicting the remaining length of time for the test pass is useful in terms of the schedule outcome.

In Figure 17-8, the test passes get shorter as the QA team finds fewer defects. For this product, the three test passes use a total of 19 work days, and the first test pass is 6 days long. A gap exists between passes 1 and 2 to provide time to repair defects.

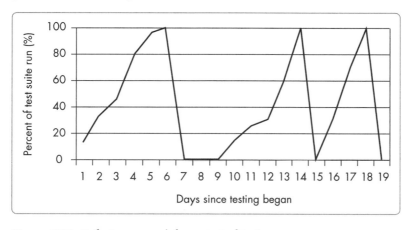

Figure 17-8: Defects per week from start of testing

Defects Found in Test Passes

The number of *defects found in each test pass* is useful to chart. The first pass testing is predictive of the post-release quality as well as testing cycle time. If the same post-release techniques just described are used prerelease, you can predict the defects that QA will find.

Defects Repaired per Week During Testing

A graph showing the number of *defects repaired per week during testing* is another useful tool. If you plot repaired defects alongside defects found, the curve will follow the defects-found curve but be delayed. The time difference between the two curves represents the average delay in making repairs. Figure 17-9 shows about a one-week delay from defect identification to repair. This can be predictive of what to expect in the next round of testing.

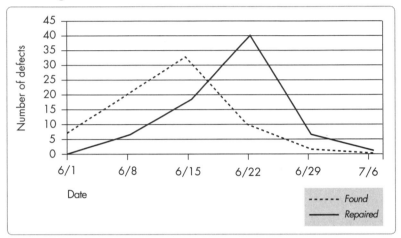

Figure 17-9: Defects found and repaired per week of testing

The measurements presented here can help you prepare for defect identification and repair. Ultimately, you need to select the right set of metrics that fit your product's requirements.

The Impact of Defects on Quality and Productivity

The quality culture of the QA and engineering teams can be the key driver to overall quality and QA productivity for a small company. The quality of the code leaving engineering at the start of testing and the quality of the defect repairs drive the culture of the teams and the company. Unfortunately, many engineers do not give either of these issues enough thought.

A product's defect count as it enters the testing phase defines the quality of the shipped product and the schedule. The quality of the product is proportional to the quality of the product entering testing, because testing finds percentages of problems, not a fixed number of defects regardless of how many exist. Defect counts at the start of testing affect the schedule by adding to the overall cycle time for the testing team. Defects require identification and repair time, and large numbers of defects require more test passes to ensure quality code.

You can observe the effect of defect count at the start of testing on the total test schedule. Table 17-5 shows an example that compares starting defect counts of 300, 40, and 10 entering testing against the number of test passes. In all cases, assume that engineers will repair 85 percent of the defects properly, but they will repair 15 percent improperly, and these defects will require more work. Notice how starting with 300 defects requires four test passes to achieve zero defects. Starting with 40 defects needs three test passes. Starting with 10 defects requires two test passes. This illustrates how the initial defect count can have a big impact on schedule.

Table 17-5: Defect Reduction vs. Testing Passes with 15 Percent Error Rate

Testing stage	300 start #	40 start #	10 start #
Pass 1 end count	45	6	2
Pass 2 end count	7	1	0
Pass 3 end count	1	0	0
Pass 4 end count	0	0	0

Also important is the quality of the repairs. Repair quality can be measured in the *test pass reduction rate*—the percent of identified defects that are not properly fixed and new failures that are caused directly by the repair. It is fair to characterize an organization by its correct repair rate or, conversely, by the repair failure rate. For example, a 25 percent failure rate indicates a sloppy organization in which engineers do not check their work or communicate with QA. A reasonably well-run organization should have a failure rate of 10 percent or lower. A 5 percent (1 failure in 20) organization is performing very well indeed: Development engineers are working closely with QA engineers before implementing a repair to make sure they understand the problem. Engineers are also checking their work to avoid introducing new problems.

Let's take a look at another example. Assume engineering builds 100 defects into a project that QA finds in the first test pass. Each pass takes a week because a full regression test is undertaken on each pass to catch side effects of defect repairs. Consider the simple scenario shown in Table 17-6 with three different repair rates, 25 percent, 10 percent, and 5 percent, starting at 100 defects.

Table 17-6: Repair Failure Rate vs. Testing Passes

Stages	25% repair failure rate	10% repair failure rate	5% repair failure rate
Start count	100	100	100
Pass 1 end count	25	10	5
Pass 2 end count	6	1	0
Pass 3 end count	2	0	0
Pass 4 end count	0	0	0

The outcomes of the three approaches are considerably different. The 25 percent team takes four test passes before the product is ready to ship. The 10 percent team takes three passes. The 5 percent team takes two passes through the code for success. If each pass takes 5 days, then the 5 percent team takes 10 days less than the 25 percent team for the same initial defect count. In practice, the time difference is even greater, because this example does not include engineering time to *make* the repairs. If you assume 20 percent of a day spent per defect found and 5 days per test pass, you get the data illustrated in Table 17-7.

Table 17-7: Total Time vs. Different Repair Failure Rate

Stages	25% repair failure rate		10% repair failure rate		5% repair failure rate	
	Defect Count	Time (days)	Defect Count	Time (days)	Defect Count	Time (days)
Start count	100		100		100	
Pass 1	25	5.0	10	5.0	5	5.0
Pass 1 repairs		5.0		2.0		1.0
Pass 2	6	5.0	1	5.0	0	5.0
Pass 2 repairs		1.3		0.2		
Pass 3	2	5.0	0	5.0		
Pass 3 repairs		0.3				
Pass 4	0	5.0				
Total days		26.6		17.2		11.0

Wow! The team with a 5 percent repair failure rate closes a release 15 days faster than the team with a 25 percent rate. The time savings are much larger as the size of the project increases. You can clearly see that driving a positive engineering attitude toward defects entering the testing phase does cut schedule time and reduces post-release defects.

Additional Reading

Here is some additional reading on topics presented in this chapter:

Code Complete: A Practical Handbook of Software Construction, by Steve McConnell (Microsoft Press, 2004)

Controlling Software Projects: Management, Measurement, and Estimates, by Tom DeMarco (Yourdon Press, 1986)

Effective Software Test Automation: Developing an Automated Software Testing Tool, by Kanglin Li and Mengqi Wu (Sybex, 2004)

High Quality Low Cost Software Inspections, by Ronald A. Radice (Paradoxicon Publishing, 2004)

Introduction to the Personal Software Process, by Watts S. Humphrey (Addison-Wesley Professional, 1996)

Software Inspection, by Tom Gilb and Dorothy Graham (Addison-Wesley Professional, 1993)

Software Release Methodology, by Michael E. Bays (Prentice Hall, 1999)

PART V

PLANNING THE FUTURE

A key role for the development manager is planning the future of the company's product and company technology. At many small firms, planning is limited because of lack of time to take on the task. Even though day-to-day activities can be overwhelming, you should set aside some time on a regular basis to plan for the future.

This section discusses approaches and methods to help you make forward-looking planning more systematic. It includes techniques for selecting projects, project estimation and planning, and general technology planning.

18

SETTING THE DIRECTION

The development manager must oversee the product and technical directions for the development team; he also works with marketing to set the product direction for the company. Developing the direction should be a collaborative effort that involves the technical leaders of the sales, marketing, and development teams. Important considerations in setting product direction include market requirements, customer requirements, industry technical direction, and company needs.

If you fail to set the direction, the direction will be set for you by default. Without specific direction, engineers can be influenced and motivated by factors that are not particularly business focused, such as the thrill of working with new technologies or approaches or rewriting code rather than reusing it. Engineers also have strong preferences for particular software and systems, and they may select third-party packages based on short-term utility while not considering long-term costs, effect on quality, and business risks.

If you're new to the company, take a look at how development made technology decisions in the past before you set the direction for the future. Try to understand the reasoning behind past decisions. Think about choices of language, operating systems, computers, third-party software, and data formats. Consider past "create-versus-buy" decisions. Knowing how decisions were made in the past can help you understand any biases of the team and will give you ideas for improving the technical decision-making going forward. In some cases, the reasons for past decisions may not be clear—but this should not prevent you from documenting decisions now or in the future.

You cannot set technical direction in a vacuum. As you consider a strategy, review it with the executive team and encourage input and support. Decisions are affected by high- and low-priority issues, with trade-offs and compromises being common. Proper communication with the executive team ensures that everyone is aware of the big picture, including its pros and cons.

As the technical leader, your decisions in setting the future technical direction require that you consider five elements: Listen to the market, create a whole product, defuse hidden technical time bombs, plan for required technical overhauls, and optimize customer setup.

Listen to the Market

As you plan a product and technology direction, consider the requirements of current customers and the current and future market.

Sales, marketing, and customer service teams can help you learn more about your customers' interests. Meet with customers. Spend time observing as users work with your product; this can provide great insight into how you might improve the product. Ask customers about their concerns, their future plans for using the product, and their ideas for new features. To appreciate the big picture, you can compile data gathered from multiple customers.

Current customers can provide great evolutionary advice about your product, and potential new customers can help identify key features that are missing. As most small companies grow by acquiring new customers and selling more products to current customers, looking ahead to new customers' needs should be an important part of your planning efforts. If you focus only on current customers' needs, you can run the risk of over-customizing your product to suit a smaller potential market. The product marketing team should regularly examine your company's markets, talking to current and potential customers. This information allows the team to identify different groups of customers with similar problems. For each group, the marketing team can examine the value a potential solution would bring, and the development team can determine practicality and potential costs of solutions. With different options identified, marketing can set the product direction.

This may sound like a straightforward process, but it often involves multiple iterations and examination of different ideas to isolate those with the best potential for the next product offering. With the cooperation of marketing and engineering, this process can occur in a systematic way.

As you examine potential markets, stretch your current product in different dimensions to consider potential for new opportunities. Some new opportunities require simplifying your product and offering it packaged at a lower price. Other opportunities require new specialized features. Still other opportunities include different industry "verticals"—meaning that your product can be used to solve a similar set of problems for a different industry.

Tackling new market verticals should not be considered lightly. Be prepared for a larger effort. Entering a new market vertical usually involves considerably more work than expanding a product line in an existing vertical—not just in customer sales efforts, but also in learning the problems and concerns of the new industry. The development team needs technical expertise in the requirements of the new industry before a new product is designed and built. Part of your planning should be to account for the engineering training time required to attack new verticals.

Investigating the product's future is an ongoing task for the development manager and others, and planning for the future should not be limited to an annual strategic planning session. These discussions provide valuable information that should be considered at least once a quarter. Failing to discuss the product future regularly can add huge time lags into planning processes and can make the product's (and company's) future less dynamic and less successful.

Create a Whole Product

As discussed in earlier chapters, the *whole product* concept[1] describes not only providing a software product that customers want to buy, but providing a complete solution to the customers' problems and needs. A whole product includes the software, customer services, technical support, appropriate technical interfaces, ease of integration with other tools, ease of installation, and a forward-looking plan. A development manager cannot focus solely on the product software. Instead, look at what it takes to expand the software into a whole product, with a focus on interfaces, integration with other tools, and ease of customer implementation.

If the costs and effort required to assist customers with implementation of your product are high, you should examine this area carefully and often. Small company sales are influenced by customer implementation difficulties and costs. Customers find enterprise systems difficult to implement in general, so a simplified system will attract sales. Company management can neglect to attack product implementation improvements early enough in the company's growth cycle. High implementation costs will stall out a small company's growth.

Some software categories require extensive numbers of interfaces to different systems to be accepted by the market. The next new interfaces are not necessarily as fun to implement as a new product feature, but they can result in high sales value. Examine your interface needs early with marketing and plan for growth.

For some software products, direct interfaces with other tools are essential for success. As with interfaces, this is not a glamour area for software engineering, but it is essential for maximizing your product's value for the customer and its overall success.

---

[1] The whole product concept is the topic of the book *Crossing the Chasm* by Geoffrey A. Moore and is also covered in marketing texts.

Looking ahead often requires marketing binoculars to identify future directions. However, sometimes it requires donning a flak jacket and looking for hidden problems.

Defuse Technical Time Bombs

Some past technology decisions might be ticking time bombs that will go off when you least expect it. These *technology time bombs* are caused by technical choices at the beginning of product development that result in problems that explode in the future. Engineers can create such problems by focusing on a quick product construction while ignoring the long-term effects of their choices. In addition, engineers making technical choices can have personal biases that might not represent the best long-term business choices for the current situation.

Technology time bombs have different delay times and different effects when they explode. Knowing what to look for as a development manager can help you spot these issues early enough so that the problem does not leave your company unable to support its customers. Consider the following areas when reviewing your technology and looking for potential problems:

How standard is the data format chosen for communicating with customers? Does it add to customer costs when they integrate with your system?
> Sometimes data formats are not specified at the outset of the project, so the engineering team will use the most convenient format, which might prove to be very inconvenient for future customers.

Did the team build code for a software component, even though a reasonable commercial component was available?
> This is referred to as "the not invented here syndrome." Some engineers want to re-create components for their own education or so that they have complete control over the code.

Was an uncommon language used in your product's construction?
> This can result in difficulty finding and hiring appropriate replacement engineers. As a small growing company, actively avoid this problem, since use of common languages should be the norm.

But uncommon languages may be used when a technologist has a personal interest in or preference for them.

What are the reasons behind key technology choices?
Sometimes technology is chosen for familiarity or for learning purposes, not because it is the best choice.

How thoroughly has QA checked the API input error checking? Is the coverage solid?
Both engineering and QA often conduct inadequate error checking with application programming interfaces. Because of the complexity of most APIs, making complete tests and checks can be difficult.

Does the product have major features that current customers do not use?
If this is the case, and if the features do get used eventually, you should expect customers to uncover new problems.

How scalable is the data layer, front end, and middle layer?
As the customer base increases, speed issues often appear in server-based software.

Has anyone reviewed the system hardware choices for scalability?
For software used on a server, development often focuses first on getting the functionality right and considers scalability later. Early testing of software scalability and recommended hardware is a good idea.

How does third-party code performance scale with system volume increases? Has another customer of the third-party code used it on a system with the volume you are expecting?
Sometimes scaling problems are tied to third-party packages incorporated into your system. Don't assume that these packages have been properly tested for higher speeds and customer loads.

What are third-party code licensing costs when volume is high?
Licensing of some components can include a painful price increase as more customers are brought online. Understand the per-customer and scaling costs for use of any third-party package.

What is the reliability and quality of third-party code?

As quality of commercial software code varies considerably, carefully review third-party code during testing; don't assume it's okay.

Finding and defusing technical time bombs before they explode requires some detective work. All aspects of your product's construction must be examined, including compatibility, scalability, quality, vendor reliability, and long-term costs. Although avoiding a blowup might not always be possible, minimizing the effects usually is.

Some technical choices can present serious technical flaws that are not easily repaired. When this happens, you might need to make major changes to the code base. It may be time for a technology overhaul.

Plan a Technology Overhaul

A *technology overhaul* involves the replacement of major sections of the current code or redesigning the product's architecture, while keeping the functionality of the code roughly the same. A new technology may be required to solve systematic design flaws. Consider an overhaul in response to major issues that cannot be fixed gradually along with new development.

The need for an overhaul can often occur on a legacy system you inherited. On the other hand, an overhaul can be a nightmare for a development manager who supervised building the system in the first place. In either case, explain to your boss and peers why the choices were made in the first place and why significant changes need to be made now.

Time and resources are always scarce in small companies, so competition for them can be intense. If you don't get peer and management buy-in, dealing with expensive problems that are not easily visible and do not produce short-term visible results can result in misunderstandings and mistrust.

Also consider the impact of an overhaul on your customers. These changes might (and often do) force changes in the customer's operations or technology. For example, your changes might require that the customer purchase a new third-party application, such as database software. You must consider the customer impact before starting the work and offer your customers sufficient notice of upcoming changes.

How the overhaul is handled depends on the projected cost and business needs. If the overhaul is "minor" and development can complete it in a single focused release over a three- to six-month period, implementing the changes at once makes the most sense. It will require the support of marketing and sales, because a release that does not improve the product features can cause problems with sales growth. You will need a strong business case for performing a technology overhaul, as doing so will displace other important product work.

If the changes are not minor and cannot fit into a single short-term cycle, your choices are more difficult. A one- to two-year overhaul project rarely makes business sense for a small company. It leaves the company's product features static for too long. The time delay of the overhaul invites a large amount of risk from competition and from loss of momentum with existing and future customers.

One approach for an overhaul is to map out the effort by major sections per release. This can be difficult to coordinate along with normal releases and will drag out the effort over a longer time if additional staff is not available. Another approach is to build the new system in parallel with work supporting the existing system. This can be logically simpler but requires extra staff and infrastructure that you may need to scale back at the end of the effort.

In summary, when you believe a technology overhaul is needed, you must create and present a clear business case for it and continue to push the issue toward resolution. Don't wait until the system blows up and hurts your product and customers.

Optimize Customer Setup

Although shrink-wrapped, mass-produced software is sold "as is," many products and services require additional setup procedures before the customer can realize the full potential of the software. Companies that sell products that require or benefit from setup efforts often overlook the costs of such operations. If these costs are ignored, optimizing the customer setup is usually ignored as well.

Creating a great product that is expensive to deploy per customer may not be problematic if your customer base is small, since the costs in such a case could also be small. But as your customer base grows, so do the costs of these extra efforts—with increasing customizations, rollout times, and rollout costs. Most small companies cannot afford large time delays or high development costs with each new customer, and problems with implementation and setup can cause loss of sales, as more potential customers hear about problems associated with your product.

If customers are willing to pay for customization of your product, sales with more customization options might be viable. However, a product that requires heavy customization per customer means that your development staff must grow as sales increase. Such an approach defines a consulting business model, which requires a different consideration of costs, sales, and expenses than required for a one-size-fits-all software package.

Combining a consulting business model with a software product business model is a difficult task for a single software company. Customers will always try to push down the price of the custom coding or will expect it to be free with an expensive product. This will make the customization more of a cost than a sale for your company. Therefore, you must minimize customization efforts and costs early on, before the company's growth phase.

If customization is part of the company's business plan, create a separate group or business unit for customization efforts, with different price requirements determined for the product and service parts of the business. Top-level agreements about how concessions will be made will simplify the sales process when customers place pressure on the product or service element of a sale.

Whether paid for or not, delays from sale to rollout add time before a new customer can become a paying customer. Large delays during a growth phase will hurt your company's cash flow and ability to grow, even if the company has all the customers it wants. Growth strains cash flow because your company must spend cash well in advance of receiving payment from customers, and the current cash input will be less than the cash output.

The higher the growth rate and longer the delay from costs to revenues, the higher the profit required on past sales to sustain the company without outside investment. This situation is even worse for the software as a service

(SaaS) model, in which customers pay your company over time instead of providing a lump sum payment.

Rollout and customization requirements affect not only the development team, but also the operations, support, documentation, and project management teams. The development team can usually find ways to help reduce the costs and delays that other teams face if developers focus on the most important problems.

If your business model requires customization to get users up and running, look for ways to optimize this process before you are inundated with orders. To cut time and costs, first figure out the current rollout time and cost per new customer. The process of calculating the costs will require that you examine the steps and the process to identify multiple ways of reducing time or minimizing error.

Other solutions vary for cutting times and cost depending on the analysis. Here are some examples:

- Change the bundling and scope of the product to reduce rollout times and costs.

- Do not target customers who by their nature require the most customization.[2] This could mean pursuing mid-sized companies instead of large companies, which expect more attention and customization with large software purchases. Large companies have the financial influence to demand free customizations while squeezing you on price. You can mitigate this effect by creating new features that also enhance the product for the general market, but avoid making such rationalizations if they are not truly the case. From a business risk perspective, a CEO often prefers several smaller sales over one large sale. More sales can reduce risk if something goes wrong with a deal. However, the CEO's strategy may prefer large sales over smaller ones if company credibility will benefit from large account references.

---

[2] An exception is the case in which your company's business strategy is focused on a mixed product/service market geared toward large customers. Make sure your company has deep pockets, as the sales and delivery cycles can be long in this situation.

- Simplify the customer's integration efforts by writing a software program that automates the process. If the customer has to manipulate old data to use your system, make the process as automated as possible and part of your standard offering.

- Standardize your customization offerings to reduce deployment time. Instead of allowing full customization, include a few standard customizations and make them as simple as possible. This principle can apply to professional service organizations as well. Creating frameworks, methods, and standard customizations that speed up the deployment can greatly improve the company's profits. The basic rule boils down to "create once, sell many times."

- Create a customization or integration group that focuses on improving customer implementations by reducing their costs and shortening their deployment time. This group will scale up with sales increases as the company grows.

19

PRODUCT ROADMAP AND STRATEGY

Strategic planning requires more than sales predictions and a financial plan—it requires a product strategy and a product roadmap based on thoughtful analysis of where the company began, where it is heading in the future, and how it plans to get there. The development manager plays a critical role in the process by producing a realistic product roadmap that sets the course and coordinates business needs with development, marketing, sales, and other team strategies.

Senior management must look continuously at the road ahead while remembering the paths the company has already taken. As a senior manager, you must watch your step to avoid pitfalls while focusing on the horizon that leads to your company's future.

After you have determined your destination, planned your route, and scouted out the immediate path, you can complete a short-term (less than one year), middle-term (one to three years), and long-term (three to six years) strategic plan.

MISSING THE MIDDLE

At my company, I clearly observed the split between short-term and longer-term planning. The managers had no interest in aligning the two. Politics dictated the short-term tactics; investors wanted to see movement in selected areas. Management sold the long-term plan to investors as it showed a rosy future. Part of the reason for not aligning the two plans in the middle may have been management cynicism. If they built out the middle-term plan and saw a big gap between the longer-term promises and the direction they were heading, they could not tell investors they believed in the longer-term financial models.

Development met the short-term goals over the next nine months, but the company did not succeed in stepping toward its longer-term goal because management had no plan to get there.

—Project management director

Failing to see the short-term path in front of you can get you stuck in a hole, while a lack of long-term vision can leave you wandering; however, a common and dangerous problem at a small company is missing the middle term: No plan for getting from here to there (the destination) is determined and regularly updated. Without a complete strategic plan that includes the middle, you may seize short-term opportunities that lead away from longer term goals. Non-strategic short-term choices do not build on each other to increase corporate value. Instead, these choices bring in short-term revenue at the expense of future potential.

Creating a full strategic plan that includes a middle-term plan takes an executive team effort. The team will need to consider many aspects to provide a solution that meets the company goals, including the product roadmap, company finances, expected sales, and company staffing plan.

Even more important than creating the plan is reviewing it quarterly and making adjustments as needed. Many companies create strategic plans once a year and then file them away rather than updating them regularly. The process of replanning provides the real value in strategic planning, not the plan itself.

From a development leadership perspective, you will find it challenging to hold to the high road rather than go with the flow. It takes a bit of political skill to convince others that some short-term choices can be detrimental in the long term. However, don't simply and quietly accept short-term product choices that won't get your company where it wants to go; make your opinion heard on the big issues.

With this information in mind, let's look at the planning area in which development has the largest influence and concerns—the *product roadmap*.

Creating a Product Roadmap

Product roadmaps are usually developed with marketing to define the evolution of the product line(s) over time, and they focus on the major shifts that impact the product and its market. The roadmap must not be a marketing fantasy; it must be based on realistic development assumptions about a product course that is reasonable to achieve and that produces the product the company and its customers expect. Creating a product roadmap requires that you have a solid understanding of the current product goals, along with its flaws and limitations that can affect the course.

Start with the marketing strategy and consider several major product options. Also consider other major efforts that the company expects development to undertake, such as develop projects that improve productivity, repair faulty systems, close customer deals, and improve corporate image. All company project efforts should be considered while creating the product roadmap.

Let's look at a straightforward approach to comparing different options.

Evaluating Choices

Cost-benefit (CB) analysis is a classic tool with both formal and informal definitions. In this section, the discussion is not financially formal but uses a variation on the calculation to account for probability of seeing the benefit. CB analysis is used to determine which projects will create the most revenue. This analysis is underutilized in the software market because of the complexities in estimating potential benefits of any investment and the ability to accurately forecast the costs of vaguely stated objectives. However, CB analysis can be an effective sorting tool for small software companies.

Performing CB calculations on future product proposals offers insight into which projects are most likely to succeed. More important, these calculations can identify projects that *will fail*. CB calculations can reflect the overall management team's judgment about what will happen during each product cycle, and they also allow you to compare potential successes of multiple projects. This information is valuable to consider when thinking about future product planning.

Cost-benefit calculations can be wrong, but the relative values for projects proposed are likely to be close to actual relative values. You can use these calculations to make comparative choices on new project proposals. Some projects improve customer experience or simplify an internal task, but they need to be evaluated against all other projects and the returns compared before they can be selected.

Projects come in multiple types: *Revenue* projects bring in money. *Productivity* projects can improve the effectiveness of the team so they lower costs and improve services. *Required* projects describe projects with an external mandate—such as projects based on federal regulations for medical software companies and Year 2000 software upgrades. *Risk Reduction* projects reduce the chance of a disruption of your business. *Image* projects improve the company's image but do not increase revenue directly. Typically, small growing companies avoid image projects because the revenue is either zero or very difficult to define, but in some cases the right image project can be key to company success.

In small companies, revenue is usually emphasized. Some companies focus only on revenue and ignore productivity and risk reduction until after problems become acute. Should revenue always trump productivity and risk projections? The short answer is no—revenue can dominate but it should not always win. Failure to consider risk reduction or productivity issues can be fatal to a small growing company, because both risk and productivity issues increase as the company grows.

Many small companies do not use cost-benefit analysis to investigate future projects, relying instead on executive instinct or voting selection processes. Both instinct and voting can easily produce less-then-optimum results, however, when appropriate information hasn't been gathered. They also are subject to individual biases that may not be in the best interest of the company.

In general, cost-benefit analysis isn't the end-all solution, but it can offer good advice on what makes sense when planning an organization's future.

PROJECT SELECTION BY SALES

At my company, year-long projects were voted on by a sales staff of about 12. The company needed to make three sales for the product to break even on development costs. Most sales people knew of only a single potential sale for the project in their region, so they had a strong incentive to place their vote where the next sale would occur, even if they knew that the company could sell only one product.

My company needed a stronger marketing department to survey the sales people and talk to customers. This would have let them determine the overall market for each customer and then select products with the highest potential sales over a three-year period. Instead, we made big choices with little foresight and with no review of what happened.

—Engineering director

Cost-Benefit Calculation

When estimating the CB for a project, consider it in the context of all projects to ensure consistency. All project analyses should be weighted similarly for crucial factors.

One crucial factor is the time frame for the analysis—the length of time considered for benefits, risks, and costs. The choice of time frame can vary based on the type of business and on the size of the company's projects, with larger projects requiring longer time frames. For most small software businesses, using two or three years for the analysis works well. Use the time frame consistently for all projects you analyze.

The next step is to evaluate the time and expenses on the project for your standard time frame. This estimate will vary depending on the type of effort defined earlier: revenue, productivity, requirements, risk, and image projects. Then, for different types of projects, consider the financial benefits versus the probability (odds) of achieving those benefits. For a revenue project, you can estimate the total sales expected. For a risk reduction project, calculate the odds of the risk being realized and the financial penalty of the risk happening (the negative benefit). For a productivity project, look at the benefit of saved time and money versus any probability of not realizing this benefit. For required projects, do not calculate the benefit, but do estimate the costs; then assign a CB value to add at the top of the list. For image projects, calculating the benefits can be very difficult, but getting the best guess down on paper is useful.

With all of this information in hand, you can calculate the CB for a project using this formula:

$$CB = Benefit\ dollar\ value \times Probability\ of\ benefit \div Benefit\ dollar\ cost$$

For example, if a revenue project is projected to have $1 million in sales over three years (benefit) with probability of sales success estimated at 70 percent and a cost of $200,000, then the CB is 3.5 ($1,000,000 × 0.70 ÷ $200,000). Alternatively, a risk reduction project with a cost of $1,000 to solve a problem that could cost $50,000 with a probability of 5 percent would have a CB of 2.5 ($50,000 × 0.05 ÷ $1,000).

NOTE   *CB is a unitless value, as it divides money by money. Strictly speaking, financial calculations use "present value of money," found by discounting the value of future money when comparing it to money in the present. However, for most one- to three-year engineering projects, the estimates are so rough that adding the present value calculation is not necessary.*

Cost-Benefit Comparisons

You can compare several types of projects using a CB approach. For all project types, estimating the cost is not as difficult as calculating the benefits of the project and the likelihood of experiencing those benefits. If you systematically create the estimates and then record them, you can make comparisons between project estimates made months apart. As new information becomes available, you can update the CB information. Although required projects are different from optional projects (in that you *must* do the required projects), they typically have a zero or low revenue benefit. Enter this information and set the CB to a large number such as 100 to ensure that these projects appear at the top of the CB list. Add a note indicating mandated task completion dates.

You can add all of the project information into a spreadsheet or chart. Table 19-1 illustrates a simple example that lets you compare different projects side by side. At the top of the table is a required project, with an artificial CB that forces it to the top of the list (of course, this doesn't mean that its true CB is 100).

Table 19-1: CB Table Example

Description	CB 3yr	Total cost $K	Probability	Benefit $K	Weighed benefit $K	Type	Notes
HIPAA requirements	100[*]	$40	100%	$0	$0	Required	By Jan.
Release process time reduction	8.6	$23	100%	$200	$200	Process	
Add web interface	5.0	$50	50%	$500	$250	Revenue	
Multiple system backup	5.0	$100	10%	$5,000	$500	Risk	

[*] Set to 100—not calculated

An ordered CB table can provide insight into the relative importance of tasks, but it shouldn't be used directly as a task planning or sequencing mechanism. Once the team reviews the table and makes project choices, task scheduling can begin. In some cases, required tasks will be scheduled after desirable projects with large benefit-cost ratios.

WARNING *CB is very easy to fudge to make a project look better. Take a skeptical view of all numbers and test the underlying assumptions.*

When reviewing calculated CB, perform a "smell test": If a product has a very high CB (greater than 10), retest the assumptions. If a product has a CB of 2 or less, be skeptical of the benefits and costs. As these are rough estimates, it would be easy for such a project to turn into a loser if the costs escalate and the benefits are lower. In general, look for projects that have CB values of 3 or more. In all cases, keep the assumptions and CB available in a table even if the project looks like a loser. As potential projects often seem to come up again in 6 to 12 months, you can revisit earlier assumptions to see what might have changed.

Creating One-Page Assessments

A useful adjunct to CB is the *one-page assessment,* which describes the underlying project at a high level and includes many of the assumptions. The one-page assessment is a useful tool that complements cost-benefit analysis. Each assessment provides a quick overview of the proposed project, its costs, and its benefits. The executive team can review the assessments along with the CB project summary table when determining which projects to authorize. The one-page assessment is the initial guide to whether the team should investigate the project further. It is also handy months later if an executive team member asks for information about a particular project's assessment.

Anyone on the executive team can collect the information for the one-page assessments; however, most of the assessments will require that the information be collected from several different executives. Marketing and engineering should be consulted for all assessments.

A typical one-page assessment describes these items:

- Title (at top)
- Author
- Date
- Version
- Type of project (keyword)
- Description (including dependencies)
- Benefit (statement of reason for doing project)
- Costs (in dollars and labor)
- Timeline
- Recommendations

Figure 19-1 shows a sample template for a one-page assessment.

TITLE

Instructions: Replace all italic text with entered values

Author: *Author's name here*
Date: *Date created*
Version: *Version #*

Type of Project: *Revenue, Productivity, Risk Reduction, Image, Required*

Description
Add a few lines describing the effort. The description will be a business description for the executive team. List dependencies on other projects.

Benefit
Add a statement explaining the reason for this effort—the justification. Describe benefits, including sales dollars and units, productivity, and risk reduction. Use numerical values. If unknown, provide a range that is your best estimate. Benefits in revenue or productivity will note how long before these benefits occur.

Costs
Briefly list the potential costs in dollars and hours. Break down hours by team performing the work. Ranges of estimated costs along with the most likely costs are useful.

Timeline
Describe potential timelines for completing this effort with caveats and options.

Recommendation
Describe your recommendations for this effort in 3 to 4 lines.

Figure 19-1: Template for a one-page assessment

Project Components

When you're preparing one-page assessments, some projects will contain multiple smaller projects. If you determine that the smaller projects can be broken down into independent projects, consider breaking them up before performing the final analysis.

Sometimes projects can be divided into smaller portions that can be easily analyzed. For large projects that span a year, for example, consider breaking them up into blocks of functionalities that offer distinct values to the customer. For each component, perform a cost-benefit calculation specifically focused on the perceived value of the product to the customer with only that functionality. This analysis approach is more difficult than project cost-benefit calculations, because calculating the financial return for pieces of functionality can be an abstract concept. However, discussing with marketing the relative value versus cost for functional blocks offers considerable utility, since it forces marketing to prioritize and record the effective values of different feature sets. Allowing marketing or management to indicate that all features must be included in the product in no particular order before it has any value lowers the project's chance for success.

Collecting the effective value of subcomponents will involve discussions with multiple customers to understand how they perceive the value of the product. After these discussions, write down the relative values of the subcomponents; this information can be very useful in the future. Management and new customers can often drive new feature requests into the product without considering the impact these may have on other planned features. A broader perspective lets the team choose implementation sequences that benefit your company the most.

Additional Reading

Here is some additional reading on topics presented in this chapter:

> *The Entrepreneur's Manual: Business Start-Ups, Spin-Offs, and Innovative Management*, by Richard M. White (Chilton Book Co., 1997)

> *Maximizing ROI on Software Development*, by Vijay Sikka (Auerbach Publications, 2004)

> *Software by Numbers: Low-Risk, High-Return Development*, by Mark Denne and Jane Cleland-Huang (Prentice Hall PTR, 2003)

> *Strategy Pure & Simple II: How Winning Companies Dominate Their Competitors*, by Michel Robert (McGraw-Hill, 1997)

20

GOING FORWARD

If you have read straight through this book, you have covered a lot of ground. With so much information to consider, the path forward can seem daunting. Fortunately, you have a guidebook on hand to help you find your way.

If you are a new manager, don't worry if that feeling of being lost in the woods is still with you. At ground level, the trees look similar and they all block your view, but don't wander around the forest floor hoping to find yourself somewhere you want to be. Instead, change your perspective regularly—climb a tree to get above the forest so you can view the landscape. A manager needs to be able to see the big picture and understand how his or her hard work relates to it. Consequently, make a regular effort to revisit the high-level view of your company and your development efforts. If you don't like what you see, make changes. To sum it up: Stop, assess, and then act.

A little retrospective thinking can also help. Think about where you've been and where you are now. If you like people, software, technology, and management, your job should be exciting and fun overall. If you haven't felt that way in a while, shake yourself awake and ask why work isn't energizing. This will lead you to change either where you are spending your time, what you are prioritizing, or how you are leading. It can also lead you away from your current company.

Remember that being the development manager isn't about ego, job perks, being in charge, or other direct benefits to you. It's about you guiding your team to success. Good management means supporting your team, helping development staff grow, treating team members fairly, and helping the business along. Treating others well may not always advance your career, but it will make you a good manager who earns the respect of your team, boss, co-workers, and ultimately yourself. And that will make the journey worthwhile.

SOFTWARE COMPANY STRUCTURE

Structuring the organizational aspects of a growing software company requires that you understand the tasks that the company needs to perform. When the company first starts, the leadership often distributes the tasks among the staff. As the company grows, these tasks will also grow in size and number, and new employees will need to be hired. As new employees are hired, the organization of the company will shift, and roles will become more specialized.

This appendix illustrates how company structure changes as a company grows. To illustrate the changes, some key small company sizes are examined along with their associated organizational structures. The companies described are modeled after small software product companies, rather than software contracting firms. Although the descriptions are detailed, they are not intended to define the only ways to structure a small company—in practice, other organizational structures can also be used successfully.

The sizes of companies discussed here are as follows:

- One-person software company
- Two-person software company
- Twelve-person software company
- Fifty-person software company
- Hundred-plus–person software company

The first four examples illustrate a functional/hierarchical[1] organization, as it is the most common structure for smaller firms. A hundred-plus–person software company often uses other organizational structures. Although you don't need to wait until your company has more than 100 people on staff to reorganize, the pressure that occurs at that point becomes large enough that the issue of an effective organization becomes particularly pressing.

Company Tasks

To understand companies of different sizes, you must first consider the business and software development tasks that are required to create a working software company. These tasks fall into two general categories: business tasks and software life cycle tasks. *Software life cycle tasks* include work needed to develop a viable software product and maintain it after development. *Business tasks* enable software development and keep the business financially viable—from getting the funding to paying the bills, hiring staff, and managing the effort.

The following lists of business and software life cycle tasks are not intended to be all encompassing, but they do cover tasks common to software companies of different sizes.

---

[1] Described in earlier chapters, a functional organization segments work by functions (for example, marketing, sales, engineering, accounting) while a hierarchical organization uses a top-down delegation of authority.

Business Tasks

- Acquire funding

- Maintain financial accounts

- Deal with government regulations

- Handle human resources issues

- Supervise staff

- Sell products or services

- Plan for the future

- Purchase, maintain, and support computers and systems

- Manage, estimate, and track projects

- Define technical policies and processes

Software Life Cycle Tasks

- Define product

- Design architecture

- Write and debug code

- Test product and assure quality

- Package software

- Release software

- Support customer

- Create technical documentation

Keep these types of work tasks in mind as we examine companies of different sizes, starting with the one-person company.

Typical One-Person Company

In a one-person company, the owner-operator does everything, from the business tasks to the development tasks. To succeed, this person must either be technically savvy with business skills or a businessperson who contracts out technical development. Some people can successfully sustain this type of company for a while, but most find that wearing two hats is very difficult and requires too many skills.

Some technical people run successful one-person, one-product companies with no interest in expansion. This structure can work acceptably well for a niche product that has very limited growth potential. But if the product has significant potential, other companies will eventually move into the market, and competition can pose challenges to the one-person company.

Typical Two-Person Company

A businessperson and a technical person can effectively run a two-employee software company with an appropriate division of labor. The technical person (often the chief technology officer, or CTO) handles all the operations and engineering, and the businessperson (often the president) handles running the business. The two must collaborate extensively.

The task requirements are about the same as those of a one-person company, but the software development tasks and some technical tasks that are not strictly development oriented (such as keeping the hardware in proper working order) go to the CTO. Everything else falls to the president. The tasks are split as follows:

President—the businessperson

- Acquire funding
- Maintain financial accounts
- Deal with government regulations
- Handle human resources issues
- Sell products or services
- Support customer relations
- Plan for the future

CTO—the technical person

- Purchase, maintain, and support computers and systems
- Manage, estimate, and track projects
- Define technical policies and processes
- Create technical documentation
- Define product
- Design architecture
- Write and debug code
- Test product and assure quality
- Package software
- Release software
- Support customers technically
- Plan for the future

As a company succeeds and grows larger, task sizes increase until more employees are hired to handle the load. Which tasks grow fastest with sales growth varies depending on the product and industry. Common functional areas that experience rapid staff growth as revenue grows are sales, customer support, and engineering. Engineering efforts can increase rapidly as the company grows, because customers often want customized features as part of the sale.

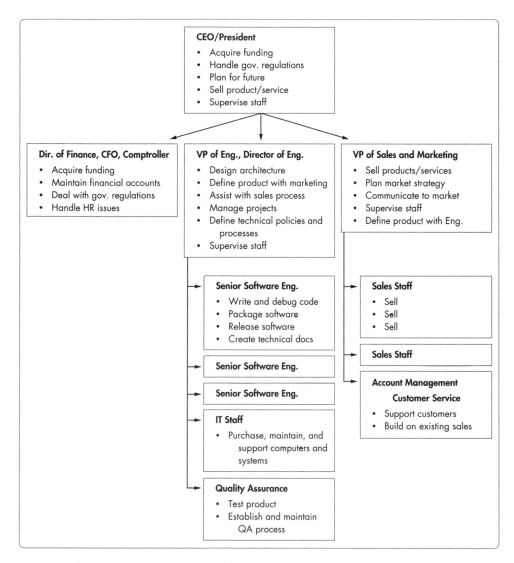

Figure A-1: Example of a 12-person software company

Twelve-Person Software Company

At the 12-employee level, the software company is a small team. Employees are assigned some specialized tasks by function, which adds to the overall organizational efficiency. Administrative and support tasks are usually assigned first, but there is usually some overlap in roles and tasks for everyone in a small firm.

As the company size is small, all employees talk to each other constantly. Everyone has a good understanding of what other team members are doing, with the possible exception of the software engineers, who are heavily focused on building the software.

Figure A-1 illustrates an example 12-person company organized along functional lines. The figure shows each staff person by title. Common employee tasks for each function are shown as bullet points on the first instance of the function. A number of different arrangements of responsibilities are possible with a 12-person company; one common variation is whether product definition is dominated by engineering or the sales and marketing person. Another variation is splitting the sales and marketing role between two people.

Twenty-four to Fifty-Person Software Company

As a software company grows larger than 12, staff is usually added to fill out functions. A 24-employee company will likely feature the same key functional areas used in a 12-employee company. The CEO or president may separate marketing from sales and HR from finance at this level. For the software-as-a-service model, the company may require an operations department. The following departments would be appropriate in this size of company:

- CEO
- Finance
- Sales
- Marketing
- HR
- Development (includes QA and documentation)
- Operations

As the company approaches 50 employees, the CEO will fill out all the functional areas with separate staff and management. The functional areas are more likely to be distinct, reporting to the CEO. In a 50-person company, engineers have more specialization (such as a build and release engineer) as some functions can add to efficiency at a lower cost.

Compared to a 12-person company, a 50-person company does not enjoy the continuous communication experienced by a small team. Too many communication paths are available with 50 people for everyone to keep in touch daily (that's 1,275 potential two-way conversations).

Figure A-2 illustrates a sample 50-person company organized along functional lines. This example does not portray a "perfect" company organization but illustrates a common one. In this example, the number

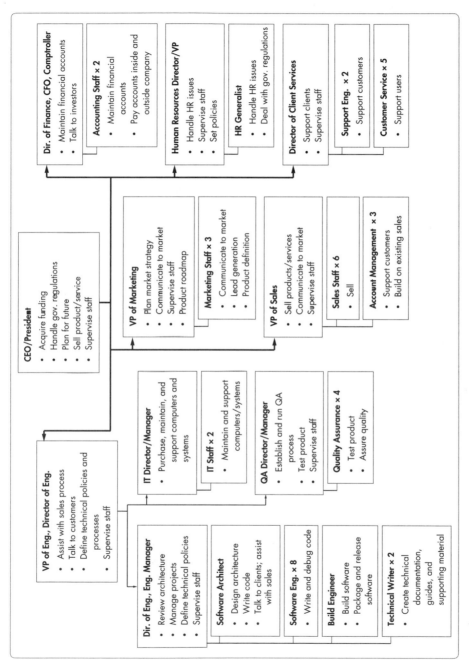

Figure A-2: An example of a 50-employee company

of people in a particular staff position is shown by the × *N* notation. For example, × 8 would indicate that eight people hold this position.

Notice in this example that customer service and account management are separate. Customer service will support the user of the product, while account management will support the purchaser of the software. For many products, the user and purchaser are different entities, and even when the same person handles both tasks, different support skills are required for each.

Numbers of staff for each team and corporate structure vary considerably at the 50-person company size, often depending on the product offered, the industry, overall goals of the company, background of the CEO, and specific short-term needs of the company. For example, for product companies with a stronger emphasis on quality, the ratio of quality team to engineering staff will be closer to 1:1. In some firms, this ratio can be as high as 10:1 engineers to QA, but this is definitely not recommended.

Hundred-Plus–Person Software Company

At the 100-plus–employee size, the company requires large functional teams that experience communication fragmented by function. Employees do not know everyone else in the company. Communication is strong within the functional areas, but it is weaker between functional teams.

As companies grow to one hundred employees or more, management usually considers different methods of restructuring the organization. The CEO can choose multiple organizational approaches but typically chooses a straight hierarchy, a matrix structure, or segmenting by small product teams.

As companies grow, communication that worked with fewer staff ceases to work well. In a small company, instant messaging (IM), many rapid emails, yelling over the cube walls, or walking to someone's desk every time you have a question works well. In a larger company, however, such approaches can overwhelm employees with too much noise and too many communications from too many sources.

Managers sometimes try to shield their employees, demanding that all communications go up the ladder and back down so management can triage. This can seem isolating, as it creates workgroup "silos." This approach is an inefficient way to get work done.

Let's consider several different approaches to organizing a larger software company. Structured approaches include a hierarchy, a matrix, many small product teams, and a flexible product team. For all of these approaches, bear in mind the main functions of management: organizing work for sale (such as project work), supporting individual employees (mentoring and coaching), and improving the overall organization (process improvement and hiring).

Hierarchical Structure

A *hierarchical structure* for a company has each person reporting to a single manager. In a hierarchy, a clear chain of command exists. A hierarchy divides tasks by functional area. In each area, a manager controls the function.

Figure A-3 illustrates a simplified company hierarchy.

A hierarchical structure has some advantages over other structures. First, a hierarchy offers a clear chain of command. The top management makes directives and sends them down the management chain. Second, management can reduce communication paths by creating separate functional teams, which

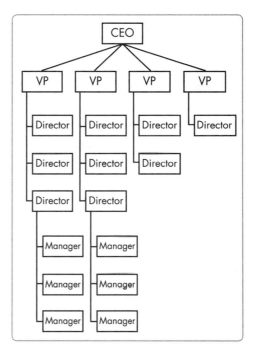

Figure A-3: Company hierarchy example

reduces communication noise. The different functional teams communicate mostly internally at a smaller scale, while inter-team communication is reduced. In addition, functional areas can optimize internal workflow.

On the other hand, many problems can exist in a hierarchical structure. First, each manager can optimize his or her department to the detriment of the overall company. This happens because each functional team is part of a production chain required to deliver the product or service, but each team is managed independently. As each functional manager is focused on the efficiency of his or her team, the manager may not focus on the efficiency of the organization as a whole. For example, a functional team can push part of its work onto the next team by reducing the scope of what it delivers, completing it with poor quality, or completing 80 percent of the work and promising that the rest will come later. These tactics make it appear as though the team has completed a milestone on time so the statistics look good, but such approaches lower the overall efficiency of the company.

In addition, work is often backed up in functional areas because of staff limitations, a non-project focus, and different priorities for different teams. For example, if five projects are active, but only two QA engineers are on staff, situations may occur when all five projects require the full-time attention of the two QA engineers at the same time. This results in the delay of three or more projects.

Finally, project communication between different functional areas is slower and less reliable, if it happens at all. Depending on the company culture, many inter-team discussions go up to the top of the hierarchy and then back down in another functional area.

With these key deficiencies in functional and hierarchical organizations, companies often use other organizational structures. This is especially true in companies with large numbers of projects.

Matrix Organizations

A *matrix structure* solves some of the problems of a hierarchical structure. It supports project management as well as functional management. Both project managers and functional managers have authority in their respective roles: the project manager for the project development, and the functional managers for supplying staff, mentoring the team, and setting processes and polices.

Companies select a matrix structure based on many factors, including company size, company culture, and business requirements. Companies with less rigid cultures, many projects, and the need for speed often use a matrix structure. With the project managers driving the individual projects, efforts are less likely to stall out or fall into an "information hole."

Consider different variations of the authority given to the hierarchical management versus project management. One solution is to split the authority between the functional management and the project management in half. However, how much authority senior management gives project managers versus functional managers varies considerably from company to company. Project managers dominate at some companies, while executives give project managers little authority but all the responsibility at others. Authority can be split in a company with a cooperative culture, and this proves to be an effective combination.

The classic matrix organizational chart shows split authority with dotted lines from the project managers. When drawn, the organization chart resembles a grid or matrix—hence the name. Figure A-4 shows a sample matrix organization.

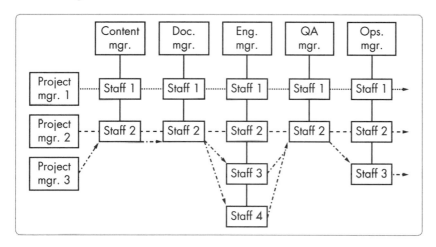

Figure A-4: Example of a matrix organization

Many effective methods can be used to split the authority of the functional manager from that of the project manager. One approach is to give the functional manager authority to set standards and choose staff. The functional manager defines how a project will be completed in general, sets the standards for success, and ensures that the projects are meeting a high standard. The project managers get to drive the projects with staff and focus on project success.

Matrix organizations do have problems, however. Staff employees can get contradictory instructions from direct managers and project managers. Who is actually "the boss" is not always clear, which can lead to politics and infighting between project managers and functional managers if the company culture is pushy.

In addition, matrix organizations can lead to significant morale problems. If the functional managers have most of the authority, project managers may believe they have all the responsibility but no control and will be demoralized. The reverse situation can happen as well in companies that have strong project management but weak functional management.

Finally, projects often collide in functional groups—multiple projects need the same staff to meet their timelines, forcing each project manager to demand top priority for particular projects. Often, the functional manager must make the call on the priorities of competing projects. Project collision can be time consuming to resolve and avoid because of the defused authority. Priority discussions can be much more difficult in matrix companies than in hierarchical companies.

Neither matrix management nor hierarchical structures are ideal. Finding the right combination of functional and project control can work reasonably well. However, keeping development organizations as small as is practical and then giving them independence is often the best approach.

Small Product Team

One alternative to large hierarchical or functional organizations is the *small product team*. The company organizes each product team around individual products and provides functional support for each. Management empowers the team to make all of the decisions about the product. In a 100-person company, the product team will be relatively small, and this is its advantage: It has scaled down a piece of the company to the small company structure.

Product teams excel at creating products that are revolutionary—products that break the existing models of how they are built and used. Developing products that are upgrades to existing ones works well in existing organizations; trying to build revolutionary products in the same product group will encounter roadblocks that will greatly impede progress, including limiting processes, working with older use models, being compelled in the overall profit/loss structure, changing team attitudes toward risk, and creating problems related to change. Separating revolutionary product teams into their own product groups enables the new team to drive the new product area to success.

Figure A-5 illustrates an example structure for the small product team. Note that the CEO splits off some functions to report directly to him or her. Typically, HR and Finance will still report directly to the CEO. Sometimes the CEO will also choose sales to be a corporate activity.

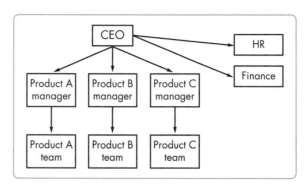

Figure A-5: Small product team

The structure of product teams will vary: It can be functional, matrix, or flexible based on what the product manager wants. However, the team will include roles for sales, development, operations, marketing, and other product-related functions. Each product team consists of sufficient team members to handle all the functions needed for the product. This does not mean that the team consists of a team member from each functional discipline. A team member could handle more than one functional area, for example, such as programming and QA. In this structure, upper management works to define overall strategy and provides support as needed for each of the product teams. This approach works for software products that small- to medium-sized teams can create and support. Teams can create products effectively and with more enthusiasm because they have more control over their particular tasks. This approach avoids the prioritization and communication disadvantages of the functional or matrix organization and is favored by many team members.

The small product team approach can have disadvantages, too. It is often necessary to "overstaff" some areas to create the product teams, for example. A product line may require only one-third of a marketing person's time, but a full-time person is assigned. Small product teams can also have problems with coordinating their efforts with other product areas; this makes sense because each area was set up to optimize the product. In addition, cost savings may be missed through corporate purchasing of equipment and software, although this is a relatively small problem compared to the effectiveness advantages. Finally, once the team is set up, this method offers less flexibility in going after new product areas. To do so requires that a new team be formed, often by pulling people off existing successful product teams.

Overall, the small product team's disadvantages are minor compared to the advantages of a more effective organization that can produce quality software quickly. The small product team works best for companies with relatively stable products planned over a multiple-year time frame.

Flexible Project Teams

The *flexible project teams* approach can make a team nimble. As projects arrive, management chooses project team leaders based on the projects' needs. The project leaders then select teams as projects require and as team members are available. Project team membership often overlaps, with one team member belonging to other teams as each project progresses. This approach requires a higher percentage of people with project leadership abilities than other organizational structures.

The flexible project team approach works very well in companies with many varying projects that are looking for speed and flexibility. Flexible teams are empowered as they provide the opportunity to form rapidly and allow team members to make project decisions directly.

The flexible project structure requires separating the non–project management functions from the project leadership. This can be accomplished in several ways, and Figure A-6 illustrates one approach to separating the management functions of mentoring, coaching, and evaluating employees working on teams. While the project teams are flexible based on project need, the management structure stays in place as projects change. This allows employees to have a consistent relationship with their managers to work through long-term issues.

Management needs to handle process improvement in this organization as well. One approach is to assign the job to the managers who are working directly with employees. A good alternative is for management to assign flexible project teams to handle specific improvement tasks.

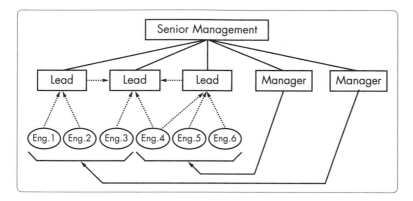

Figure A-6: Flexible project leadership

Like the others, this approach has disadvantages. A company that has few projects on a yearly basis can wind up with excessive management overhead. Also, it may be difficult to find enough engineers willing to be project team leads, although mid-career and senior engineers usually like the opportunity to lead on a part-time basis. Staff corrective action can also be more difficult with the diffused authority as compared to that in a functional-hierarchical organization.

Conclusion

Having reviewed some basic organizational structures for small companies, you might be tempted to rate them overall from best to worst. In practice, however, each can be effective, depending on your company's culture and what it is trying to do. In each case, be aware of the disadvantages of each structure and work to mitigate those problem areas.

B

INTERNATIONALIZATION

Internationalization of a website or application is more complex than it might first appear. When thinking about internationalization, an engineering team's first instinct may be to focus on translating the program's English text into another language—and how hard could that be? Instead, however, the team encounters complex problems, with many details to investigate, and some of them can remain unclear until after the company actually ships the product.

Internationalization is more than language translation, as it requires knowledge of currencies, laws, formatting, images, data structures, time-lines, and costs. The depth of work can be clarified by knowing what areas to investigate and what questions to ask. Until you have clear answers, do not provide concrete estimates. Conservative assumptions are warranted for your first internationalization project.

This appendix provides an introduction to internationalization questions and issues. It is divided into three parts: definitions, questions to ask, and some best practices. Review them all before you scope and plan your project. Better yet, find an engineer who has worked on internationalization and bring him or her into the team.

Here are some definitions of terms used in this appendix:

> **Internationalization**   This is the process of adapting your US English program for use in other countries. In general, this means dealing with other languages, laws, currencies, conventions, and graphics, among other considerations.

> **Locale**   This is the combination of language and country that uniquely identifies the information displayed by the application.

Internationalization Questions to Ask

The following questions deal with planning, the translation firm, costs, database issues, currency/dates/dimensions, and country and language issues:

- What is the long-term plan for the product's distribution internationally?

- What are the limits to the countries that might be considered?

- What languages does the company want to support in the future?

- For the countries that need to be supported, do some of them use multiple languages?

- How do language and country interact? Are a single language or multiple languages used in the same country?

- Will the company use US English for all English-speaking countries, or will it choose different versions for different countries (for example, UK English versus US English)?

- Who will be working with development to assist with the definition and support after deployment?

Translating Staffing and Costs

Translation is a continual effort. With each new release, additional translations are required. Getting clarity up front about who will pay for this additional work can save you grief later. Also, you should identify who is going to verify that the translations are correctly implemented.

- Who will perform the translation quality assurance?

- What is the strategy for maintaining the translation for future releases?

- Who will pay for future translations and maintenance?

Although it is not necessary to use an external translation firm, doing so is often a practical solution that can be better than having someone on staff perform the translation.

- How will we interact with the translation firm?

- What file format will the translation firm accept? Some firms will accept submissions only in Microsoft Word or Excel format, not in XML or another file format.

- What is the expected turnaround time for translations?

- Can we get a review of the final product?

- How will we provide context for the translator to perform the translation? The context can determine how some words and phrases are translated.

Database Considerations

Internationalization usually forces you to make changes to your program's database structure. Often new fields or different data types are required.

- How will you store the language data in your program to allow for easy updating?

- Are data format issues of concern? Software teams use several different formats for data storage including ASCII, Latin-1, UTF-8, and others. These have different bit requirements, so switching data format can have an impact on speed and data storage ability.

- How will engineering export the data to supply to the translator?

- How will the translated data be imported from the database?

- Are multilingual reports required?

Country and Language Requirements

Language requirements can involve subtleties. For example, dialects can be important, and conventions and layout can become significant issues.

- What will be the language impact on screen layout? Different languages take different length and form factors to say the same thing—for example, German words use 30 percent more space than English ones. Chinese has a different form factor altogether.

- What particular country laws are associated with the software offering?

- Who is reviewing the legal issues associated with your program or website's interactions with different countries? Consider privacy, security, and contract requirements.

- What are your plans for graphics and image changes per country? Different cultures can require that different graphics and images be used. Different countries may want different images as part of their marketing efforts. Who will select the images?

Currency Questions

Most internationalization projects involve purchases or tracking of different currencies. Consider these questions in your definition of the work:

- What currency will be used for purchases or reporting?

- How will the program display currency format? (For example, French Canada reverses the period and comma from US dollars: $2.333,44.)

- What are the currency symbols and layout?

- How will the currency be stored in the database?

- How will we report currency in data reports?

- How will the product update the currency relationship with US dollars?

Dates, Metric, and Dimension Issues

Date conventions are often not considered when internationalizing a product, but they do vary between countries. In some countries, for example, the Gregorian calendar is not the standard. US programmers may not consider metric versus English units, but that translation may be required as well.

- What date formatting is required for the countries supported?

- Does your program use units that may require conversion to the metric system?

- Do current user interface fields need to be resized to accommodate different dates, currencies, or text?

- Which calendar will be used?

- Which time zones need to be considered?

- Do time zone considerations exist for multiple users communicating between different countries?

- Does the application support the taxes required by the target country?

Best Practice Approach to Internationalization

Different solutions exist for different needs based on all the preceding questions. Here are some good general approaches to use when internationalizing.

Locales

Design the system around a *locale*. Each locale is a pairing of a country with a language to create a unique identifier. This may provide duplication of language data, but it offers the maximum amount of flexibility and avoids needing to change the code later. For example, Canada would have two locales: Canadian-English and Canadian-French. The US would have one locale: US-English.

Translation Process

Design the entire translation process in advance and write it up. The process should describe how to export, import, and translate the data. Consider the costs and turnaround time for the translators. This will help determine the future delivery schedule for your product. When engineering completes the code for a release, it can sometimes take weeks more to translate, verify, and repair. Translation mistakes and text changes are common, so assume time for iteration.

Quality Assurance

Plan a strategy for how QA will verify languages other than US English. A QA strategy will require that someone review the website or program and point out problems.

Database and Import/Export

Design the data format and database interface up front. Take the following elements into consideration when designing database changes and data exchange formats.

Select a data format for storing language information. Avoid choosing multiple formats based on history. Ideally, use a coding of UTF-8 or UTF-16 if a Kanji language is a possibility. However, in some situations, no single encoding will work for all of the countries being considered.

Use unique keywords in the program to identify different text elements. A switch in the code will select the language, which the keyword will reference from a table in the database.

Design the data import and export system in advance. Store and export not only the keywords and their English values, but also context phrases that clarify the intent for the translator. Example: *Go* could mean *press the button* or *exit*.

Translation Firm

If the translator will not support your ideal format, design a method of automatically converting it to the preferred format. For example, suppose the customer chooses the translator, but the translator supports only

Microsoft Word and Excel files. Creating special interfaces or practices for these firms may be necessary, as translation is not a one-time task.

One potential solution for the translator who wants to use only Excel is to customize the program. Excel 2003 and later versions support XML import/export if the proper template is built in advance. You can set up a template such that XML import/export is easy to perform. The process would then be as follows:

1. Your program can export an XML format.

2. The translator can read the XML into an Excel program using a standard XML template you set up.

3. The translator makes changes to specific boxes in the Excel program and returns it to you.

4. You export the XML from Excel and read it back into your program.

A convenient way to lay out a translation table in Excel is illustrated in Table B-1, showing an English-to-Wingdings (◎◎⑤⌇ↁⓄ⌇⑩) translation template. The Context column provides the translator with context if the English phrase is ambiguous.

Table B-1: English to Wingdings with Context

Unique Name	English	◎⑥④⌇ↁ⑥⌇⑩	Context
TitleAP	Accounts Payable	☞ↁↁ⑥❶⑤❶⑩	
		✓ↁ❺ↁↁ③ↂ	
EnterAP	Go	ↂ⑤❶ↂ⑨	Submit the information on the page (not physically go somewhere)
ClearAP	Clear	ↁ③ↂↁ⑨	Remove data from page (this is not about understanding or transparency)

User Interface

Plan your layout of screens and pages with flexibility to allow larger-sized text as well as photo and graphics changes. A graphics team cannot just think about the US office and English layout considerations.

Consider graphics and photos as part of the locale swapping code. Store multiple images and allow references from different locales to the desired images. Multiple locales can point to the same image.

Finally, be sure to include error messages in your translation strategy. Development staff often overlook error messages because they are not always visible.

Summary

Don't take an internationalization effort lightly, even though it may seem easy on the surface. Review with the customer all the factors presented in this appendix. The customer might surprise you with new requirements based on your questions. This approach will also raise issues with the customer about any longer-term internationalization plans. An implementation that works well in Latin-based languages may not work well in Asia, for example. It is much better to ask questions up front than to be surprised and get stuck later.

C

CORPORATE WORKFLOW DIAGRAM

This appendix describes a simple approach to drawing corporate workflow diagrams, which can be useful for understanding how a company works and for training others about the process. They can also provide great help in identifying problems and figuring out solutions.

Specific company problems can lead to investigation of workflows related to that specific problem. However, you shouldn't wait until you have a problem before you put together a clear understanding of the overall corporate workflows.

For a small company, creating a simple workflow diagram is usually sufficient. A simple workflow diagram helps you understand how the company works, from creating estimates to shipping the product. Although complex methods exist for creating and analyzing these diagrams, the benefits of complexity are mostly realized by larger companies.

A good practice is to analyze several common workflows as part of your initial corporate orientation:

- Quote and estimation process
- Order-build-invoice process
- Internally defined product development process
- Customer change order process

Creating a Simple Workflow Diagram

To create a simple workflow diagram, start by talking to people in the organization to understand how the company works. Make sure you include input from sales, marketing, operations, and finance teams as well as customers and vendors. These conversations should clarify the steps in the workflow and the expectations of individuals participating. Then grab a pencil and paper and follow these steps:

1. Create a large dashed box to represent your company.
2. Create boxes for each team in the workflow, labeling each with the team name and the function performed in parentheses.
3. Create boxes for external customers, users, and vendors.
4. Draw lines with arrows to show requests for work and work delivery paths. Add notes to arrows to indicate items delivered as needed for clarity.

Figure C-1 illustrates the building blocks used in a workflow. Although this is a fairly simple set of building blocks, it shows how you can map most workflows easily.

Workflow Example

Let's move on to an example diagram that can be used to investigate slow invoicing problems. For this example, suppose you have just joined a company that creates semi-custom web applications for US and international

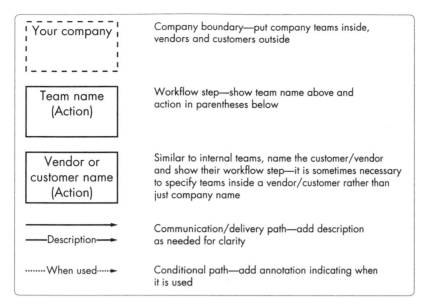

Your company	Company boundary—put company teams inside, vendors and customers outside
Team name (Action)	Workflow step—show team name above and action in parentheses below
Vendor or customer name (Action)	Similar to internal teams, name the customer/vendor and show their workflow step—it is sometimes necessary to specify teams inside a vendor/customer rather than just company name
—Description—▶	Communication/delivery path—add description as needed for clarity
⋯⋯When used⋯▶	Conditional path—add annotation indicating when it is used

Figure C-1: Building blocks of a workflow diagram

markets. You are in charge of the engineering, quality assurance, and operations teams. The company offers customized applications in a software-as-a-service (SaaS) model and hosts the applications on the company's servers. International customers want the application to be translated into the appropriate languages and want to use graphics that appeal to people in the host country.

Your boss tells you that your company has been having difficulty invoicing customers in a timely fashion and asks you to investigate. She also tells you that some finger-pointing is going on between sales, operations, and accounts payable about who's to blame for the problem.

You start by drawing a high-level diagram of your company, showing the main interactions between the functional areas. Your sketch looks like Figure C-2. With this drawing as your initial reference point, you can mark it up with the specific workflow that you are investigating. In some cases, you can zoom in on specific details of a group and prune away functions that are not relevant to your problem.

To continue your investigation, you interview people involved in the complete order-build-invoice workflow. As you are talking to individuals, you

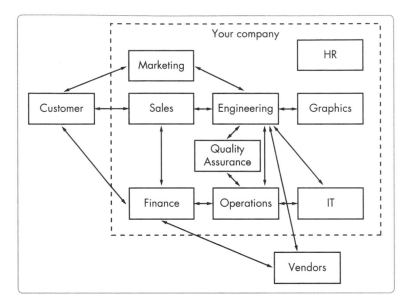

Figure C-2: High-level view of your company's major workflow

sketch out the workflow in steps and ask each of them if you have properly captured each step.

First, you talk to the sales team; they tell you that they receive orders from the customer and send a copy of the order over to finance, the accounts billable group, engineering, and operations.

Next, you talk with engineering and learn that they receive the orders and then create the web application, working with other teams. To complete an order, the engineering team needs to use the services of a translation vendor and the graphics team. Engineering also works with QA to complete the website. Engineering has to ask purchasing for translation vendor support. The translation vendor gets requests directly from your purchasing group in finance while finance's accounts payable team looks for payment.

Next, you talk to QA. QA tests the website and requests corrections from engineering. When QA determines that the website is acceptable, they send the information to operations for deployment.

Next you talk to operations team members, whose jobs seem cut and dried. Operations receives the website from QA and deploys it. Operations also lets accounts billable know when a website goes up, but because no particular order number is used in the process, operations sends over a general description of the site and a date deployed. As you are leaving the operations area, the operations manager also tells you that he gets no advance notice of orders and really has to scramble to schedule deployment work.

Finally, you talk with the accounts billable and accounts payable groups in finance. They tell a different story. Too often the accounts billable team has to ask sales for an order when it comes in. They also have difficulty understanding whom to bill when operations puts up a website, because they don't have a purchase order number from operations. So they have to call sales, operations, and sometimes engineering to figure it out.

All of this information is too confusing in the abstract, so you revise your high-level diagram to focus on the specifics of this workflow. You revise your sketch to remove groups not involved and to add specific subgroups when appropriate. Then, you add actions to each group to illustrate what they do in the workflow. Your diagram looks like Figure C-3.

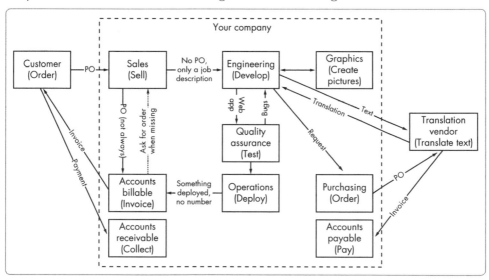

Figure C-3: Example order-build-invoice workflow diagram

From the diagram, you can follow the workflow of the purchase order. With the diagram, it is easier to see that the gap occurs between sales, accounts billable, and operations. The diagram also makes it easier to experiment with potential solutions.

One approach is to get agreement from sales always to send order information to both accounts billable and operations. Operations now has the reference order number and some notice of the order being completed by engineering. Operations is then required to attached the order number to the deployment notice given to accounts payable. Operations will also be the backup check if it finds a web deployment but no corresponding order from sales—operations can talk to sales directly to request the order and have enough information to identify the appropriate order. Figure C-4 illustrates the addition of sales supplying the customer order to operations not shown in Figure C-3.

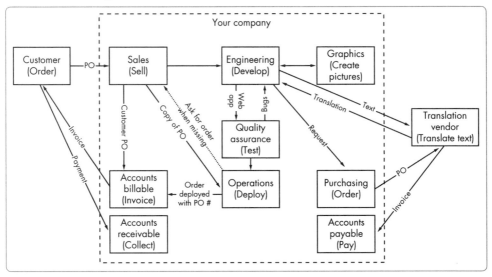

Figure C-4: Revised order-build-invoice workflow

Although this is a simple example, workflow diagrams can also be used to resolve more complex workflow issues. They are useful while training new employees, as well.

Simple workflow diagrams are easy to construct and provide a method for visualizing and improving workflows in your company.

INDEX

code
    artifacts, 101–102
    automated testing of, 314
    custom, 106, 111
    managers writing, 62–63
    modules, disorganized, 106
    reusing prototype, 95
collaboration
    executive team, 201
    interdepartmental, 59–61, 184–186
    marketing and engineering, 97–99
    office organization and, 58–59
    product definition through, 86–89
    promoting culture of, 178–179
comments, file check-in, 144
communication
    with boss, 193–196
    vs. concentration, 56–58, 61
    with customers, 204–206
    with executive team, 200–201
    interdepartmental, 59–61
    office layout and, 58–59
    organizational structure and, 366,
        368, 369, 370
    skills, evaluating, 71
    team management and, 33–37
company culture
    candidate selection and, 69
    corporate style, 179
    engineering team,
        perceptions of, 188
    interteam problem resolution and,
        184–186
    management style, 180
    meetings and, 180–184
    new jobs and, 19
    peer relationships, 186–187
    understanding and influencing,
        177–179
company growth. See also
        organizational structure
    customization costs and, 344–347

interdepartmental relations and,
        184–185
    meeting style and, 180–181
    quality assurance staffing and, 308
    role of development managers
        and, 1–2
    stages, 3
    system scalability and,
        158–160, 342
company image, 110, 352, 354
company values
    new jobs and, 19
    ranking table, 321
    release planning and, 110, 119
compartmentalization, 181. See also
        organizational structure
complaints, 37
component identification numbers,
        127–128
conference rooms, 58
confidence, importance of, 198–199
confidentiality, 31–32
conflict resolution, 37–39, 197–198
content management systems, 142
conversations and office organization,
        58–59
corporate culture. See company culture
corporate style, 179
corporate values. See company values
corporate workflow diagrams, 22–23,
        385–390
cost-benefit (CB) analysis, 351–356
co-workers, getting to know, 16–17
Crystal Clear, 276
currency and internationalization,
        380–381
customers
    defects found by, 328–329
    early releases and, 114–115
    getting to know, 21–22

impact of retiring software on,
117–118
perception of product, 100–104
as a resource for future planning,
338–340
sales and proposals, 206–212
satisfaction of, 203–206
customer support, 93, 103, 212–213
customer-use models, 102
customization, 106, 111, 344–347

D

daily stand-up meetings, 35
data
automated testing for, 314
collection meetings, 183
reporting and analysis, 169–171
retiring software and
customer's, 118
warehouses, 170–171
database design and
internationalization,
379–380, 382
dates and internationalization, 381
decision branching in process
modeling, 289, 290
decision drivers for ranking defects,
320–321
decision-making meetings, 183
defects, product
customer perceptions and, 100–101
customer status updates on, 122
failure mode analysis, 160–162
impact on quality and productivity,
330–333
quality assurance metrics, 324–330
ranking and selecting, 319–324
tools for tracking, 149–151,
309–312
delays, project, 237–238, 246–248
delegation, 12

dependencies, 249
dependent component
numbering, 128
detail managers, 180
development managers
promoting software engineers to,
61–63
role and definition of, 1–2
starting jobs. *See* new jobs, starting
development processes, 239–240,
267–270
ad hoc, 270, 276
agile, 275–279
customizing, 279–280
improving, 287–288, 295–299
introduction and enforcement,
281–284
iterative, 273
modeling, 288–295
selecting, 281
spiral, 274–275
test- and model-driven, 279
waterfall, 270–273
development teams
candidate selection. *See* candidate
selection
effective. *See* effectiveness in
development teams
management of. *See* managing
development teams
new managers of. *See* new jobs,
starting
promoting respect for, 188
development tools assessment,
133–135
backups, 134, 135–140
build methods, 145–147
defect tracking, 149–151, 309–312
release process, 147–149
selection, 151–154, 240
source control versioning, 142–145
user interface prototyping, 95–96

G

Gantt chart programs, 220, 249–255
Gentleman Farmer example, 130–131
Git, 144
Givemeabreakfarming Software
     example, 130–131
goals
     coaching and individuals', 40–42
     project, 234–235
     understanding boss's, 193–194
growing
     companies. *See* company growth
     development teams. *See* candidate
          selection; effectiveness in
          development teams
     relationships. *See* relationships
GUIs (graphical user interfaces). *See*
     user interfaces (UIs)

H

handshake annual review, 49
hidden product features, 101
hierarchical organizational structure,
     369–370
high-trust behaviors, 28–29
hiring. *See* candidate selection
hit-and-run interviews, 78
honeymoon period, 13
human factors engineers, 96–97
humor, 63

I

image projects, 352, 354
import/export design and
     internationalization, 382
incremental backups, 137–138
independent component
     numbering, 128
informal conversations, 200

information
     gathering in new jobs, 14–16, 17–18
     presentation meetings, 183
intellectual property (IP), 20, 133–135,
     157–158
interaction framework for
     projects, 239
international support, 377–378
     assessment of, 171–172
     best practices, 381–384
     considerations, 378–381
interruptions, software engineer,
     56–58, 61
interviews, 74–79
IP (intellectual property), 20, 133–135,
     157–158
isolating development teams, 61
iterative development process, 273
iterative steps in process models,
     289, 290

J

JUnit, 314

K

kickoff meetings, 242–243
knowledge questions, 67

L

languages, foreign, 380. *See also*
     translation (language)
late performance reviews, 48
legacy code, 106–107
legal issues, 117, 380
lightweight development processes,
     269–270, 275
limited releases, 113, 115
locales in internationalization, 381
localization. *See* international support

tracking product defects, 149–151,
    309–312
tracking projects, 245–246
    change control process, 259–261
    guidelines for project
        management, 246–248
    maintenance and overhead,
        229–230
    making scheduling predictions and
        alterations, 257–259
    risk management, 261–264
    software approaches for, 249–257
    time tracking, 226–229
training
    continuing, for team members,
        39–40
    development process, 282
    internal staff on software
        updates, 122
    in new jobs, 13–14
    release process cross-, 148
trait evaluation of job candidates,
    67–73
translation (language), 379, 382–383
trust, 26–29, 87–88, 178–179, 193

U

UIs (user interfaces). *See* user
    interfaces
unplanned and unsupported features,
    102–104
urgent issues, 11–13
usability engineers, 96–97
use cases
    in API documentation, 167
    in product definition, 90
user interfaces (UIs)
    automated testing, 314
    defect ranking, 320, 321
    designing, 96–97
    internationalization and, 383–384
    prototyping tools, 95–96

V

vacation time and calculating
    overhead, 230
values. *See* company values
verbal estimates, 226
version identification, 121,
    124–129, 128

W

waterfall development processes,
    270–273
weekly project status meetings, 35
weighting defect rankings, 322–324,
    326–329
white box testing, 314
whole product concept, 91–93,
    340–341
wikis, 141–142
workflow, corporate business, 22–23,
    385–390
work habits and preferences,
    evaluating, 70
work hours, estimating, 218–219,
    256. *See also* calendar days,
    estimating
work skills training, 39
writing and delivering estimates,
    224–226
writing skills, evaluating, 71
written estimates, 222–226

X

XP (extreme programming), 276–277

More No-Nonsense Books from

no starch press

THE ART OF DEBUGGING WITH GDB, DDD, AND ECLIPSE

by NORMAN MATLOFF *and* PETER JAY SALZMAN

The Art of Debugging illustrates the use of three of the most popular debugging tools on Linux/Unix platforms: GDB, DDD, and Eclipse. In addition to offering specific advice for debugging with each tool, authors Norm Matloff and Pete Salzman cover general strategies for improving the process of finding and fixing coding errors, including how to inspect variables and data structures, understand segmentation faults and core dumps, and figure out why your program crashes or throws exceptions. You'll also learn how to use features like catchpoints, convenience variables, and artificial arrays and become familiar with ways to avoid common debugging pitfalls.

SEPTEMBER 2008, 280 PP., $39.95
ISBN 978-1-59327-174-9

CODE CRAFT

The Practice of Writing Excellent Code

by PETE GOODLIFFE

Code Craft shows how to move beyond writing correct code to writing excellent code. The book covers many code-writing concerns, including code presentation style, variable naming, error handling, and security, as well as the wider issues of programming in the real world, such as good teamwork, development processes, and documentation. *Code Craft* presents language-agnostic advice that is relevant to all developers, from an author with extensive practical experience.

DECEMBER 2006, 624 PP., $44.95
ISBN 978-1-59327-119-0

WICKED COOL RUBY SCRIPTS

Useful Scripts That Solve Difficult Problems

by STEVE PUGH

Wicked Cool Ruby Scripts provides carefully selected Ruby scripts that are immediately useful. With this book, you'll learn how to streamline administrative tasks like renaming files, disabling processes, and changing permissions. After you get your feet wet creating basic scripts, author Steve Pugh will show you how to create powerful Web crawlers, security scripts, full-fledged libraries and applications, and much more. For each script you'll get the raw code followed by an explanation of how it really works, as well as instructions for how to run the script and suggestions for customizing it. *Wicked Cool Ruby Scripts* will save you from the tedium of repetitive tasks and give you back the time it would take to write scripts from scratch.

DECEMBER 2008, 216 PP., $29.95
ISBN 978-1-59327-182-4

WRITE GREAT CODE, VOLUME 1

Understanding the Machine

by RANDALL HYDE

Write Great Code, Volume 1: Understanding the Machine explains the fundamental concepts of low-level computation in a friendly, language-independent fashion. Covering topics like binary arithmetic, bit operations, I/O, memory access and more, author and professor Randall Hyde illustrates machine organization without requiring a mastery of assembly language. Readers can also expect to learn about floating-point, numeric, and character representation; constants and types; Boolean logic; CPU and instruction set architecture; and how compilers work. This is the perfect book for high-level programmers ready to move from good to great.

NOVEMBER 2004, 488 PP., $39.95
ISBN 978-1-59327-003-2

WRITE GREAT CODE, VOLUME 2

Thinking Low-Level, Writing High-Level

by RANDALL HYDE

Write Great Code, Volume 2: Thinking Low-Level, Writing High-Level shows software engineers what too many college and university courses don't: how compilers translate high-level language statements and data structures into machine code. Armed with this knowledge, you will be better informed about choosing the high-level structures that will help the compiler produce superior machine code.

MARCH 2006, 640 PP., $44.95
ISBN 978-1-59327-065-0

PHONE:
800.420.7240 OR
415.863.9900
MONDAY THROUGH FRIDAY,
9 AM TO 5 PM (PST)

FAX:
415.863.9950
24 HOURS A DAY,
7 DAYS A WEEK

EMAIL:
SALES@NOSTARCH.COM

WEB:
WWW.NOSTARCH.COM

MAIL:
NO STARCH PRESS
555 DE HARO ST, SUITE 250
SAN FRANCISCO, CA 94107
USA

The Electronic Frontier Foundation (EFF) is the leading organization defending civil liberties in the digital world. We defend free speech on the Internet, fight illegal surveillance, promote the rights of innovators to develop new digital technologies, and work to ensure that the rights and freedoms we enjoy are enhanced — rather than eroded — as our use of technology grows.

PRIVACY EFF has sued telecom giant AT&T for giving the NSA unfettered access to the private communications of millions of their customers. eff.org/nsa

FREE SPEECH EFF's Coders' Rights Project is defending the rights of programmers and security researchers to publish their findings without fear of legal challenges. eff.org/freespeech

INNOVATION EFF's Patent Busting Project challenges overbroad patents that threaten technological innovation. eff.org/patent

FAIR USE EFF is fighting prohibitive standards that would take away your right to receive and use over-the-air television broadcasts any way you choose. eff.org/IP/fairuse

TRANSPARENCY EFF has developed the Switzerland Network Testing Tool to give individuals the tools to test for covert traffic filtering. eff.org/transparency

INTERNATIONAL EFF is working to ensure that international treaties do not restrict our free speech, privacy or digital consumer rights. eff.org/global

EFF.ORG

ELECTRONIC FRONTIER FOUNDATION

Protecting Rights and Promoting Freedom on the Electronic Frontier

EFF is a member-supported organization. Join Now! www.eff.org/support

COLOPHON

The fonts used in *Growing Software* are New Baskerville, Futura, and Dogma.

The book was printed and bound at Malloy Incorporated in Ann Arbor, Michigan. The paper is Glatfelter Spring Forge 60# Eggshell, which is certified by the Sustainable Forestry Initiative (SFI).

UPDATES

Visit *http://www.nostarch.com/growingsoftware.htm* for examples, templates, updates, errata, and other information.